Expressive HANDMADE BOOKS

Alisa Golden

Sterling Publishing Co., Inc
New York

Designed by Wanda Kossak
Photographs by Sibila Savage
Art projects and diagrams by the author unless otherwise indicated.

To convert inches to centimeters, multiply by 2.54.
To convert inches to millimeters, multiply by 25.4.

Library of Congress Cataloging-in-Publication Data

Golden, Alisa J.
Expressive handmade books / Alisa Golden.
p. cm.
Includes index.
ISBN 1-4027-2051-3
1. Book design–Handbooks, manuals, etc.
2 Bookbinding–Handbooks, manuals, etc. I. Title

Z116.A3G64 2005
686.3'02–dc22

2005048961

2 4 6 8 10 9 7 5 3 1

Published by Sterling Publishing Co., Inc.
387 Park Avenue South, New York, NY 10016

Distributed in Canada by Sterling Publishing
c/o Canadian Manda Group, 165 Dufferin Street
Toronto, Ontario, Canada M6K 3H6
Distributed in Great Britain by Chrysalis Books Group PLC
The Chrysalis Building, Bramley Road, London W10 6SP, England
Distributed in Australia by Capricorn Link (Australia) Pty. Ltd.
P.O. Box 704, Windsor, NSW 2756, Australia

Printed in China

Sterling ISBN 1-4027-2051-3

For information about custom editions, special sales, premium and
corporate purchases, please contact Sterling Special Sales
Department at 800-805-5489 or specialsales@sterlingpub.com.

CONTENTS

Chapter Three

Dreams, Flags, and More Accordions 48

Chapter Four

Side Bindings and Sewn Signatures 75

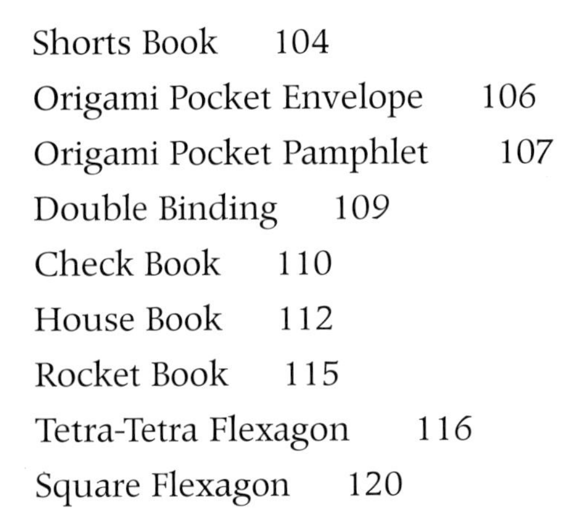

Chapter Five

Folds and Twists: Books with Multiple Paths 103

Chapter Six

Covers and Closures: Keeping It All Together 123

Chapter Seven

Sorting Through the Big Box 143

PREFACE

Books in Ezra's memory, 2003
Back row (left to right): *Four Tea Cups; Confused Living: A Jumble Book; In My LIving Room; A Black Ribbon*
Front row (left to right): *One Word; Rain Check, Where, Oh Where*

Although I have been making book art for twenty years, for the past ten my focus has been on book structures. I use the form to enhance the content or to indicate the concept to the reader. Initially I taught every structure I knew. But that wasn't enough. My students didn't want to repeat the class but they wanted to keep coming. I then had to learn more to teach more. I couldn't find one book that had all the structures I liked, so eventually I sent out queries to publishers, and Sterling accepted my first book, *Creating Handmade Books.*

After the book was published, someone called me and said, "I love all these little books but how can I make them be more than just fetishes?" Content has always been foremost when I think about making a book; usually I assume that I need a text before I can begin, so I do all the writing first. I had wanted to address content more thoroughly in my first how-to book, but I had already run over my page limit.

Just when that book was published, my son had a heart attack, which left him brain injured. Our lives changed quickly and drastically. I couldn't make art. I couldn't write. I sat still all day long watching him and ended up drawing pictures of him and everything else in the hospital to pass the time until he became responsive again. I was creating something, but that wasn't work I wanted to share. I wrote short stories as he got better. Nurses came and went. One nurse died. In the middle of daily life how could art matter? On the other hand, I couldn't stop making things or I felt like I would explode.

I wrote to Sterling and asked if they wanted a second book, which they did. I threw myself into the unemotional world of ordered instructions and precise diagrams. I had to make models, but I was having trouble creating things myself. My own ideas were too hard to work with; I felt like all I had to share was pain. Still, I pushed my way through the process and made *No Moon Tonight*, the title was from the three words my son had said the night before his injury. My themes developed: acceptance, sacrifice, compassion. I made *Oh, Great Chicken,* another book with a heavy subject. I finished the second how-to, *Unique Handmade Books*, then I felt stranded. I still wasn't making many books. I was having trouble expressing myself.

My friend Nan told me about spiders in her telephone box and, a few days later, related a dream in which everyone had a spider but that she was missing hers. I liked the connection between daily life and her dream and created *Wind, Wire & Web* based on her stories. I liked this book, but it wasn't exactly my story. Where was my story? My mind tossed and turned words around, but they wouldn't fit together to satisfy me. I couldn't focus.

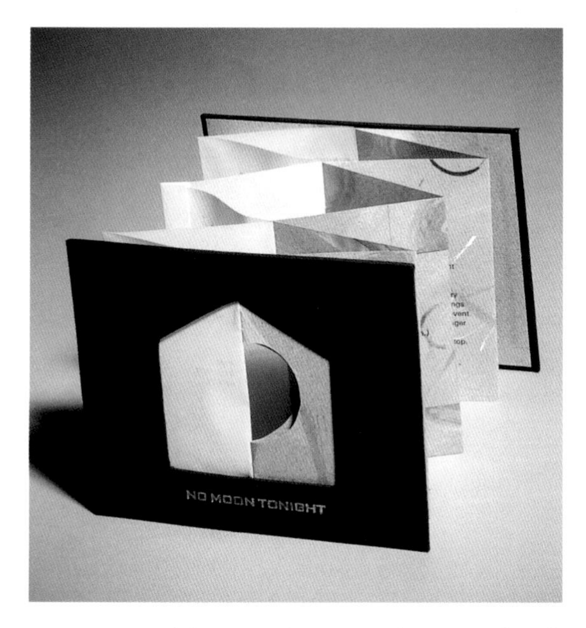

No Moon Tonight, 1999; letterpress from wood and metal type on painted paper; back-to-back accordion; edition of 35; 6¾" × 5⅛" (photo by Jim Hair)

Oh, Great Chicken, 2000; letterpress on painted paper; edition of 15; 2¾" × 7¼" circle accordion book in 3½" × 8" × 1" folded box

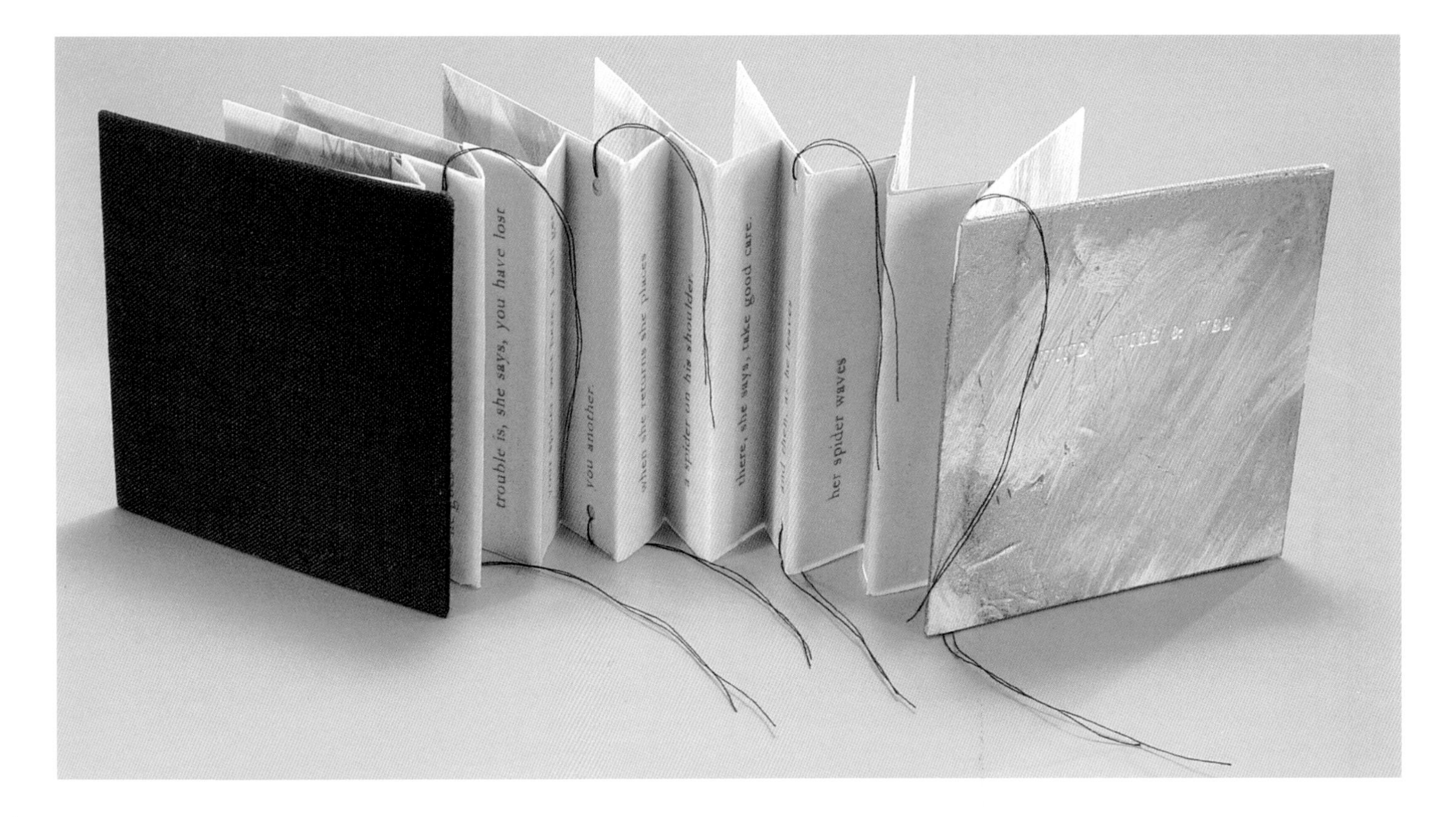

Wind, Wire & Web, 2000; letterpress on painted and stenciled paper, threads; single-flag book; edition of 45; 3" × 3"

I switched media. I taught myself how to make monotypes with water-based ink. I painted with the ink on a piece of Plexiglas, then let it dry. After misting a piece of paper with water, I pressed the damp paper onto the plate, then carefully peeled back the paper. Accustomed to making multiples of things, I got eleven Plexiglas plates so I could work on several prints at once and finish them in a day or two. They were bright and colorful. I didn't have to think. I worked intuitively. For the first time, I accepted the word "beauty" in what I was striving for. I was finally feeling happier.

Books kept calling to me. After twenty years of making books, I am always thinking books. I tried the monotypes in the book-within-a-book *Three Month Diary* and *No Sign of a Dress* (more heavy content), and put a monotype in *Ram's Horns*. Making large numbers of similar monotypes was a production I didn't like.

I tried to write again but the poetry was labored and felt clunky. I wasn't getting the magical feeling from either writing or reading the poems. Abandoned by the writing muse, I went back to image making.

Nine months went by. It was time to make another book. I didn't have a text. I had no idea what I wanted to say. I pasted objects to the back of nine old linoleum blocks with gel medium. I worked as if I were making monotypes: creating all nine at once. I cut linoleum blocks to print first, to add color. Then I printed the collagraphs on top. The layers formed many bright colors. I liked them. I looked into each one and got inspired to write. It is an

Cat and Couch Potatoes, 2001; monotype

old trick, to look at a picture and write about it, but I had never done it with my own work before. This time, I found I had plenty to say. There was a whole world I was not addressing, which included the delight I felt about my daughter as well as the joy when working with my son. I discovered I could still feel happiness if I just focused on small daily events. Some of

Three Month Diary & No Sign of a Dress, 2001; letterpress, handwritten text, monotypes; multiple signature on ribbons, 8¾" × 11" and single- flag book, 3" × 5"; edition of 8

Three Month Diary & *No Sign of a Dress* (detail)

Ram's Horns, 2001; letterpress and mixed media; three single signatures sewn to an endpaper; edition of 7; 5" × 5¾"

Lightning Strikes a Butterfly, 2002; letterpress, collagraphs, linoleum cuts; side bound; edition of 27; 6¼" × 8¼"

these events became the book, *Lightning Strikes a Butterfly.* Working with my own images was much more powerful than an assignment to create a poem about a museum's masterpiece. I had discovered a new way of working that enabled me to write and make books again in a style that I liked. My daughter, Mollie, touched me with her expressive clarinet playing. My son, Ezra, happily attended school in a wheelchair: his smile and love inspired me.

One Word, 2003; typewriter, handwriting, solar prints; flower-fold book; unique; 4¼" × 4¼"

Ezra died unexpectedly from cardiac arrest when he was six, in the summer of 2003. In the four weeks that followed, I made seven one-of-a-kind books just about Ezra. By working through my grief in book form I was able to keep hold of him a little while longer. I thought of holding him and the things we did together. He had rarely cried. I cried a lot as I made each of the seven books: *Where, Oh Where; Rain Check; In My Living Room; Four Tea Cups; A Black Ribbon; One Word; Confused Living: A Jumble Book.*

After a month I decided to try to turn my attention outward. But looking out at the world made me look inward as well. Overcoming loss and holding onto memories through making art are now my primary themes. I'm interested in how we can transform our (sometimes painful) experiences into something new, perhaps even something beautiful, that others can understand.

Having spent most of my life making art under what most people would consider "normal" circumstances, I found that when confronted by obstacles, I adapted how I worked. I have made art for pleasure; I have made art compulsively in crisis; I have made art in grief to relieve pain. I know what it feels like to be blocked and I discovered techniques that help me begin again. I realized that many people have different reasons for making art and that they work in different ways. All of these personal changes alerted me to a different style of teaching: the desire to dig more deeply and find out what moves people, what their memories tell about them, and how they can accept or change themselves through their art. The chapters that follow closely resemble my approach in class.

This book is dedicated to Ezra's memory. It is also dedicated to my husband, Michael, and to our daughter, Mollie.

Acknowledgments

I'd like to thank Heath Frost for inviting me to give a talk for the Book User's Group at the San Francisco Center for the Book. I came home that night and began typing up what I had said, then realized I had a topic and material for this new how-to, which I had not planned to write. Thanks to all the people who came and listened and also to Steve Woodall for recommending me.

It was a pleasure, once again, to work with photographer Sibila Savage.

Many thanks to the people who enthusiastically tested my instructions and gave good advice: Nina Ciani, Abigail Craig, Alexandra Crichlow, Tori Crichlow-Debro, Betsy Davids, Heath Frost, Michael Henninger, Diane Johnson, Norma Lydon, Peter McCormick, Damon-Eugene Rich, Emily Rosenberg, Zona Sage, Judy Sarna, Val Simonetti, Dona Snow, Geraldine Stokes, and Emily Marks, Nan Wishner, and Louise Yale.

With every book structure, I try to give an explanation of where I learned it. Many structures are passed around informally, and the source is not remembered. Bookmaking then becomes like a folk craft, where the ideas are shared, developed, adapted, and re-created simultaneously. I am most grateful to the respectful and thoughtful style of my own teacher, Betsy Davids.

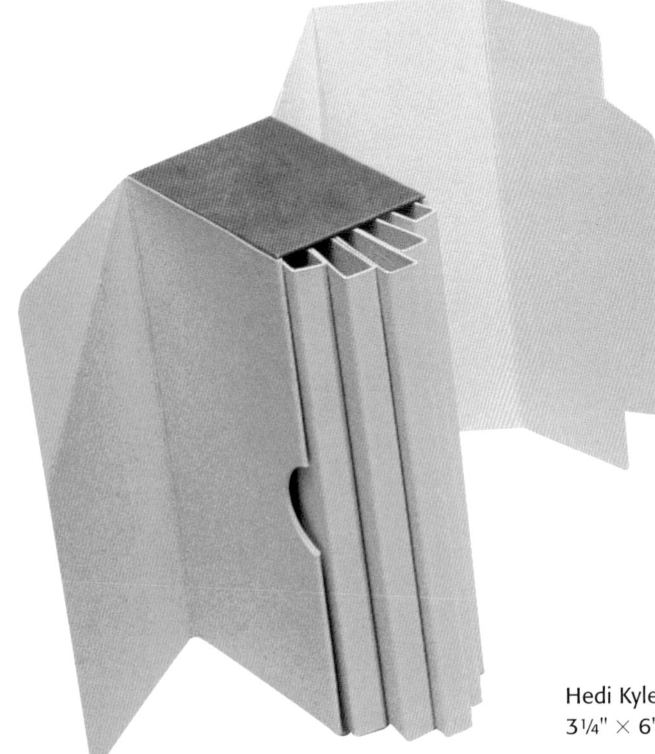

Hedi Kyle: Multi-Section Slipcase Model, 1997; book cloth, dyed Tyvek, boards; 3¼" × 6" (photo by Paul Warchol)

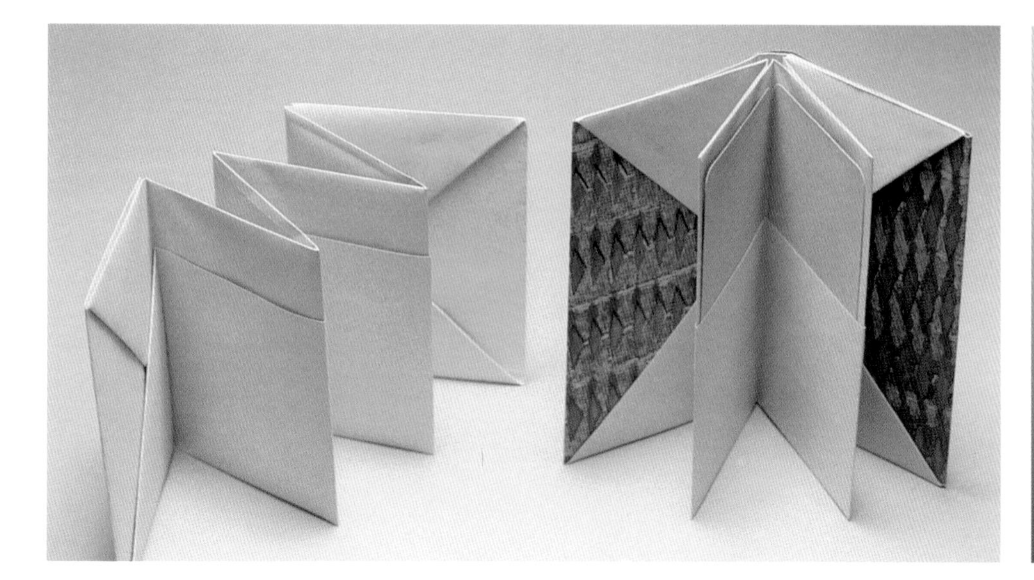

Hedi Kyle: Pocket Folder Model, 1997; paper; 4" × 7" (photo by Paul Warchol)

Keith Smith: *Book Number 15, Janson's History of Art, Revised,* 1970; found book altered by adding collage from photo offset reproductions; 9¼ × 11¾ × 2" (photo by K. Smith)

The earliest teachers and developers of new structures in the field are widely regarded as Hedi Kyle and Keith Smith. In the past decade Edward Hutchins has enthusiastically and quickly created and shared many more, and he happily teaches them wherever he goes. Katherine Ng and Bonnie Thompson Norman also generously share with me what they create and learn. Many other individuals have contributed as well, and I extend a hearty thank-you to all.

Chapter One

WAYS TO BEGIN

Workspace on top of cutting mat
Top row: watercolor pencils
Second row: waxed macramé cord, linen thread and bookbinding needle, beeswax, binder clip, Japanese screw punch
Third row: bone folder, superfine black pen, pencil, stencil brush, assorted papers, X-Acto knife, awl, scissors
Bottom: metal ruler

When you are making art, you are interpreting the world and reweaving it in your own style. The trick is to find your own style of telling the story. Your style will depend on what is important to you. If accuracy is important to you, you might try to describe something as precisely as you can. Perhaps you want to capture a moment and communicate it as realistically as possible. On the other hand, you may want to convey a feeling that is hard to describe; you might use metaphors or colors to share your mood, connecting something abstract (the feeling) to something concrete (the colors or objects). This is how you create culture. You are creating a world for both the reader and yourself. Where do you want to go? Think about your journey as you choose what to make into a book. First, you need thinking time. What are you curious about?

Find something that interests you today. Take a walk. Birds, overheard conversations, and the shapes of houses are among the things that may stimulate your interest. A few words in a newspaper article may also be a catalyst for a bigger idea. If emotions are propelling you, do some writing, drawing, or painting to address your feelings.

Research your interest and gather more information. Often the dictionary definition of a word has an unexpected fact included with it. Make sketches, gather photographs, assemble the materials that will support your original idea or feeling.

Perhaps you are feeling blocked. You are aimless and don't know where to go. There are too many roads or all the roads are washed away. What can you do? Turn off your internal editor. Some small voice is telling you that you aren't doing something *enough.* You aren't focusing *enough.* You aren't writing well *enough.* It doesn't matter *enough.* Shake that voice loose. Send it away until you finish writing or designing your project. Only then should you look at the work critically. For now, work from within. Work from your heart.

A few years ago, I asked Ken Rignall, a former printmaking teacher of mine, what he was doing. When I was in school, he used to make prints of fruit. They were exceptional, but they were always fruit. He said he was painting.

"What are you painting?" I asked, thinking about the fruit.

"Anything! It doesn't matter." He gestured expansively toward the sky.

At the time I just thought how free that sounded, but didn't think about it again until I began worrying about my own work. I was having trouble beginning any kind of project. I kept hearing, "Anything" in my head and decided to let go of my desire to make *Something Important* and just make *Something.* "Anything" turns out to be the correct answer. Make *Anything* and it will be *Something.* When you work, your style and your mood will shine through, no matter what you make. If you have strong emotions they will be apparent, no matter what the actual subject matter. A vague feeling of, "Oh, I'd like to write" probably won't be enough. Focus on what you feel strongly about, and just begin.

If your mind won't let go to let you write, try picking a time when you are the sleepiest. I've found passages in my journal that I don't really remember writing. Often I can use these passages as a catalyst for a final piece. I usually have a subject in mind when I write these bits.

May Sarton wrote *Coming into Eighty: New Poems,* a whole book of poetry, because her cat woke her at two every morning; the ideas she scribbled at that time, without the usual daily distractions, became poems she treasured.

Once you have a kernel of an idea, a motivating desire to express something, you have begun the process of making a book. All that you need to do is explore your idea through practice. Let your hands move, and your mind will follow.

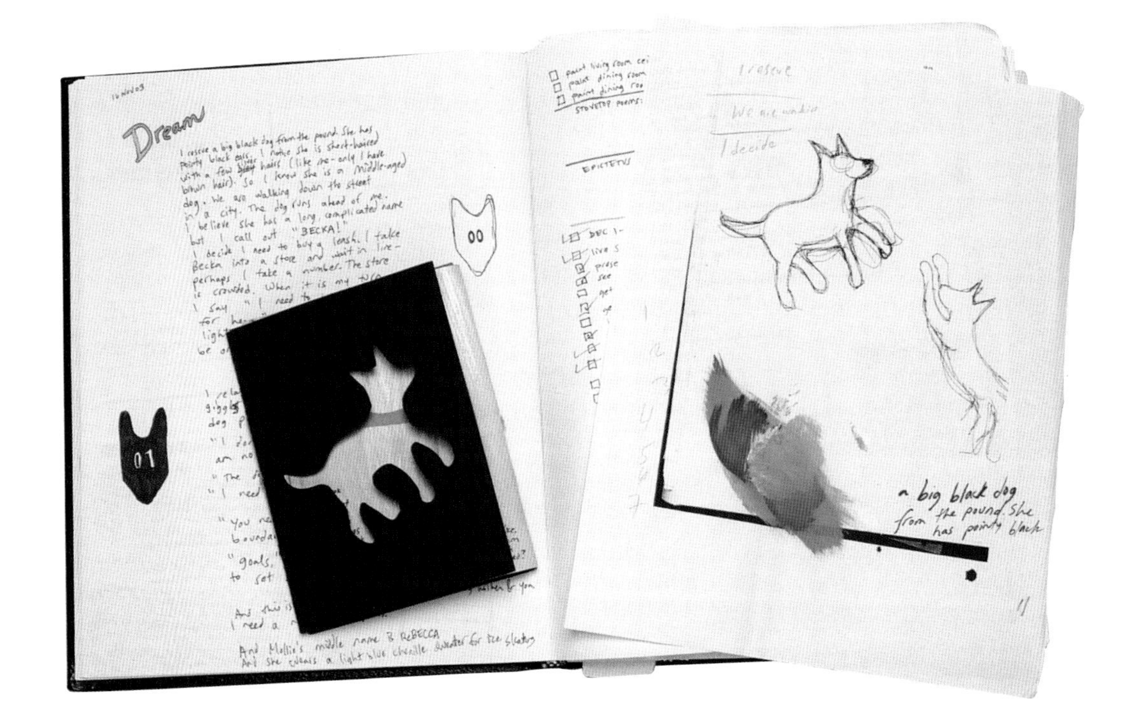

Journal with notes and *Blue Leash for a Black Dog*, 2004

Beginning with Form

Try choosing a form that will enhance your content and help tell your story, giving more meaning to what you have to say. Or use materials that reflect the content in a subtle way; try using watercolors in a book about the sea, for example. Use matches or crayons when making a book about fire.

You can start with any kind of materials so that you understand the process, but you will be more satisfied if you use good materials for the final project. I call this preliminary step "sketching," even though I am not drawing. Part of the sketching procedure may include printer paper and clear tape, materials I seldom use. As you stick things onto pages of a crudely made structure, your interior monologue will go something like: "Okay, I'll put this paragraph on this page and draw a little picture there." Sketching the book is a cautious approach. On the other hand, I often learn something surprising by just taking the materials in hand and charging ahead.

When you have a rough sketch that satisfies you, make a mock-up, or dummy, of your final project, using the paper and some of the materials you plan to use. At this stage you will find out whether the paper is too thick or thin, whether the inks bleed or are sticky, and discover other irritants of this nature.

About Tools and Materials

In every culture and throughout history, people have used the materials that were most easily available to them to make books; those near rivers used clay, for example. Whatever you do, you will be happier if you use tools and materials suited to your task. If you wish to make art that will last longer than a few years, school glue, tape, and construction paper simply won't hold up. The glue warps, the tape yellows, and the paper tears easily. When you can, use glue and wheat paste that are formulated for book-making.

Even within the realm of art papers there is thrift and extravagance. For the books I describe in the chapters that follow, you may be decorating the paper, so a good quality, inexpensive paper is appropriate. If the cost still seems out of your budget, decide what your goals are. Change your medium if you need to.

Tools for Bookbinding

Having a physical place where you can sit down at any time and make something is just as important as having ideas, journals, and tools. Find a place that can remain permanently your spot. The larger your work area, the larger the book you can make. Most of the structures in this book are small and can be made in an area approximately three feet by two feet. If you don't have a permanent spot, put all the tools in one box or bin so they are convenient and easy to get to. The quicker the set-up time, the more time you will have to create something fun. The following is a list of suggested tools:

- self-healing cutting mat
- #1 X-Acto or art knife and a package of spare #11 blades
- utility knife with retractable blade and spare blades (to cut boards)
- bookbinding needle, or a package of repair needles that contains a strong needle with a medium-size eye
- waxed linen thread, macramé thread, and/or strong thread that doesn't stretch or break when you pull on it; and a small cake of beeswax or a candle stub
- sharp scissors

- pencil and pencil sharpener
- metal ruler (12" is good for most projects, 24" is handy to help you cut large sheets of paper)
- awl or ice pick
- binder clip, small bulldog clip, or paper clips
- self-adhesive linen tape (often used for framing)
- bone folder (bone or plastic, with two flat sides and at least one pointed end)
- PVA (polyvinyl acetate, a glue especially for bookbinding)
- 3⁄16" spacing bar (look in a hardware store for this, usually made of metal) or a one-foot length of 3⁄16" dowel (so you won't have to measure the space between boards for a hardcover binding)
- wide-mouthed plastic container, such as a cottage-cheese container
- stack of old magazines or catalogs (to use as scrap paper when gluing)
- glue brush or stencil brush (flat bottomed, round, approximately 1"–2" in diameter)
- waxed paper
- 2–10 Masonite boards, smooth on both sides (to help flatten the projects)
- heavy book or dictionary to put on top of the boards to help flatten the projects

Useful Media for Writing and Making Images

Your own handwriting is unique, expressive, and suitable for many kinds of projects. To vary the design of your pages, add stamped or stenciled words or images. If you are using archival paper to make your books, you may want to use pens with archival ink or other archival media. In this case, archival usually means lightfast and waterproof. Here are some suggestions:

- rubber-stamp alphabets and stamp pads (pigment, not dye)
- alphabet stencils (several sizes and styles from 1⁄4" to 2", cardboard and plastic)
- archival pens such as Sakura Gelly Roll, Sakura Pigma Micron pens, or Faber-Castell Pitt artist pens (superfine or brush)
- acrylic gesso (white or other colors)
- acrylic inks and variety of brushes (inexpensive 1" and 2" wide; flat brushes and stencil brushes)
- acrylic heavy gel medium (gloss)

Assorted stencils and books, 2003–04: *Word Book Encyclopaedia, Maine Journal, Tell Yell, Again*

About Paper

Since you will be carefully crafting a book, choosing the right paper is important. You want to make something that will withstand handling and not fall apart over time. For this reason I suggest that you use papers that are created to endure, such as those made out of cotton rag, or kozo, also known as mulberry bark fiber. Other fine papers that are specified as "archival" or "acid-free" may be used. Be aware that products in general can have these labels, but no law guarantees that they will be as they claim. They are, however, certain to be better than wrapping paper and newsprint, which rapidly turn yellow and become brittle. You are taking time to create a handmade book, so choose materials that will support your efforts.

Word Book Encyclopaedia, 2003; stencils, ink, Thai mulberry paper; ledger-style side binding; unique; 3¼" × 7½"

Almost all papers have a grain, or direction in which they can be folded or torn most easily. Test the grain by gently attempting to fold the paper both horizontally and vertically; one way you will notice less resistance. The grain runs parallel to the easiest fold. Books generally need to have the grain of the paper running parallel to the spine. If the paper has no distinguishable grain, it is fine to use it either way. Handmade papers have no grain. "Grained short" means that the grain runs parallel to the shortest side of the paper. "Grained long" means that the grain runs parallel to the longest side of the paper.

For each project, you will find the size of the paper followed by (short) for grained short or (long) for grained long.

Ultralightweight Paper

20–45 grams per square meter
Feather-light papers are beautiful and come in many decorative colors and styles but they are not very durable over time. They fold, wrinkle, and tear easily. It is difficult to use adhesives or wet media with them. Even so, you can adhere them to other stronger papers to cover boards for an interesting layered effect. I glued little words between layers of paper for *Word Book Encyclopaedia.*
Types: Thai Unryu, Thai Mulberry, glassine
Suggested uses: folded double for side-bound books, adhered to a lightweight or medium-weight paper to cover boards; sew glassine into books: adhesives other than a glue stick are not recommended for glassine

Egg Hunts a Bird, 2004; acrylic inks and gesso, handmade stencils; multiple-signature binding; unique; 5¼" × 7⅛"

Lightweight Paper

45–85 grams per square meter
These papers work very well when covering boards. They are often patterned or colored and make nice endpapers, or endsheets. Print or decorate the solid-colored sheets according to your own color or pattern preference. They accept rubber-stamp ink and acrylic inks or gesso. Unless otherwise noted, they are a shade of white.
Types: Lama Li Bright (Lokta paper, many colors), Owara Mulberry, Kochi, Kozo, Mingei-Shi, Kitakata, Yatsuo, 20-lb. bond paper, origami paper
Suggested uses: endpapers, folded double for side-bound books, covering boards

Medium-weight or Text-weight

85–160 grams per square meter
These papers have the same feel as papers found in a store-bought hard-cover novel. They are opaque and can be folded repeatedly. In a sewn Western-style book you can use four sheets per signature. Use single unfolded sheets for an Asian-style side-bound book. The colored papers are slightly heavier and are commonly used as endpapers even in commercially printed books. The colored papers are frequently referred to as "pastel papers," for use with chalks.

Wood and Marble Pocket Model, 2004; acrylic inks, gesso, distressed board covers; pocket flag book; unique; 4" × 5¾"

Types: Rives lightweight, 100% cotton résumé paper, Superfine Text, Nideggan, Frankfurt, Arches Wove Text (Velin Arches), 24-lb. bond paper, glossy magazine pages
Colored papers: Canson Mi-Teintes (not fadeproof), German Ingres, Fabriano Tiziano, Nideggan (straw-colored only), Rives lightweight
Suggested uses: text for a sewn book, single sheets in a side-bound book

These Trees, 2003: acrylic inks and gesso, brush pens; circle accordion; unique; 5" × 5½"

Heavyweight

160–300 grams per square meter
Use heavyweight paper for the outer wrapper of a softcover book. It accepts inks, paints, and adhesives well without buckling. It is strong enough to support collages or photographs. Look for it in the printmaking and watercolor sections of art supply stores or art supply catalogs. The papers come in a limited selection of pale colors and, occasionally, black. For small books, an alternative to heavyweight printmaking watercolor paper is 65 lb. (175 grams per square meter) commercial cover stock.
Types: Lenox (white only), Rising Stonehenge, Somerset, 90-lb. Fabriano Artistico watercolor paper, Arches cover, Rives BFK
Suggested uses: accordion-folded books, circle accordions, soft covers, text paper of a pamphlet with only two pages

These Trees, 2003; open

Book Cloth

An easy way to give a hardcover book an important appearance is to use book cloth. Book cloth is a treated cloth that has paper adhered to one side, which makes it easier to handle than cloth alone. Glue does not seep through the weave. You can mark it and see the markings. It has a medium weight and it is quite durable. When working with book cloth you will need to use wheat paste only or a mixture of paste and PVA; PVA alone can leave shiny spots on it.

Book cloth itself is not magic, but it transforms a book, making it look more like something you might get in a standard bookstore. This may or may not be the effect you desire. As always, choose your material to enhance and support your message.

Boards

Boards for use in bookmaking are usually made of layers of thick paper. Two-ply or 4-ply museum boards are 100% cotton, archival, and do not yellow, so I prefer them. But you may also use book or Davey board or illustration board. Poster board is not archival or thick enough by itself for larger books, but you could use it for the split-board binding or for

Z10: Scrabble Album, 2003; photographs, gel pen; single signature; unique; 7¼" × 5"

miniature books. The larger the book, the thicker the board needs to be. For a larger book you might use Davey board, also called book board; it is made from sulfite pulp that has been buffered to help resist acids in the environment, and residue from your hands.

Measuring

To make a satisfactory book you need to be precise when you measure. It is true that these projects include a lot of numbers. Covers and pages need to align. Box lids need to fit. Measure carefully and you will be happy with the construction results.

Scoring, Folding, Cutting

Before you make a score, mark your paper lightly with a very sharp pencil. Make one mark at each end of where you want the score. Use a ruler and line up the marks. Then, with the pointed end of a bone folder, your thumbnail, or a butter knife, press a line into the paper, using the ruler as a guide.

You can fold paper with or without scoring it first. If you need to fold paper exactly in half, there is no need to score, unless the paper is of an extremely heavy weight. Match two corners and align the edges of the paper that are perpendicular to the desired fold. Press down and hold the corners. With the side of your other hand or a bone folder, smooth and crease the paper from the corner diagonally toward the fold. Work progressively toward the top of the paper. The bone folder is useful to make tight finishing creases.

Frequently, the directions say, "fold widthwise" or "fold lengthwise." This means that the fold is parallel to the width or to the length of the paper.

Always use a metal ruler as a guide when you cut paper: plastic and wood can become nicked by the knife and give a wobbly cut. Cork-backed rulers don't slip, but be aware of the extra thickness from the cork. Press firmly on the ruler and keep your fingers behind the edge! You may find it easier to make cuts while you are standing.

To protect your work surface, you will need a self-healing cutting mat under your project. You can use cardboard instead, but it doesn't last long. Use a sharp knife. Don't try to be thrifty with your knife blades; a sharp blade is always best for a clean cut. You will need a large package of extra blades; once the tip has broken off, the blade should be replaced.

If you really like working with paper, think about investing in a paper cutter. A 24" cutter is invaluable when working with the 22" × 30" paper, and may be sturdy enough to cut museum boards as well. A smaller, 12" cutter with a rotating blade is also handy, and you can replace the blades easily when they become dull. Whatever cutter you purchase, make sure it has a ruler printed on it; you can measure and cut at the same time, leaving less chance for error and irritation. A grid and clamping bar are also handy.

Adhesives

Only specific types of adhesives should be used when you are making a handmade book, assuming that you want it to endure over time. Always decant small amounts of liquid adhesives like PVA and paste into a separate container or onto a paper plate. Don't dip your brush into the main batch. Hairs from the brush or fibers from your papers or cloth can get into the adhesive and cause mold to grow, which is not desirable.

Before You Glue

When working with liquid adhesives such as paste or PVA, to avoid spots and sticky messes, you need to pay careful attention to make sure that the glue is going only where you want it to go. First, you need a magazine or catalog with glossy pages. Take out the staples. Arrange the sheets in front of you as if you were dealing cards: make one slightly overlapping layer from two sheets, then put another layer atop the first. Give yourself two to four layers, depending on how many pieces of your book project need to be glued. Put a small amount (approximately ¼–½ cup or 50–100 ml) of your paste or glue on a paper plate. Take out your stencil brush. Get a damp cloth or paper towel ready in case you get glue on your fingers. Now you have your materials.

Before you begin, be aware of the location of the brush, the glue, and the damp cloth. You don't want to inadvertently dip your project into them. Once you begin applying the glue, keep close watch on any glue that gets onto the glossy scrap paper. Once glue is on the scrap paper, slide the scrap paper out carefully, crumple it up, and discard it. Always fold or crumple it first so that the glue is on the inside. A small bit of glue on the scrap paper can easily smudge your book, making a sad little spot. You can walk down a crowded street without bumping into people because you know where your body is in space and you know where the other people are; so, too, you need to be aware of where your glue is in relation to your project. Work as cleanly as you can.

PVA: Polyvinyl Acetate

PVA, a white glue, is especially formulated to dry fast and be flexible. It often contains a preservative, which discourages mold from growing in your project. While it looks like the school glue you can buy in the supermarket, it has much less water in it. PVA can be bought at many art supply or bookbinding supply stores and through catalogs. Use it when you are gluing small areas. Spread it thinly and evenly with a stencil brush or a piece of board to prevent bulges in your paper. It is not possible to reposition your project should you make an alignment mistake, so work swiftly and carefully. A mistaken dot of glue on book cloth cannot be removed without leaving a shiny spot in its place. However, once you feel confident with adhesives you can use this glue in almost any situation. Mix it with wheat paste to give it more time to dry and allow you to work a bit more slowly.

Wheat Paste

Use wheat paste when gluing paper to boards, book cloth to boards, or when backing cloth. The advantage of wheat paste is that it dries more slowly, allowing you to reposition your boards if needed. If you get a spot of paste on your paper that shouldn't be there, you have time to wipe it off. Just watch out for water spots. Mix wheat paste with PVA to make it tackier, more flexible, and dry faster.

I mix my own wheat paste from a powder that I buy from Daniel Smith, Inc. in Seattle, Washington. You need clean water and a clean pint container. Add one teaspoon of powder at a time to the water and stir well between additions. It may be slightly lumpy. Keep adding powder until you reach the thickness that you can spread with a brush but that doesn't run. The paste thickens after about thirty minutes, so start by making it slightly thinner than you need. You can strain it with a small metal kitchen strainer, if you wish, but don't use this strainer for food. You can also brush the lumps to the side if you work from a paper plate.

Mounting Paper

Occasionally you will have a project that calls for an ultralightweight paper to be backed by a lightweight or medium-weight paper for strength. For example, a translucent paper with swirling colored fibers really would look great as your cover, but it is too fragile for this purpose. To add strength, apply wheat paste or a PVA/paste mixture to the stronger sheet. Leave the stronger sheet on the table. Pick up the ultralightweight paper and hold it in a "U"-shape, centering this sheet on top of the sticky sheet. Gently lower

Left: *Three Birds*, 2001; monotype; 6" × 8"
Right: *Cloud Over Absence*, 2003–04; blank album; pieced and quilted cover; unique; 12" × 14" × ¾"

the top sheet in place. Place waxed paper over the two sheets of paper; press and smooth out gently. Either remove the waxed paper and let the decorative papers air-dry or place a Masonite board on top.

Backing Cloth

Backing cloth is similar to mounting paper but uses paste only, no PVA. Another difference is that you will work on a surface that can be damp, such as a kitchen counter or plastic-coated table or tablecloth. Wash and iron your cloth first if it has any deep creases. Wrinkles are okay. Put your cloth right-side down. Using a spray bottle, spray a light mist of water over the cloth. Smooth it out. Apply paste to a piece of lightweight paper, such as mulberry. Carefully pick up this sticky, lightweight paper, hold it in a "U"-shape, paste-side down, and center the sheet on top of the cloth. Gently lower the paper in place. Place waxed paper over the paper-backed cloth; press and smooth out gently with your hands, a bone folder, or a baren, a wide, flat smoothing tool usually used for printing woodcuts by hand. You may be able to smooth it out without the waxed paper.

Keeping the Paper Flat

After you use an adhesive, put the book or papers under a heavy weight to dry. The pressure helps ensure that all surfaces will stick together and that the paper will dry flat. Always place waxed paper between the boards and whatever you have glued. For books, make sure that you use waxed paper between the endpapers and the text block so that the pages won't stick together and the moisture from the glue doesn't cause the pages to buckle. Use smooth-sided Masonite boards on top and below your project, then place a heavy book or brick on top of the boards. For a deep box, you can try putting smaller weights on the bottom, but you may just let it air-dry.

About This Book

Almost every chapter comes with its own concept, a theme that you can think about. The projects that follow may be used with that theme or with an idea of your own. A section called "Preparation" heads many of the projects to help you begin. It is not mandatory to do the preparation, but it will help you make a complete, expressive book, not just a blank book. Suggestions and materials for covers are listed at the end of each project.

It is possible that you have seen some of these structures before. I've tried to use existing structures and refine them so that they are satisfying, both to the maker and to the reader. After exploring many ways to bind a book, I see that slight variations in an established structure may be all that is needed to make a unique book. Time shows us why certain bindings thrive and others are discarded; quality of materials, ease of creation, and satisfaction to the reader are all reasons some book structures live longer than others. Most of these bindings are elegant and not too fussy. Ideally they will enhance your story but not distract from your art and writing. Sometimes the structures seem like puzzles to master; once you complete one, it may seem like time to leave it behind and move on. But the structure is only the container. It isn't a whole book. My hope is that the bindings presented are a variety of simple, intermediate, and more challenging ones, taking into account that each reader has a different level of skill or past experience.

Each project lists a different binding, but eventually you may find that one binding will work better for one of the other projects instead. All projects are suggestions for ways to work with your creative energy and your personal stories. Included here are twenty five distinctive book projects. In addition, many more variations, ideas, suggestions, and supporting techniques are provided.

This book is designed for both the absolute beginner and the serious artist looking for new inspiration. Whatever your level, this book will help you find new approaches to your work and suggest projects to help you rediscover your creativity. As you work, be bold: take risks, and try writing or drawing. You can use prepared images such as store-bought decorated paper, but you can also make your own. There is no limit to the number and variety of books you can create from your emotional experiences. You'll get an idea of how to begin to express yourself meaningfully.

Key to Diagrams

Some of the symbols used here are different from ones I have used previously. One of my testers noted that origami enthusiasts use a universal system of paper-folding symbols, written down by Akira Yoshizawa in the 1940s. At this time I am revising my symbol for "peak" (or mountain) fold and the symbol for "turn the paper over" to correspond to the origami symbols. An additional symbol for "push here," in this book, almost always indicates a time when you need to tuck a tiny bit of the paper around the corners as you cover a board with paper.

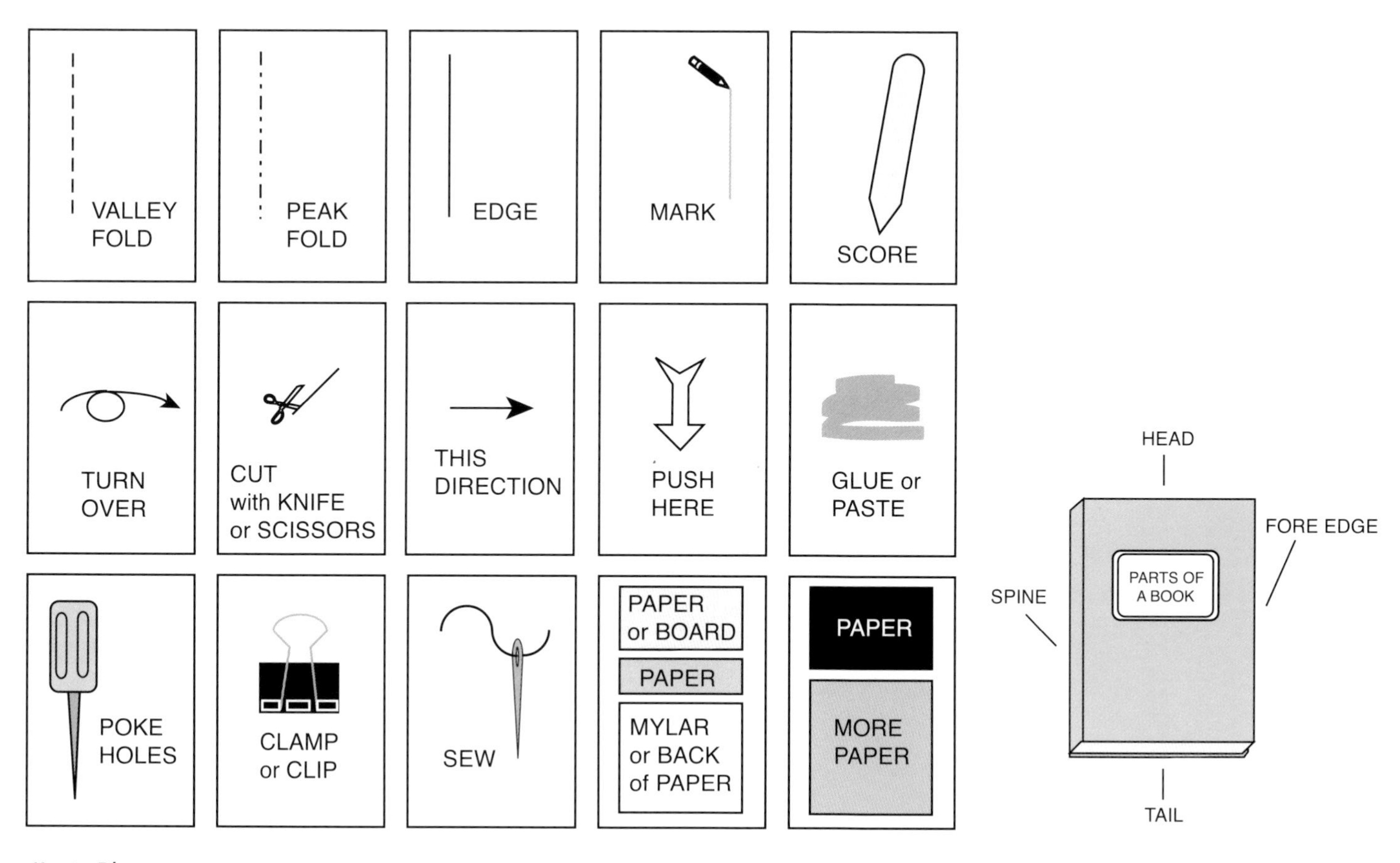

Key to Diagrams

Parts of a Book

Chapter Two

PLAY IT AGAIN: CIRCLE ACCORDIONS

Circle Accordions
Back row (left to right): *Serene; In My Living Room; Woody's Birthday Book, Sea Star*
Front row: *First Response*

A book doesn't have to be complicated to be interesting. Circle accordions require no sewing; they simply use self-adhesive linen tape to bind the pages together. Because of the thick paper and the folds, just a few pages get you a thick book. With a little paper-folding and a little tape, you can make a satisfying book in a short amount of time.

Self-adhesive linen cloth tape is made primarily for hinging mats when framing artwork, but it works well for bookbinding. The kind I buy is made by Lineco, a company that specializes in archival and acid-free materials. It is repositionable when you first work with it. The cloth stays white (unless you have painted it otherwise), and the adhesive becomes permanent over time. For reasons of economy, you may cut the $1\frac{1}{4}$" wide tape in half, lengthwise, and use strips that are $\frac{5}{8}$" wide.

Unless you are working in a school setting where cost is a major factor, consider using the cloth tape. Clear tape and masking tape turn yellow and discolor your paper. Either the adhesive loses its tack and the tape falls off or it is so sticky you will ruin the paper if you try to take it apart.

An alternative to tape is strips of paper and PVA. The advantages are: you can cut the paper to whatever size you need; you can use a colored paper to complement your book; and paper may be less expensive. Be sure to use a paper that is strong, with long fibers, like handmade paper or mulberry paper. A lightweight pastel paper may also be appropriate. In a non-archival setting, strips cut from magazines or catalogs will also work.

Once and Always: Choosing Content

How do you think about what will go into your books? Some stories are interesting the first time only. Some keep you engaged, and you keep coming back to them. You might use the circle structure to contain content of this engaging circular nature. I include the taped structures in my instructional books not only because they are so simple but because just about any theme will work with them.

A man and a woman are trying to teach a computer about jokes. They decide that there are two classifications: funny once and funny always. They realize that the element of surprise is a key ingredient. Will the listener be surprised again? This is a scene in the book *The Moon Is a Harsh Mistress* by Robert A. Heinlein. Although that book was written in 1966, the concept is still relevant today. We can relate it to book art and say that we try to make books that are "funny always." By this I mean that there are many layers to the text, images, and structure that can be revealed only after multiple readings. In short, there is always a surprise, something new to inspire you each time you return.

It is easy to make a funny-once book: a mix-and-match book or a book of rough sketches on sandpaper, for example. After the reader gets the joke, however, he or she may move right along and forget about it, like much of our disposable culture today. Even a book that is very clever and doesn't provide something new or surprising at the next look may still be endearing if enough heart and feeling were put into it from the beginning, thus transforming it into a funny-always book. A book that takes time to make deserves a message that takes time to savor.

You can create book art in at least two ways. One way is to work from a feeling and let the viewer bring his or her own experiences to the work. Another way is to plan your information carefully and present it clearly and succinctly so that the viewer has no doubt at all about what it is. You can work from your heart or from your head or somewhere in between.

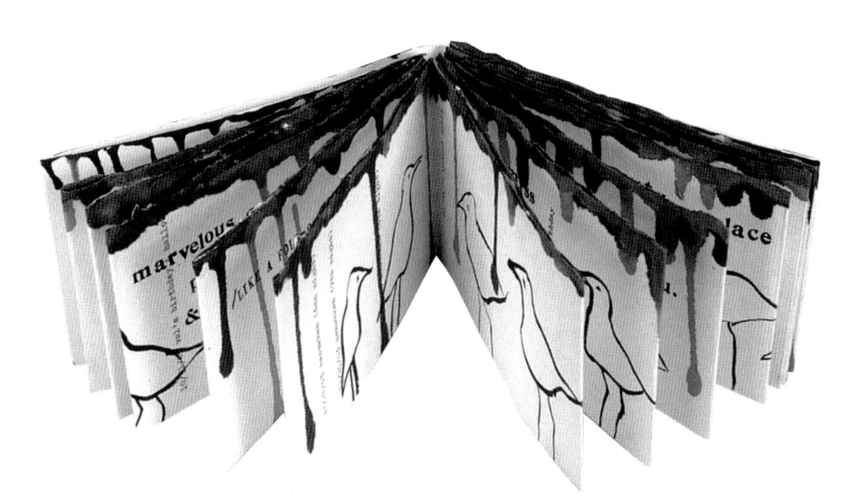

Left: *Rain Check*, 2003; typewriter, ink, rubber stamps; circle accordion; unique; 6" × 3½"
Right: *Rain Check*, open

Adding Words

If you paint the paper first with acrylic inks, you may write the words by hand or use alphabet stencils or alphabet rubber stamps to copy your words onto the pages. If your pages are dark, use white or light-colored gel pens or white rubber-stamp ink for best results.

You may choose to begin with a title page, which serves as an introduction; however, this is not necessary for a very short book. Add text where it seems appropriate. If one page looks too interesting to write upon, double up your lines and put two words/phrases on the next page. You don't have to write in straight lines; if you paint the paper first, follow the flow of your painting to produce a more organic effect.

To complete your book, make sure you put a title on the front cover. Put your name either on the front cover or inside the back cover. You could put the date, your initials, seal, or personal stamp, centered on the back cover. Another option is to add your title and last name to the spine.

Circle Accordion

Time: 30–45 minutes
For *Rain Check* I typed all the important holidays for one year on the accordion strips, then taped them together. Afterward I added the painted birds, the dribbled ink, and the rubber-stamped text. It is about the whole first year after the death of my son, Ezra, and how he would miss each of the holidays and how we would miss *him.*

My mother-in-law told me how she started repeating the word *serene* to help get to sleep, which inspired me to make the book *Serene.* To anchor each word on the page, making it less likely to float, I drew horizontal pencil lines, painted my pages like a calm ocean, and rubber-stamped a single word on each spread above a line. Each of the words is made out of letters from the word *serene.* It begins with the title, then says: "see/seer/seen/ere/serene/serene/serene." Reading it repeatedly produces a calming effect.

Tools: bone folder, pencil, 24" metal ruler, scissors or art knife and cutting mat, stencil brush
Materials: one 22" × 30" (long) sheet of printmaking or drawing paper, five 6" lengths of self-adhesive linen tape, two to four colors of regular or pearlescent acrylic ink (in blues and greens)
Example: 5¼" × 6" book

Preparation: Think about water: ocean, waves, rapids, streams, tears, rain, pools, tide pools, rivers, creeks, faucet. Choose one form of water that appeals to you.

1. Put the large paper vertically in front of you on a surface that may get messy. You can turn it the other way but be aware that if you want horizontal waves in the finished book, they will have to be parallel with the short edge of the large paper. The diagram for steps 4, 5 illustrates how the paper will be cut.
2. Use the dropper tip or dribble a little of one ink color sparingly but randomly on the paper. Use the stencil brush to brush out the puddles. Keep your water theme in mind as you cover the paper in blues and greens. You can leave white spaces. The more varied the paper becomes, the more

Serene, 2003; acrylic inks, graphite, rubber stamps; circle accordion; unique; 5¼" × 6"

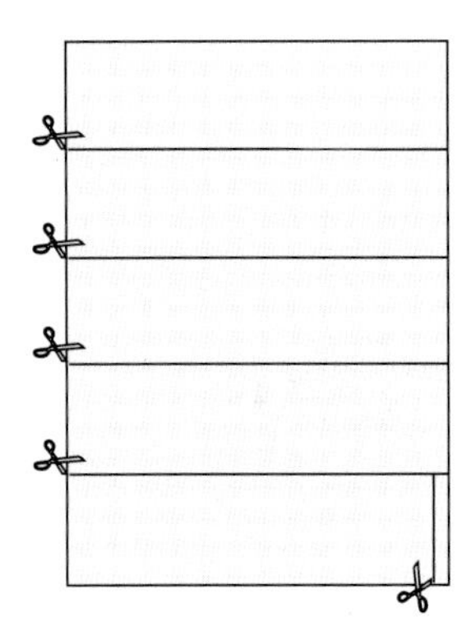
Steps 4, 5

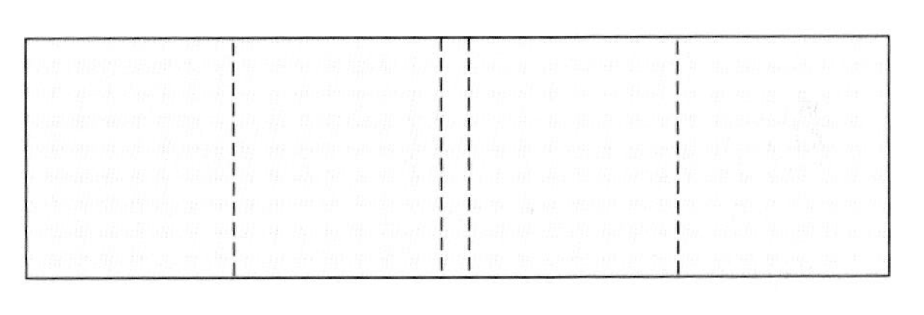
Steps 6, 7

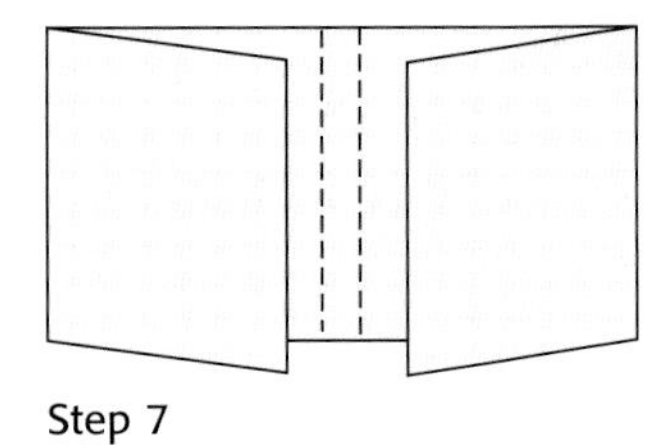
Step 7

interesting your book will be. A pattern is not necessary. Let dry. If your paper is very wet, it may take up to an hour to dry. On a warm day, or with less ink, drying time could be as short as 15 minutes.

3. While waiting for the paper to dry, make a list of at least fifteen words or phrases that describe the water, your feelings connected to this water, or anything else that relates to water or the painting you just did. Put the words/phrases in an order that appeals to you. Set the list aside.

Assembling the Book

4. Cut the large paper into 6" × 22" strips. You should have five strips.

5. Pick one strip of paper to be your cover. Cut off ½" to make it 6" × 21½".

6. Measure, mark, and score 10½" from each edge of the cover paper (on the undecorated side). You should have a ½" spine in the center.

7. Fold each edge in to the closest center fold. You may want to score the paper first at the 5¼" mark.

8. With the remaining strips, trim 1" off the edges to create four strips that are each 6" × 21".

9. Fold one strip in half, widthwise, decorations inside. Crease it well with a bone folder.

10. Keeping the paper folded, bring one open end back to the folded edge.

11. Turn the paper over and bring the other open end to the folded edge.

12. Repeat steps 9–11 for the remaining three strips.

13. Make sure the pieces of linen tape are slightly shorter than the height of your book. Trim them if necessary. Remove the backing from one piece of tape. Center the tape so that half of it attaches to the edge of the cover and half remains available and sticky.

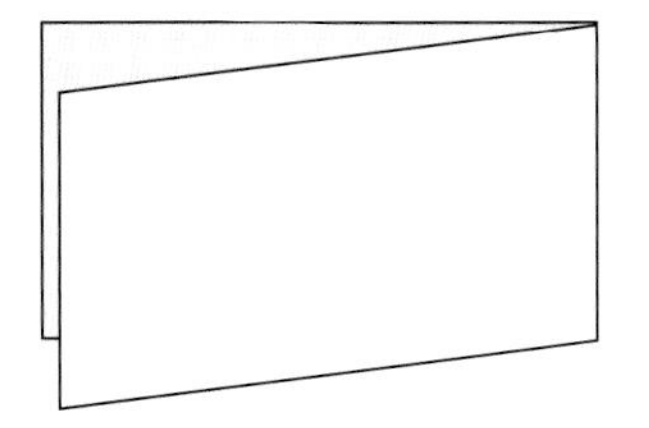
Step 9

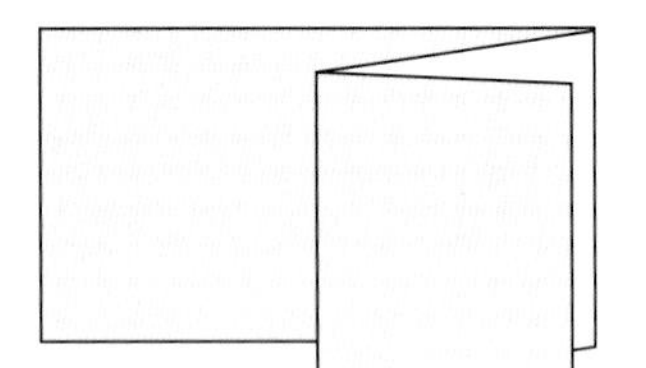
Step 10

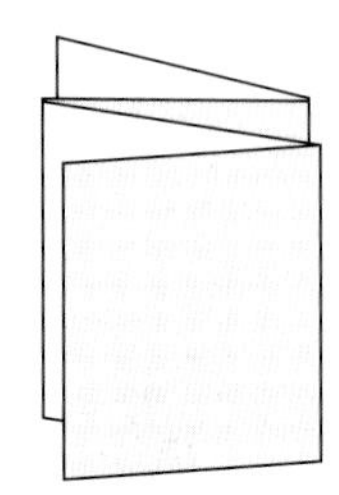
Step 11

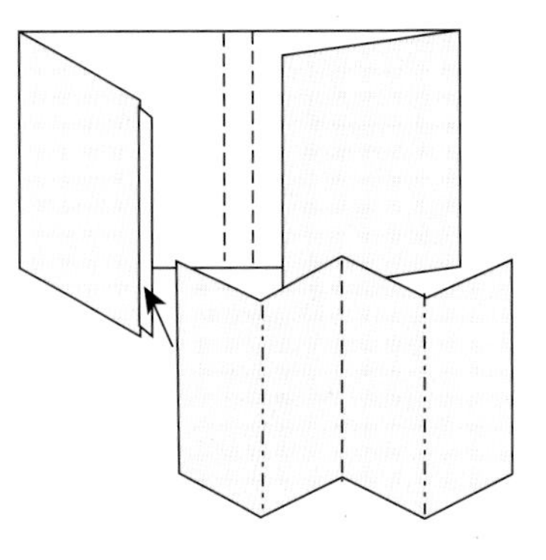
Steps 13, 14

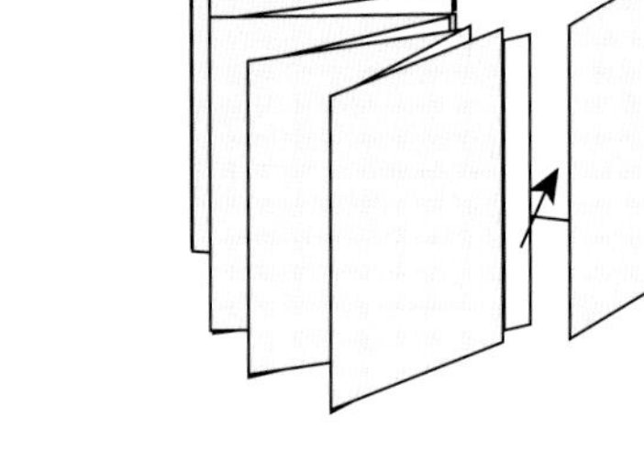
Step 15

14. Attach the next page by aligning it with the cover and pressing down on the available half of tape.
15. Continue to tape and attach pages until you get to the last one. Tape the last page to the back edge of the cover in the same manner.

Variation 1: Distressed Notebook. A circle accordion also makes a terrific 5" × 7" notebook. It is light and good for travel. The trick to this notebook is to mess up the pages ahead of time so that the bright white paper is not intimidating. You can scribble with watercolor pencils or crayons and use water to blend the marks. Draw a few parallel pencil lines here and there. Use black acrylic gesso and scribble in it. Dip a paper cup in gold gesso and make cup rings on the pages. Use stencils and add random letters and numbers. The main thing is to break in the notebook so you will actually use it. For a 5" × 7" notebook, use four pieces of heavyweight paper, 7" × 20" (short); one piece of heavy black paper for the covers, 7" × 20½" (short); five pieces of 1¼" × 6¾" self-adhesive linen tape. Follow the instructions for the Circle Accordion. When measuring the cover for the folds of step 6, mark at 10" from either end, thus allowing for a ½" spine.

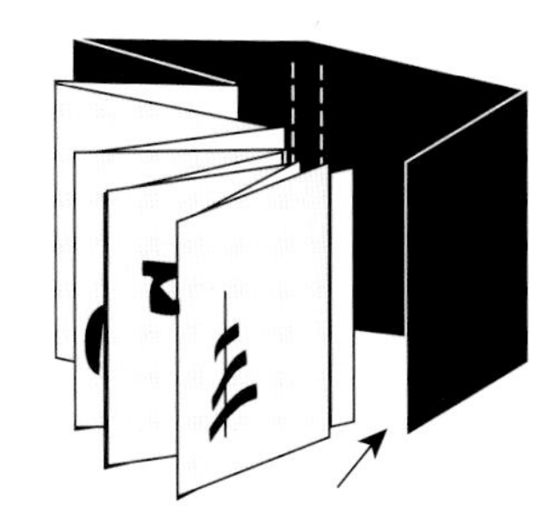

Variation 1

Distressed Notebooks, 2003–04; gesso, graphite, collage, watercolor; circle accordions; 5" × 7"

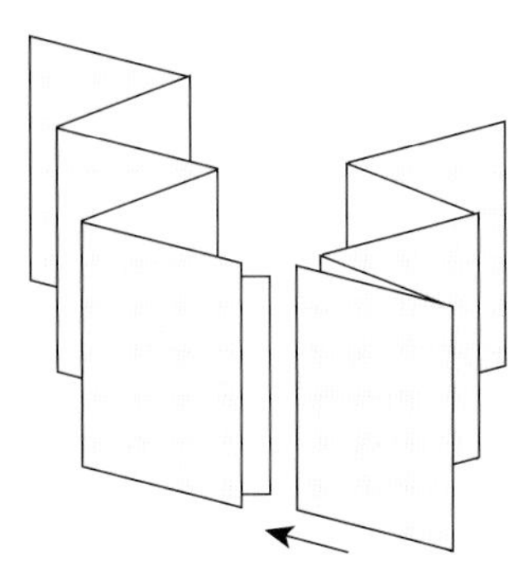

Variation 2a

Note: Make several notebooks to keep in a box. I use one notebook regularly; when I've filled it up I make a new one in a slightly different style. It is really fun to mess up the pages. Just make sure you give yourself plenty of white space in which to write. You might also paint the pages with dark inks and use a white gel pen on top of ink-painted pages. Five books of this size will fit into the Photograph or Notebook Box on page 42.

Variation 2: Circle-Star Accordion. *Sea Star* is a poem about finding a stranded starfish, putting it back in the water to live again, and watching it move so slowly. I made a sturdy portfolio to keep it protected. I painted the paper of the book to match some dyed, batiked paper someone had given me. I also glued some of the dyed paper to my painted paper as jellybean-like pebbles. Make a connection between your materials and integrate them to unify the book and make your decisions look purposeful.

Use two pieces of medium- to heavy-weight paper 5½" × 18¾" (short); two 5½" lengths of self-adhesive linen tape. Make two accordions with five panels. For each, accordion-fold one panel, then fold the other panels as if you were folding a standard four-panel accordion by measuring, marking, and scoring 3¾" from the left edge to start. The two sheets will be connected at one peak and one valley.

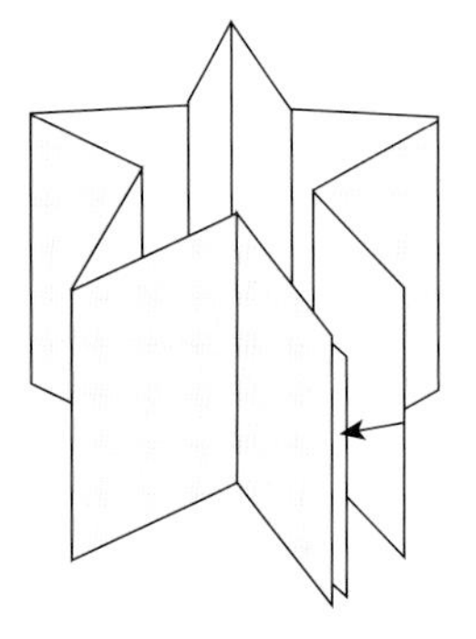

Variation 2b

Variation 3: Accordion with Irregular Panels. Instead of folding the paper into even panels, try measuring different widths, scoring, and folding the paper into irregular panels. At California College of the Arts (formerly

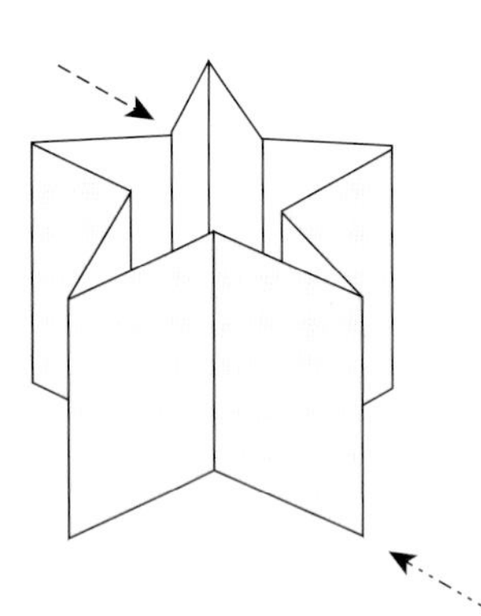

Variation 2c

Sea Star, 2003; collage, stencil, acrylic ink, batiked paper; circle-star accordion book, unique; 7½" × 5½" in portfolio, 8¼" × 6" with paper loop closure

First Response, 2003; found objects, gesso, stencil, ink; irregular accordion; unique; 7¼" × 8"

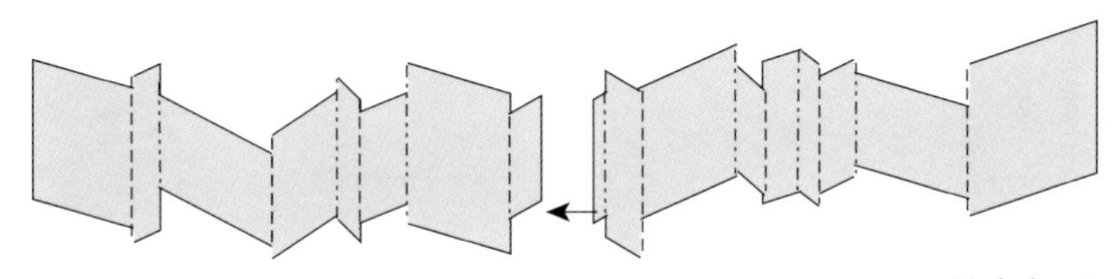

Variation 3

California College of Arts and Crafts) I went to an exhibition of the Hamaguchi Printmaking Awards and saw work by Simmin Joy Terry that quickly inspired me to make books with irregular folds. She made long, narrow prints that consisted of small rectangular images that touched only at the sides. As a result, you could not take in the entire picture at once. You started at the leftmost image and scanned to the right. It felt precisely like reading. Making a book using various sizes of image panels in place of words seemed the logical next step. *First Response* was my first response to Simmin's work as well as a personal reference to having called 911. The text is hidden on a card in a pocket. The pages are attached to a portfolio-style cover.

Circle Accordion with Pockets

Time: 60 minutes
I wanted to make a notebook as a present for my friend Woody's twenty-seventh birthday. He and his wife, Shannon, had given us a peace lily, so I painted leaves from the houseplant on one side of the paper and earth tones that I knew he liked on the other. You can also make this structure without painting the paper. Make two books with the materials listed here: one for you and one for a friend. Notice how each book is slightly different.

Tools: bone folder, pencil, 24" metal ruler, scissors or knife and cutting mat
Materials: two pieces of heavyweight paper 22" × 30" (long); one piece 22" × 14" (short); two pieces of heavyweight black paper 7" × 20¾" (short)
For the covers: ten pieces of 1¼" × 6¾" self-adhesive linen tape (five per book), acrylic inks
Example: two 5" × 7" books with eight plain sections and eight pocket sections and a ¾" spine

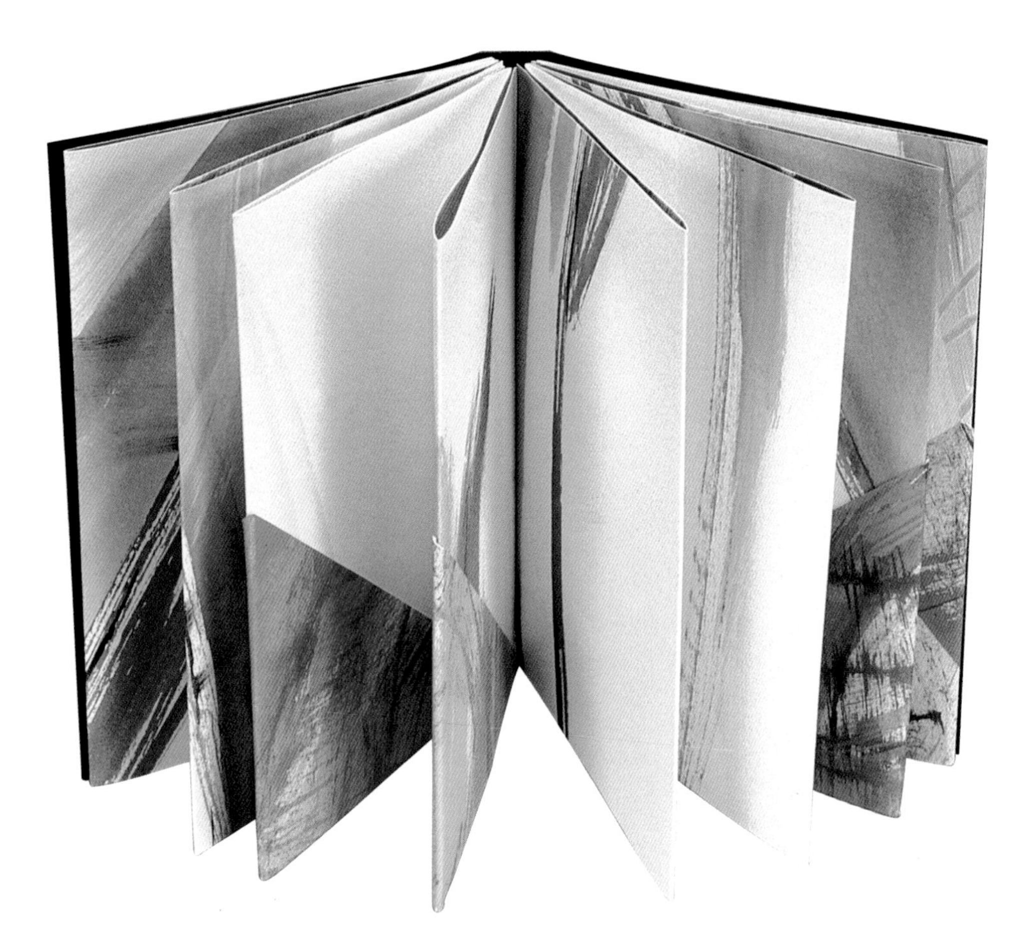

Woody's Birthday Book, 2004; acrylic inks and gesso; circle accordion with pockets; edition of two; 5" × 7"

Pocket Models, 2004; acrylic inks and gesso; circle accordion with pockets; unique; 5", 4", 3½"

Preparation: Think of someone dear to you. Imagine the colors and images this person prefers. What types of things does this person collect or have at home? What are this person's hobbies? Jot down your ideas. Keep these ideas in mind as you paint the paper.

1. Paint the white pages, front and back, with acrylic inks. Paint one side of the papers sparingly, leaving lots of white space. Let dry. Cover the other side with colors. Let dry.
2. Cut the two 22" × 30" sheets into three strips each: two 22" × 11" strips and one 22" × 7" strip, all grained short.
3. Cut the 22" × 14" sheet in half, lengthwise, to make two 22" × 7" strips.
4. Trim all eight 22"-long strips to 20" long.
5. Fold the 7" strips into accordions with four panels. Start by folding the undecorated (if applicable) side of the open paper together, then fold the open ends back to meet the folded edge. You will have 5"-wide accordion panels.

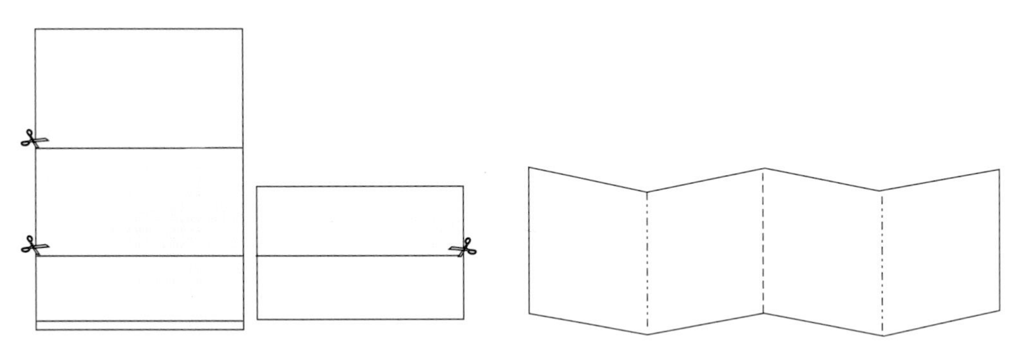

Steps 2, 3

Step 5

Swimming Fish, 2004; acrylic inks and gesso; circle accordion with pockets, case bound; unique; 5⅞ × 4⅞" × ¾"

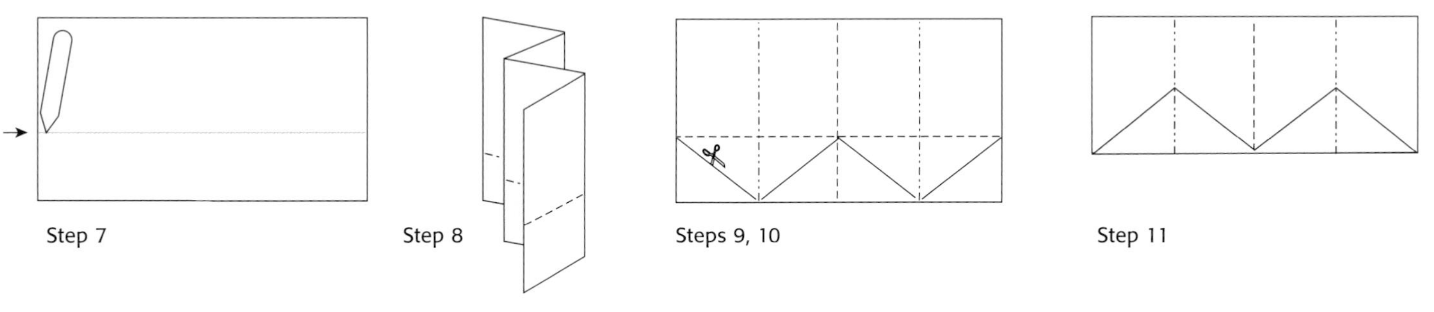

Step 7

Step 8

Steps 9, 10

Step 11

Making the Pockets

6. Arrange the 11" strips horizontally. Turn them so that the side with the least paint is up, with more of the color at the top of the strips.

7. Use the 24" ruler to measure, mark, and score a line parallel to the long side, 4" up from the bottom of each strip.

8. Fold all 11" strips into accordions with four panels. Start by folding the undecorated (if applicable) side of the paper together, then fold the open ends back to meet the folded edge. You will have 5"-wide accordion panels.

9. Open the strips. Place one strip on a cutting mat with the 4"section at the bottom. With your knife against the metal ruler for a guide, make diagonal cuts. Start from the left edge at the score, cut down to the peak fold.

10. Cut back up to the next valley fold, down to the peak fold, and back up to the right edge. You should have a zigzag shaped like a "W."

11. Fold all the triangles up along the score. Crease them to match the valley and peak folds of the flat pages: peak, valley, peak.

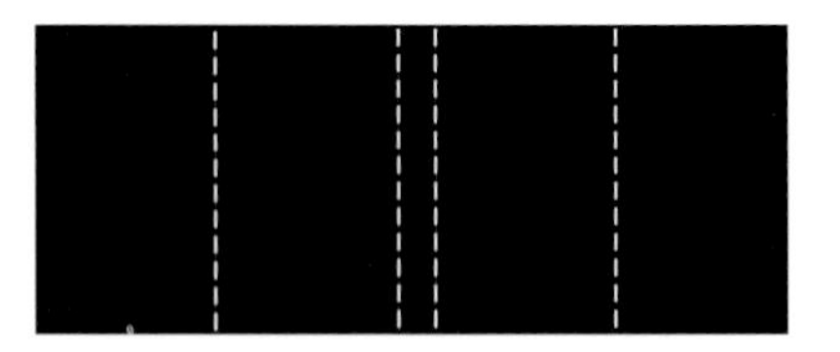

Step 12

Folding the Cover

12. Measure, mark, and score 10" from each edge of the black cover. You should have a ¾" spine in the center for a book with two pocketed strips. (If you trimmed your cover for a book with no pockets, your spine will be ½".)

13. Fold each edge in to the closest center fold. You may want to score the paper first at the 5" mark.

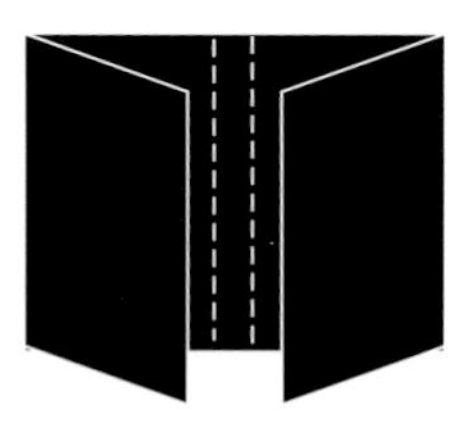

Step 13

Attaching the Pages

I alternated plain accordions with pocketed accordions, starting with a plain one. You may arrange them any way you wish as long as you use four accordions (plus the cover) for each book.

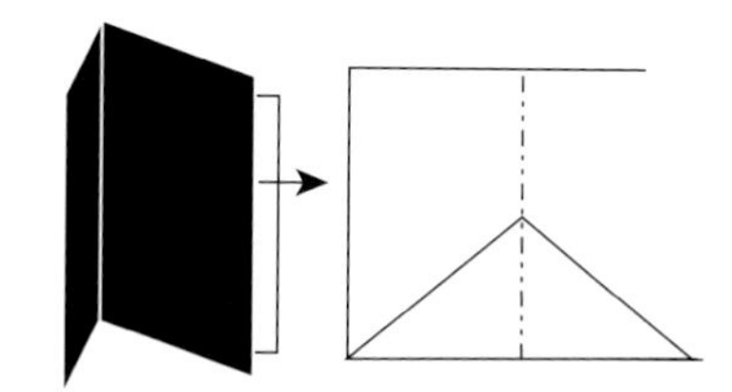

Steps 14, 15

14. Make sure the pieces of linen tape are slightly shorter than the height of your book. Trim them if necessary. Remove the backing from one piece of tape. Center the tape so that half of it attaches to the edge of the cover and half remains available and sticky.
15. Attach the next page by aligning it with the cover and pressing down on the available half of tape.
16. Continue to tape and attach pages until you get to the last one. Tape the last page to the back edge of the cover in the same manner.
17. Use a piece that you trimmed from the painted pages as a decorative image for the cover. Make sure the grain matches the long grain of the front cover by testing the smaller piece before you glue it. To test the grain, bend the small piece horizontally and vertically. Whichever way it bends more easily is the direction of the grain. If you glue it across the grain, the paper will buckle and appear wavy after it dries.
18. Repeat steps 14–17 for the second book.

Variation 1: All-Pocket Pages. Try this structure with a pocket on all pages and a 1" spine. Use two 22" × 30" sheets of heavyweight paper per book and one sheet of black paper for each cover.
Variation 2: Double Pockets. Use four sheets of paper 22" × 15" (two 22" × 30" sheets, cut in half) and fold 4" pockets both top and bottom, as in *Healing Between the Dots.*

Healing Between the Dots, 2004; drawings made with one ink line, gesso, acrylic inks; circle accordion with double pockets; unique; 5" × 7" book in 5⅝" × 7¾" × 1½" box with paper clasp hinges (box not shown)

PHOTOGRAPH OR NOTEBOOK BOX

Time: 90–120 minutes
This box holds 4" × 6" or 5" × 7" photos or cards, or it can be a container for five 5" × 7" circle accordion books or distressed notebooks. Use a lightweight paper to cover the box, inside and out, or use book cloth on the outside and a lightweight paper on the inside. Add ⅛" to the dimensions for the lid and lid cover paper if your cover paper is book cloth or of a medium weight. Construct the box first, then cover it. Use 4-ply museum board or board book to build the box. Cut boards precisely to size for best results.

Notebook Box, 2003–04;
paper, museum boards;
unique; 7½" × 5½" × 3½"

Example: 7½" × 5½" × 3½"
Tools: bone folder, pencil, 12" metal ruler, scissors, magazines or catalogs for scrap paper, PVA, brush for gluing
Materials: four strips of self-adhesive linen tape 1¼" × 5½" to reinforce the box, four strips of self-adhesive linen tape 1¼" x ½" for lid reinforcement.

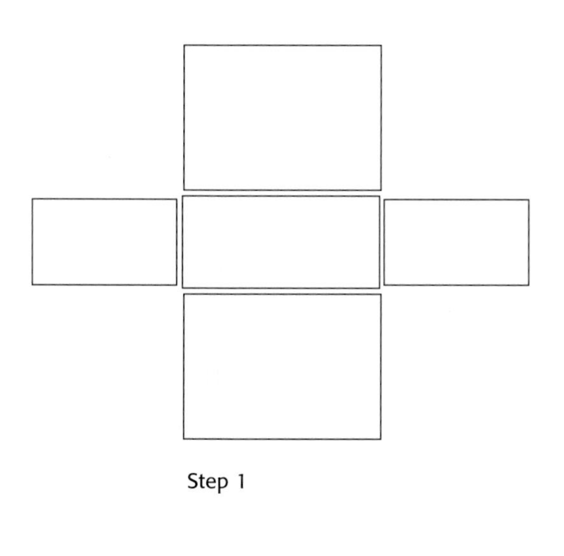

Step 1

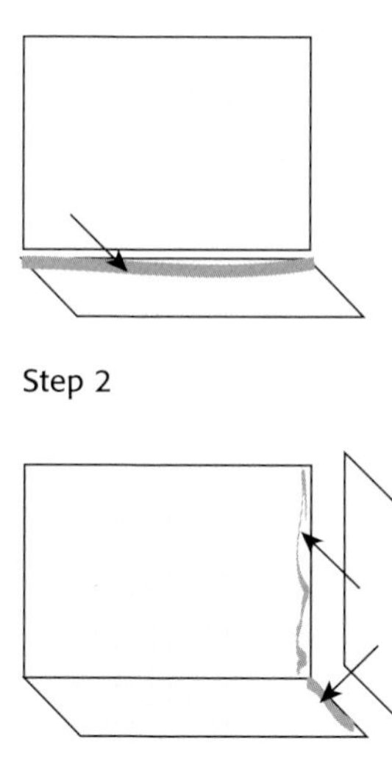

Step 2

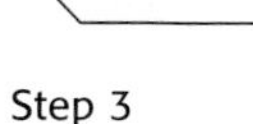

Step 3

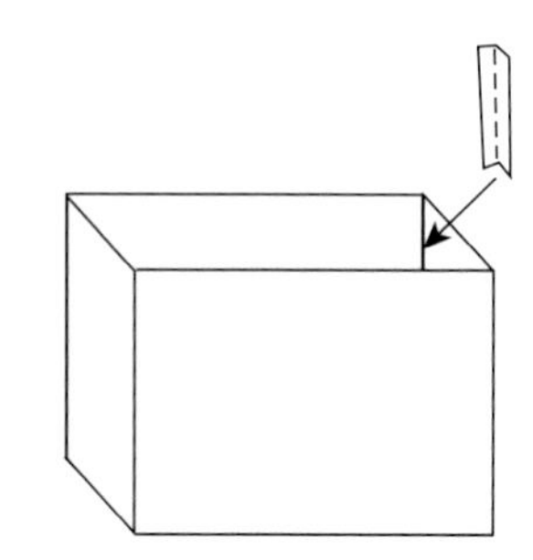

Step 5

For the base: one bottom board 7½ " × 3½" (short); two end boards 3⅜" × 5½" (long); two side boards 7½" × 5½" (short); one piece of bottom cover paper 7¼" × 3¼" (short); two pieces of end cover paper 3½" × 6½" (long); two pieces of side cover paper 8½" × 6½" (short); one piece of inner bottom paper 7¼" × 3¼" (short); two pieces of inner end papers 3¼" × 6½" (long); two pieces of inner side papers 8½" × 6½" (short)
For the lid: one top board 7¾" × 3¾" (short); two end boards 3⅝" × ½" (long); two side boards 7¾" x ½" (long); one piece of outer cover paper 10¼" × 6¼" (short); one piece of inner top paper 3½" × 7½" (short)

Building the Base

1. Place several layers of clean magazine pages on your work surface. Discard a layer whenever it gets messy or sticky. Arrange the pieces as follows: the 7½ " × 3½" bottom piece horizontally in the center (base), the 7½" × 5½" pieces to the top and bottom (sides), and the 3⅜" × 5½" pieces to the right and left (ends).

2. Apply PVA to the 7½" edge of one of the 7½" × 5½" side pieces and align it to the 7½" edge of the 7 ½" × 3½" base. Hold them briefly in place, wiping up any glue that oozes and making sure the boards are truly aligned.

3. Apply PVA to the 5½" edge of the standing (side) piece and to one 5½" edge of a 3⅜" × 5½" end piece. Also apply PVA to the 3⅜" edge of the end piece. Align the new piece with the 5½" edges touching and the 3⅜" lined up with the 7½" × 3½" base. Hold for 20 seconds or until set.

4. Continue applying PVA to the edges and aligning the pieces until all four sides are built and set. Move the base (with all sides adhered) to a clean surface.

5. Peel the backing off one of the 1¼" × 5½" strips of self-adhesive linen tape. Valley-fold it in half toward you, sticky side in back, and press it into one corner. Repeat with the other three strips and corners.

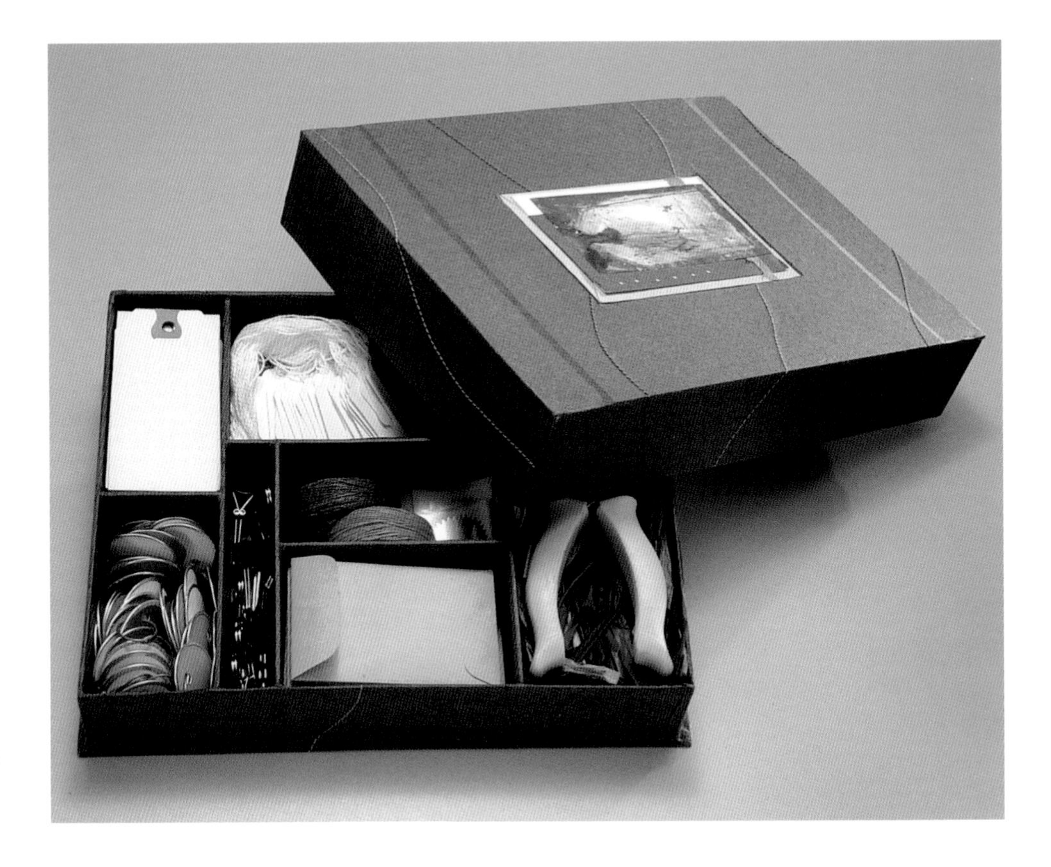

Tag Box for Val, 2001; paper, museum boards, monotype; unique; 10½" × 8½" × 2¼"

Covering the Outside of the Base

Although you need ten pieces of paper to cover the base, adhering them is quite manageable. We'll call the longer side the "side" and the narrower side the "end."

6. Arrange several layers of magazine pages for scrap paper over a portion of your work surface. Place one of the outer side cover papers (in this case, 8½" × 6½") wrong-side up on the scrap paper. Spread a thin and even coat of PVA across the entire cover paper.

7. Pick up the box and center the 7½" × 5½" side on the sticky paper. Press down. Turn the box over and smooth the cover paper down over the side of the box. There should be a ½" extension at the top, bottom, and sides of the box.

8. With scissors, cut diagonals at the corners of the cover paper, leaving ⅛" between the diagonal and the edge of the box.

9. Fold these flaps over the edges and sides, one by one. Press down firmly. It helps to turn the box so that the open top faces you.

10. Repeat steps 6–9 for the other 7½" × 5½" side.

11. The end cover papers should be slightly taller than the box but align side to side. Trim the sides if they seem to be wrapping around the right and left edges.

12. Place one of the 3½" × 6½" end cover papers wrong-side up on a clean piece of scrap paper. Spread a thin, even coat of PVA on the entire paper.

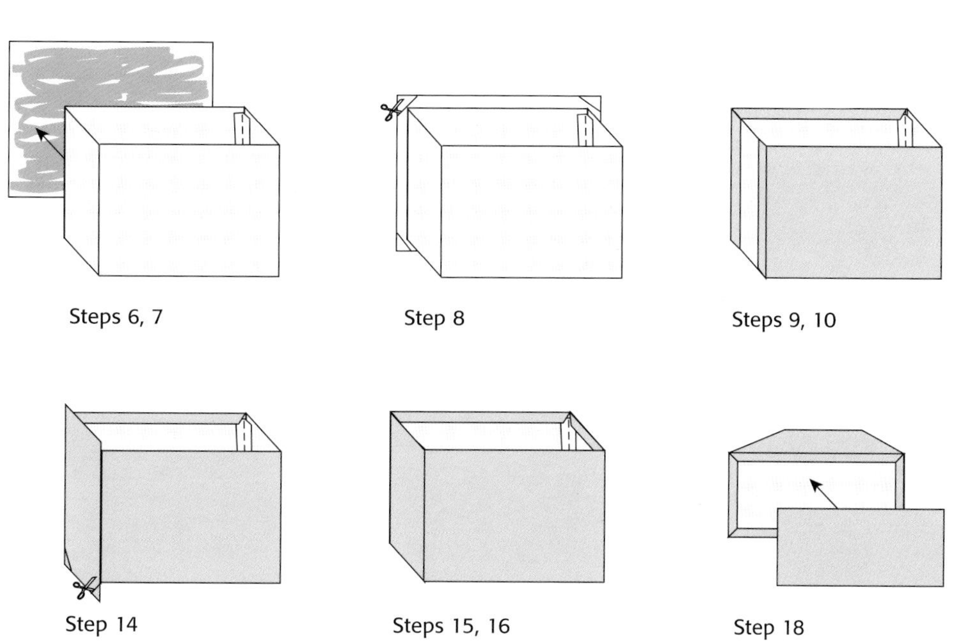

Steps 6, 7

Step 8

Steps 9, 10

Step 14

Steps 15, 16

Step 18

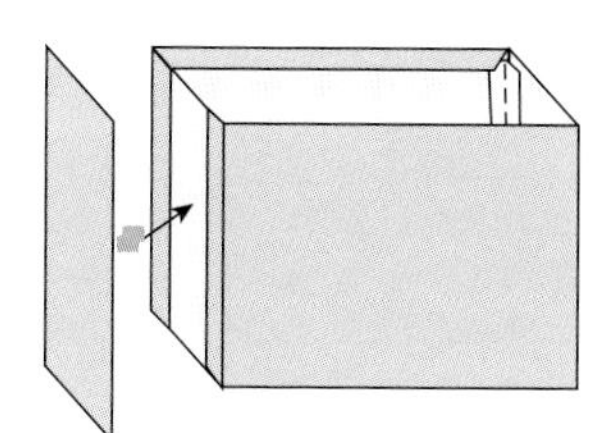

Steps 11, 12, 13

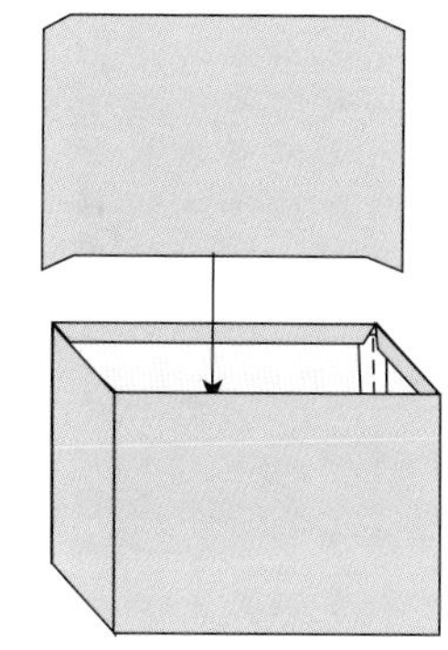

Step 20

13. Center the end of the box on the paper so that the top and bottom margins are even.
14. With scissors, cut diagonals only at the bottom corners of the cover paper, leaving 1/8" between the diagonal and the bottom of the box.
15. Fold over the flaps and press them down.
16. Repeat steps 12–15 for the other end cover paper.
17. Place the 7¼" × 3¼" bottom cover paper wrong-side up on a piece of scrap paper. Apply a thin, even coat of PVA on the entire paper.
18. Gently lift the cover paper, center it on the bottom of the box, and smooth it down.

Covering the Inside of the Base

19. Place one of the inner side cover papers (in this case, 8½" × 6½") wrong-side up on the scrap paper. Spread a thin and even coat of PVA on the entire paper.
20. Gently pick up the cover paper from the corners, arrange it slightly lower than the top edge of the box, center it side to side, and smooth it down on the inside of the box. Use the bone folder to smooth down the inner corners.
21. Repeat steps 19 and 20 for the corresponding side and for the two end papers. The two end papers should fit well side to side and can be slightly shorter than the height of the box.
22. Check that the inner bottom paper will fit inside the bottom of the box without running up the sides.
23. Apply PVA to the back of the inner bottom paper. Pick up the paper and place it inside the box on the bottom. Smooth it down with clean, dry fingers.

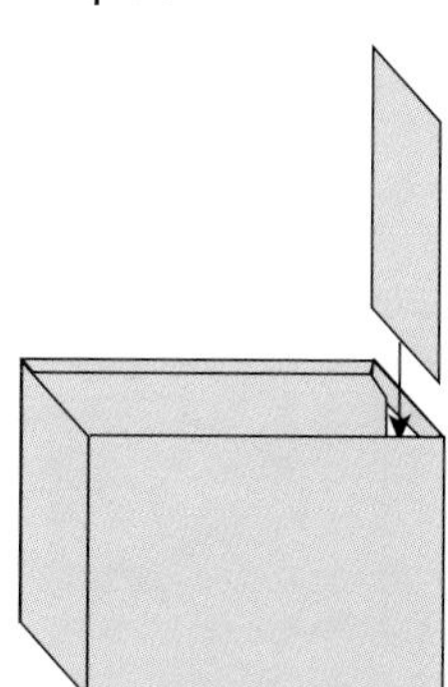

Step 21

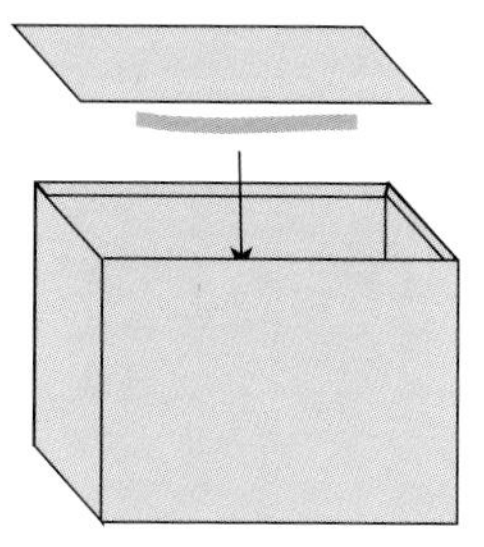

Step 23

Building the Lid

You will build the lid in the exact same manner as you built the base—matching, gluing, and aligning the sides. These sides are all ½" tall. Add strips of 1¼" x ½" self-adhesive linen tape to reinforce the corners.

Covering the Lid

This is slightly different from covering the base, since there are only two cover papers instead of ten.

1. Work on top of layered pages of magazines for scrap paper. Discard any pages as they get sticky. Place the outer cover paper wrong-side up on your work surface. Center the lid on it, open-end up.
2. With a pencil, draw around the edges.
3. Remove the lid.
4. Apply PVA to the rectangle you just drew. Affix the lid.
5. Align a ruler with one long side of the lid and use a pencil to lightly draw lines from the lid to the edges of the cover paper. Repeat for the parallel side.
6. Measure 1⁄16"–1⁄8" from the short sides of the lid and draw two parallel lines, one on each end of the lid, forming rectangles at the corners of the cover paper.
7. Cut out the corner rectangles, also cutting four tiny slits that are parallel to the long sides.
8. Apply PVA to one long flap of the cover paper and press it against the lid so that it is standing straight up. Quickly cut slits in the cover paper where it wraps around the corners, then press the paper over the edge and down inside the lid. Repeat for the other long flap.
9. Apply PVA to one short flap and wrap it over the edge and down inside the lid. Repeat for the other short flap.
10. Smooth the paper into the corners and joints with a bone folder.
11. Check that the inner paper will fit inside the lid without running up the sides. Trim it if necessary.
12. Apply PVA to the back of the inner paper. Pick up the paper and place it inside the lid on the bottom.

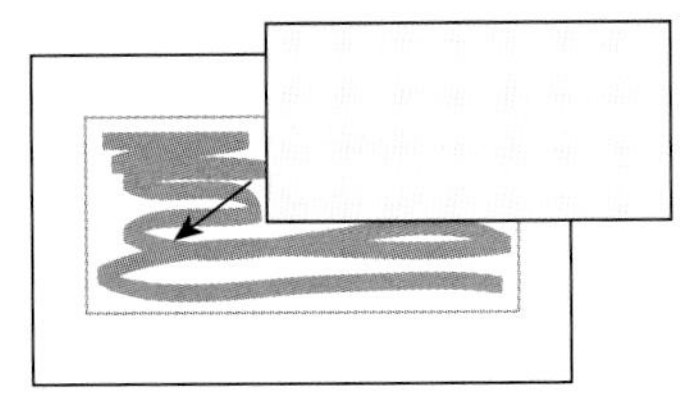

Steps 1, 2, 3, 4

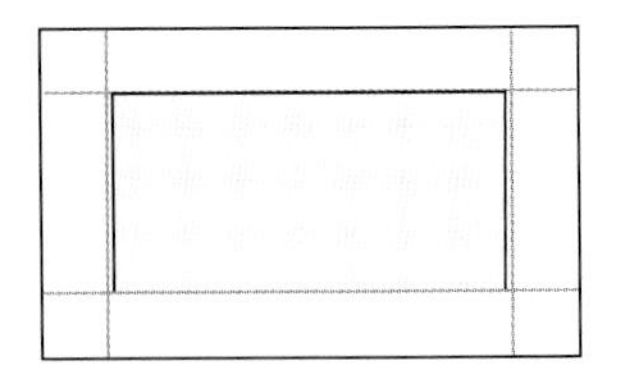

Steps 5, 6

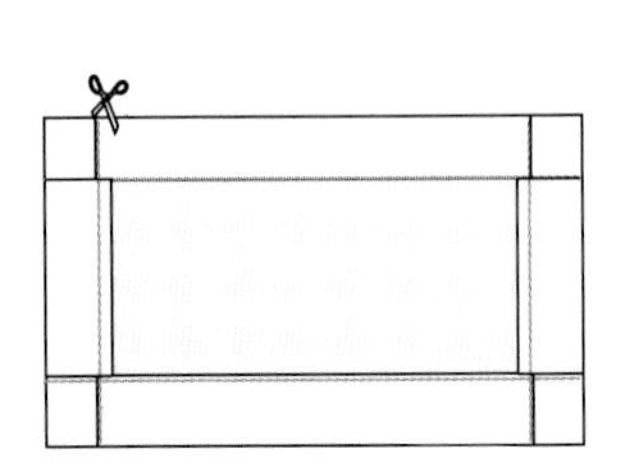

Steps 7

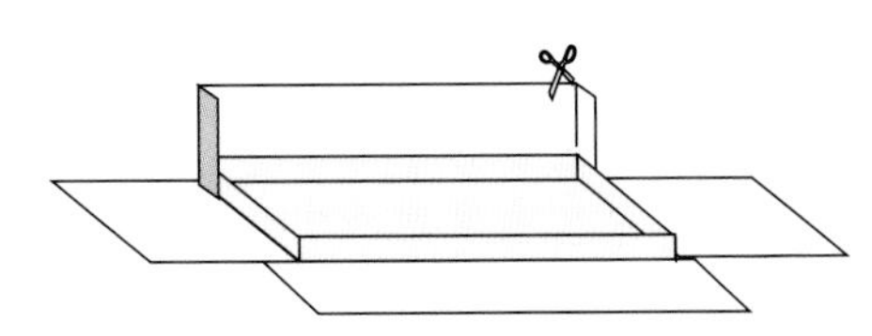

Steps 8

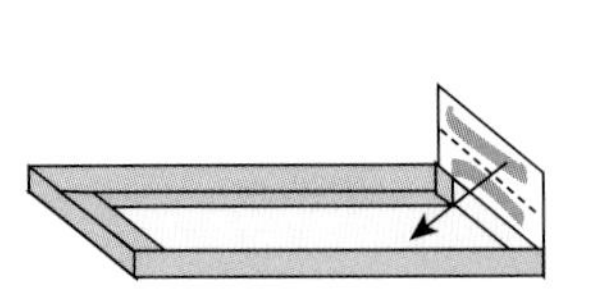

Step 9

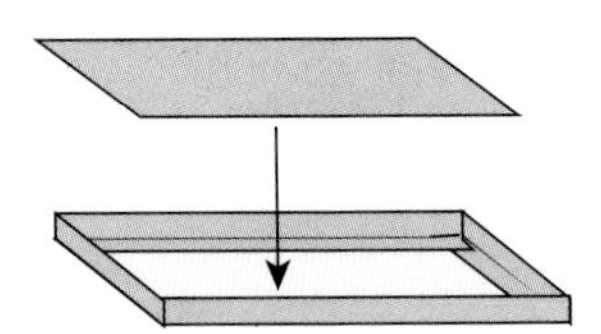

Steps 12

MAKING A BOX OF ANY SIZE

You can customize the lidded photograph or notebook box to make it any size. Smaller boxes are much easier to make, so you may want to make your box 8" or less in any direction. Determine how wide (width), how high (height), and how deep (depth) you desire the box. If you have a book already made, make sure that your box is at least ¼"–½" larger than the book all the way around. You need room to be able to get the book out of the box and you don't want the book to rub against the edges of the box. This measurements assume you are using 4-ply museum board. You may need a calculator to help you with the math. Copy this page and fill in your calculations.

WIDTH ____________ HEIGHT ____________ DEPTH ____________

Cut the boards as follows:

one box bottom = width × depth ____________
two ends = (depth – ⅛") × height ____________
two sides = width × height ____________
one box lid = (width + ¼") × (depth + ⅛") ____________
two lid ends = (depth + ⅛") × ½" ____________
two lid sides = (width + ¼") × ½" ____________

Cut the cover papers as follows:

one outer box bottom = (width – ¼") × (depth – ¼") ____________
two outer box ends = depth × (height + 1") ____________
two outer box sides = (width + 1") × (height + 1") ____________
one inner box bottom = (width – ½") × (depth – ½")____________
two inner box ends = (depth – ¼") × (height + 1") ____________
two inner box sides = (width + 1") × (height + 1") ____________
one outer lid = (width + 2¾") × (depth + 2¾") ____________
one inner lid = width × depth ____________

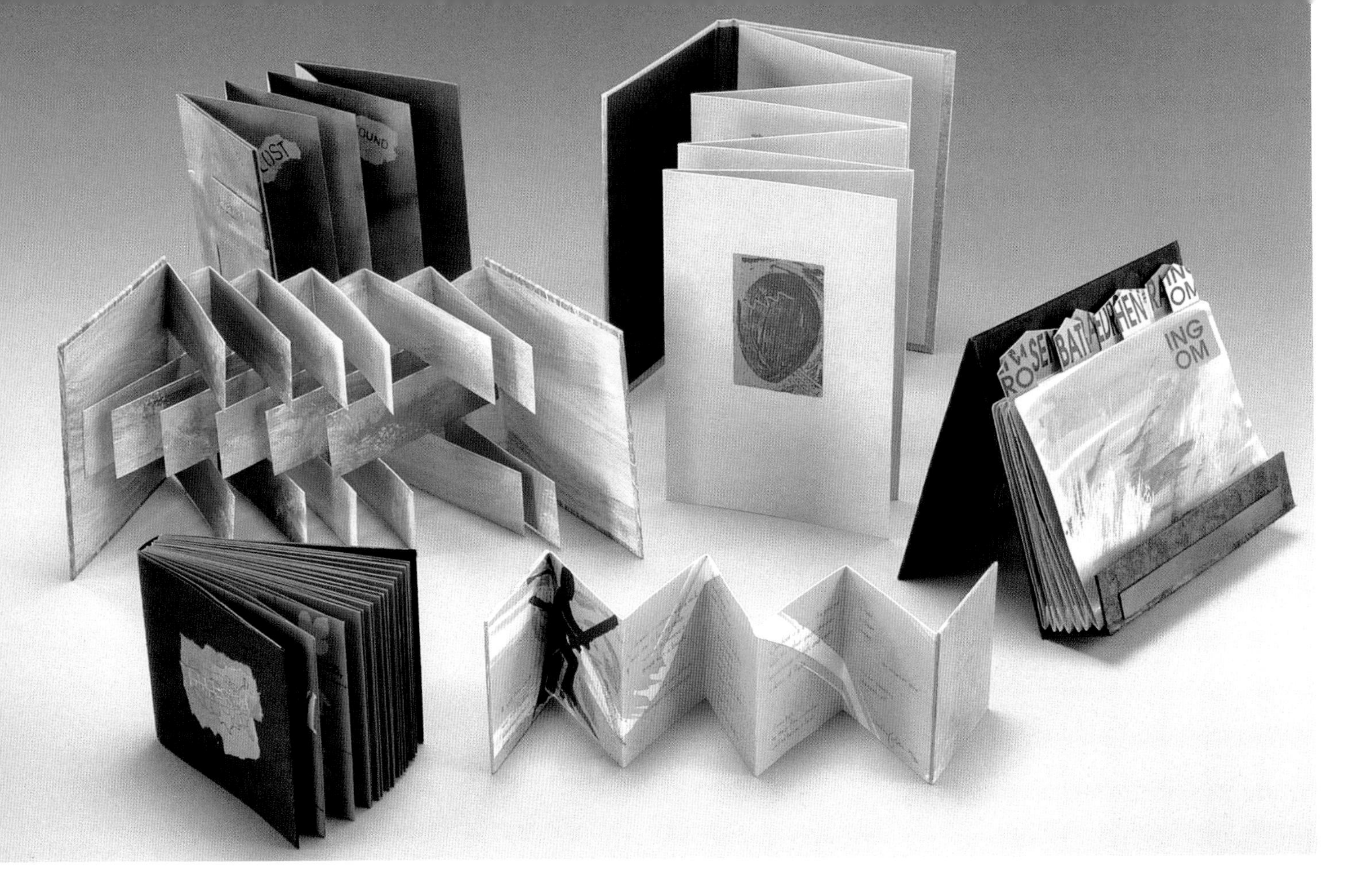

Chapter Three

Dreams, Flags, and More Accordions

Accordions
Back row (left to right): *Lost & Found; The Elephant's Lesson*
Middle row (left to right): *Just Under; House on File*
Front row (left to right): *Dream States; Not Falling/Not Moving*

I much prefer dreams when they tell a good story. Surely you've dreamed plenty of them. Do you write them down? Start by making a dream journal. Make one with a small number of pages so you can fill it easily and feel you have accomplished something. Tell yourself before you go to sleep that you are going to remember your dream and then you probably will. Keep a dream journal by your bed and write down your dreams when you awaken each morning. Sometimes I wake up thinking I had no dreams but I still jot down an image I remember. Writing down one image often reminds me of one whole dream, which reminds me of another. Keep your mind open and don't be in a hurry to dismiss anything. All of this creating and writing can help you organize your daily life and will be useful for future projects.

As you make your dream journal entries into book art, think of the voice you are using. Does writing about a dream feel different from writing a letter? Are there things you can only do in your dreams? How would you describe them so that they sound natural? A dream, like every activity in life, has a voice to it, with its own vocabulary, style, and tone.

Once you realize the tone of a dream, choose a structure to match its style. Disjointed images might be written on separate pages, cards, or flags. A longer story may need a more continuous accordion that flows from page to page. The content of the dream may dictate the style of book as well; the dream might have subplots, for which a flag with pockets would be appropriate.

Japanese Album Accordion

Time: 30–45 minutes

When I made this structure for *Dream States*, a dream journal, I intended to capture a quantity of dreams all at once. What I learned was that my dreams served both as a way to process and make sense of my daily experiences and as a reminder of things I had completely forgotten to do. In one case, I dreamed about windows for three days before I made some curtains, after which the window dreams stopped. One week is enough time to focus on this project, gather content, and fill a handmade book. To make a thick book you will be folding and gluing many sheets in a repetitive manner. You may use fewer pages, if you prefer. Doing one thing many times is good practice to help you refine your skills.

I learned this album from the book *Japanese Bookbinding: Instructions from a Master Craftsman,* by Kojiro Ikegami, in which single sheets are folded in half and then adhered at the fore edge. It is much easier to work on the pages of this book before you bind it. If you work on the pages once it is put together, you may find a page or two that wasn't completely glued to the next; just use PVA and glue it down. Glue stick is not strong enough for this structure.

After carving rubber stamps from erasers, I stamped a "dream themes" page. Each rubber stamp is an icon for a different type of dream. Later I stamped the appropriate icon next to the written account of the dream.

Give some thought to your past dreams and see what themes repeat themselves.

Some Dream Icons and Their Themes

car: transportation, no brakes, out of control
cup of tea: food, drink, friends
fig leaf: nakedness, vulnerability
ABC: school, schedule, trapped
heart: amorous, erotic, romantic
house: home, hospitality, family
skull: diseased relative appears
book: writing, reading, book art
animals: pets, zoo, transformation

Tools: bone folder, magazines or catalogs for scrap paper, PVA, small brush for gluing, waxed paper
Materials: 18 sheets text paper or colored pastel paper 3¾" × 9" (short)
Example: 3¾" × 4½" book (4⅝" with soft cover)

Dream States, 2004; rubber stamps, stencils, ink; album accordion; unique; 4½" × 3¾"

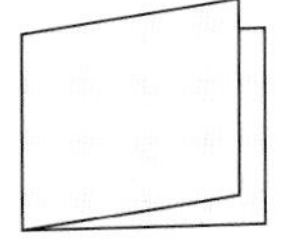

Step 1, 2

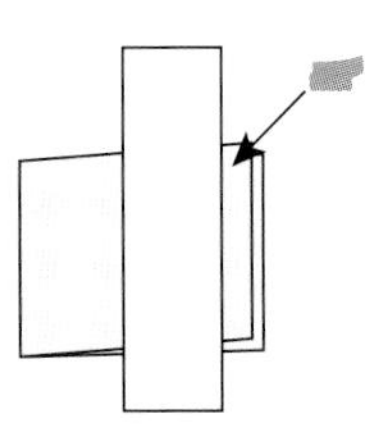

Step 4 (mask)

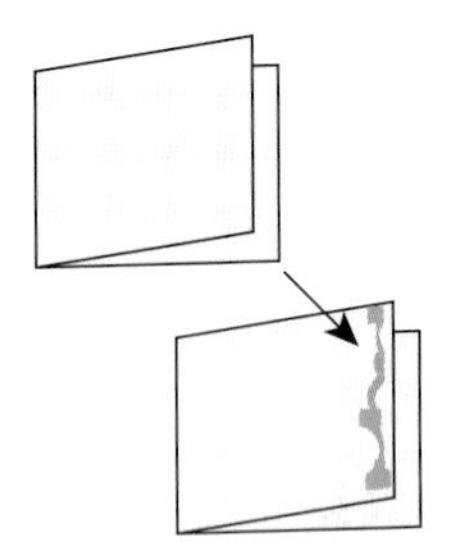

Step 6

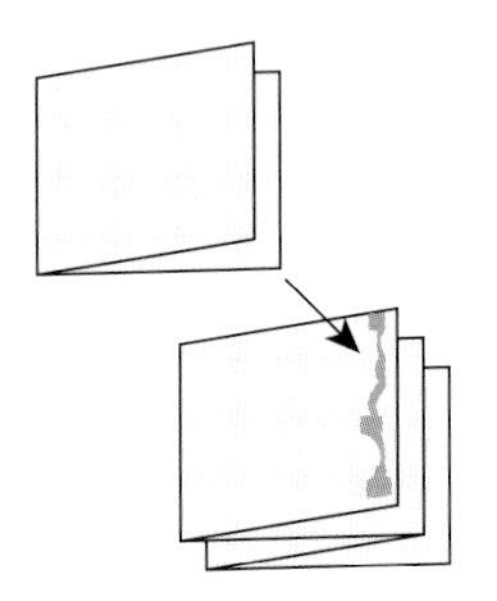

Step 7

1. Fold the pages in half, widthwise.

2. Face all of the open edges to the right.

3. You will be working from back to front. Put a sheet of scrap paper inside the last folded page.

4. Put another sheet of scrap paper as a mask vertically across the page, leaving approximately ½" visible at the fore edge. Spread the glue in a thin, flat line along this ½" wide area.

5. Remove both pieces of scrap paper and discard them, replacing the one tucked into the folded page with a sheet of waxed paper.

6. Set the next-to-last folded page on top of the exposed glue and align the edges to form the text block. Press down.

7. Repeat steps 3–5 until all the folded pages are glued together.

8. Put small pieces of waxed paper between each page. Place the entire book between two sheets of waxed paper and then between two Masonite boards. Put a heavy weight on top. Let the project dry under the weight overnight.

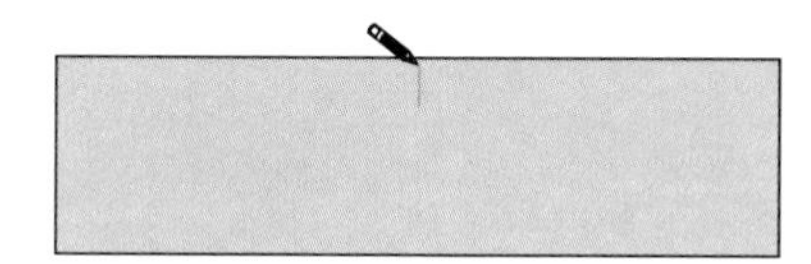

Step 10

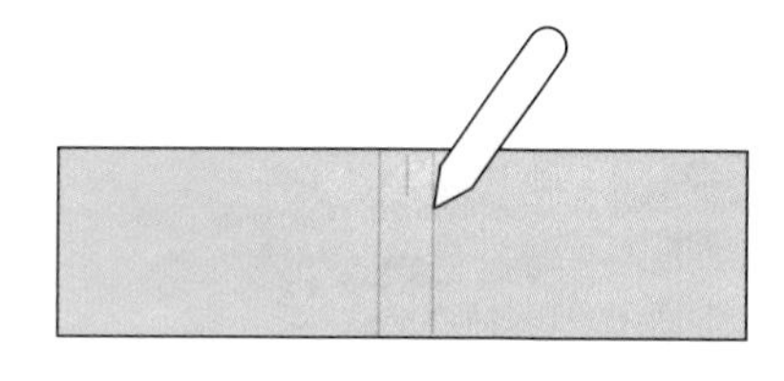

Step 11

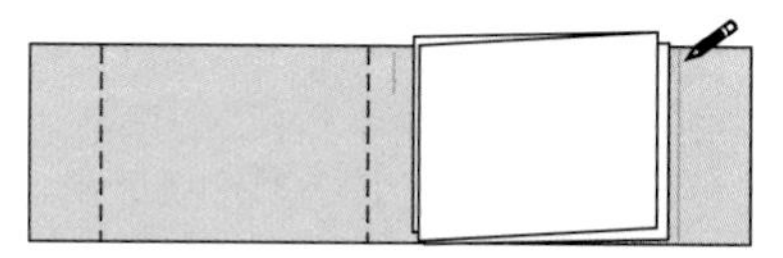

Step 12

Wraparound Soft Cover

For a cover for a book with the above dimensions, use a long piece of medium- to heavy-weight paper 3¾" wide × 13¾"–18" (short). This example has 2" front and back flaps that are glued down to the inside edges of the first and last pages. You may use flaps that are the same width as the first and last pages, if you like.

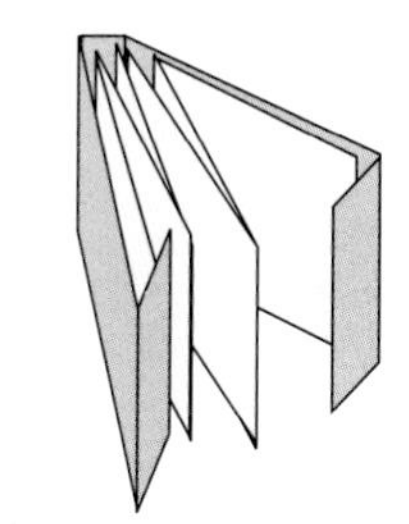

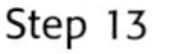
Step 13

9. Measure the thickness of your text block; this is how wide your spine should be. My example is ½". Measure on the folded (not glued) side. If the spine of the text block seems spongy, press it down a little (not tightly) and measure it while it is pressed down.
10. Measure and mark the center of the cover paper, at the top.
11. Measure, mark, and score one half the spine depth on either side of the center mark from step 10.
12. Using the text block as a guide, align it with each score in turn and make marks at the top and bottom. Score and fold at these two marks.
13. Arrange the text block inside the cover so that the first and last pages are sandwiched between the cover flaps. You may glue the cover to the text block, but the book will not open completely flat this way.

TIPS

- Make a journal, and focus for one week on remembering your dreams.
- Keep the journal by your bed and write down the dreams before you get up each morning. If you awaken during the night, try to remember the dreams then, too. Leave a space next to each scene change or dream for small 1"-square images like a rubber-stamped icon. Leave space at the top or bottom of the page for a date or a quotation from the dream.
- After you finish writing the dreams for one night, use the next page to write down what you think inspired the dreams: what is going on in your waking life, books you are reading, movies you saw, or food you ate. I call this page "analysis." You may call it "connections" or "waking life" or "hindsight," or whatever you like.
- Stamp the icons onto the pages.
- Add visual diversity to the page: use stencils or another color of pen or rubber-stamped letters to highlight a quotation from a dream or a word that describes the mood.

In My Living Room, 2003; color copy and typewriter; accordion with tapes or strips; edition of six; 4¾" × 5¾" (hard cover: pictures only), 4¼" × 5½" (soft cover: unique, with text)

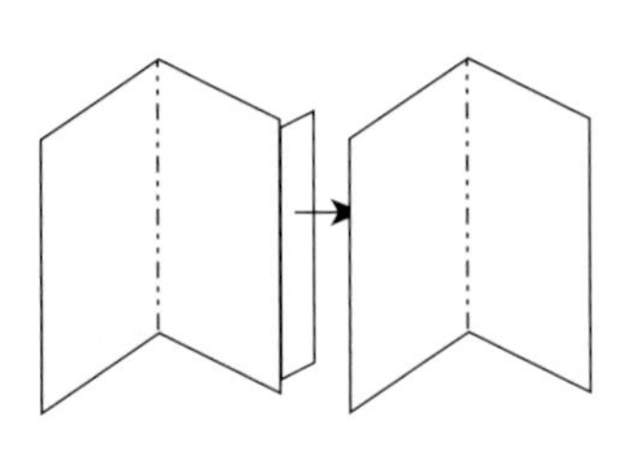

Variation with Tapes

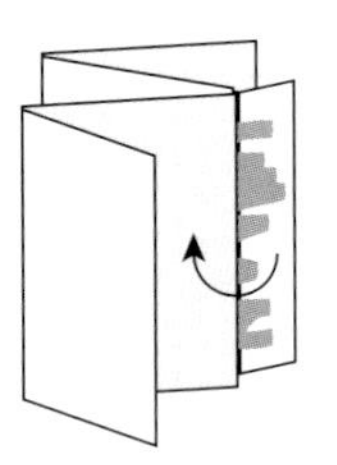

Variation with Strips

Variation: Hard Cover. A 3⁄16" spacing bar is useful when you make this hard cover. Use an outer cover paper or book cloth 5¼" × 11¼" (short); two pieces of 4-ply museum board 4½" × 4" (short); one spine piece (long) ½" × 4" *or* the depth of your text block; this is how wide your spine should be. (See the instructions on page 130 for the case binding, and page 132 for how to attach the book to the hard covers.)

Variation: Accordion with Tapes or Strips. For *In My Living Room* I attached each folded page to the next with self-adhesive linen tape at the spine. This method allows all pages to operate in typical accordion fashion, but the pages have a peak fold at the center. If you want to use pages with valley folds in the center, use decorative paper strips at the fore edge instead; to aid you in folding, use strips at least 1" wide (grained long).

SEVEN- OR EIGHT-PANELED BOOK

Time: 20 minutes for the miniature book, 30–75 minutes for larger one
It is much easier and more precise to make an accordion with eight segments, or panels, than it is to make one with seven. If you desire a book with seven panels, first fold the sheet of paper into eight sections, then cut off the last panel. By making seven panels, you have a book that opens with a valley fold from both the front and the back, giving equal weight to the content on both sides.

Standard-sized 22" × 30" printmaking or drawing paper is perfect for making a miniature book, since this paper is nearly always grained long and you will need only 22" in length. This little book is one of the quickest to make.

For a large accordion book you will need to join two sheets of paper. For *The Elephant's Lesson* I printed the dream on one side and three explanatory poems on the reverse.

Charles Hobson made a book based on a poem by Margaret Atwood. The book had nine panels and came in a custom box. After painting the box black to evoke darkness, he created a monotype of a rower to fold into the box. He wrote that "the folds of the accordion seemed to me to catch the sense of folding into and out of sleep."

Preparation: Think about the content of one dream and what words and tone work best to convey the feeling of that dream. Make a double-sided accordion that opens correctly from either side; this one has seven panels. Put a short dream on one side and your waking interpretation of it on the other. Or write the dream out in two different styles, perhaps one as a series of simple sentences or a poem and the other as your natural prose. You can make a standard eight-paneled accordion, if you prefer. For right reading on both sides of an eight-paneled accordion, rotate the contents and images 180 degrees top to bottom on the second side.

The Elephant's Lesson, 2003; letterpress, collagraphs; accordion; edition of 32; 5 3/8" × 7 3/4"

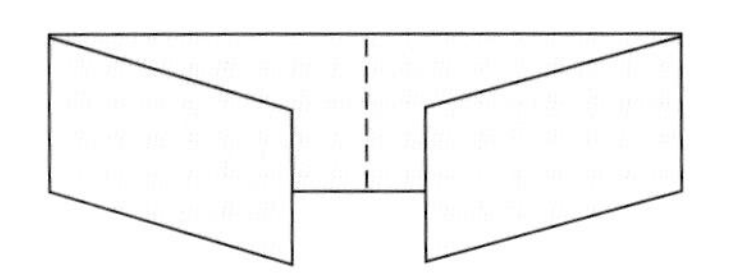

Steps 1, 2

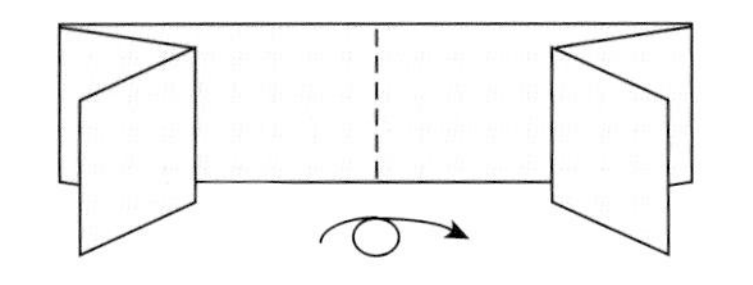

Steps 3, 4

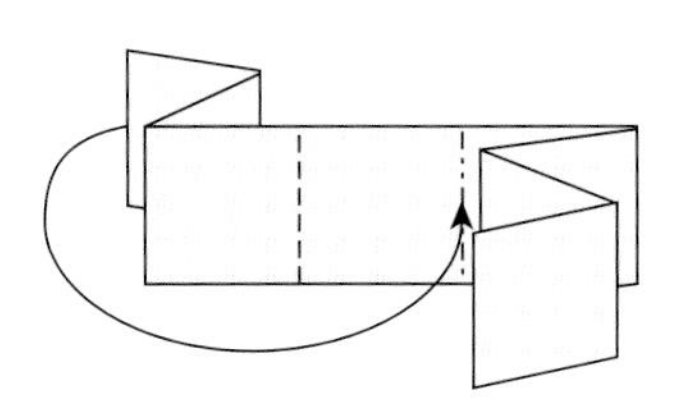

Step 5

Tools: bone folder, pencil, 24" metal ruler, scissors or art knife and cutting mat, magazines or catalogs for scrap paper, PVA, brush or piece of board for gluing

Miniature Book Materials: one piece of medium- to heavy-weight paper 2¾" × 22", two 4-ply museum boards 2¾" × 3" (long)
Example: 2¾" × 3"

Larger Book Materials: two sheets of medium- to heavy-weight paper: one sheet 7" × 21" (short), one sheet 7" × 20" (short)
Example: 5⅛" × 7¼" (with hard covers)

Making an Eight-Paneled Accordion

Use these instructions for the Miniature Book.

1. Fold the paper in half, widthwise. Open.

2. Fold the ends to the center fold, one end at a time. You will have three valley folds. Keep these new panels closed.

3. Fold the open ends back to the new folds, making sure they are aligned.

4. Turn the paper over, keeping everything folded.

5. Align the folded ends with the center fold; crease. You should now have an eight-paneled accordion with alternating peak and valley folds.

Charles Hobson: *Variation on the Word SLEEP* (text by Margaret Atwood), 1991; pastel/monotype on accordion in lacquered box; edition of 20; 5¼" × 7" × 2¼" (photo by C. Hobson)

Not Falling/Not Moving, 2002; letterpress, linoleum cuts on painted paper; seven-panel accordion; edition of 42; 2¾" × 3"

Making a Seven-Paneled Accordion

6. Cut off the last panel if you want a book with seven segments. (If you do, notice that you can now have a valley fold as the first fold on both sides.)

7. For hard covers, attach a piece of 4-ply museum board that is exactly the size of one panel to the first and last panels.

Note: For the seven-paneled accordion, only one cover will show on each side, like the book *Not Falling/Not Moving*. Or make a fully wrapped portfolio (see pages 127 and 128) and attach the back of the last panel to the right-hand board. The front panel is not attached in the book *The Elephant's Lesson* (photo on page 53).

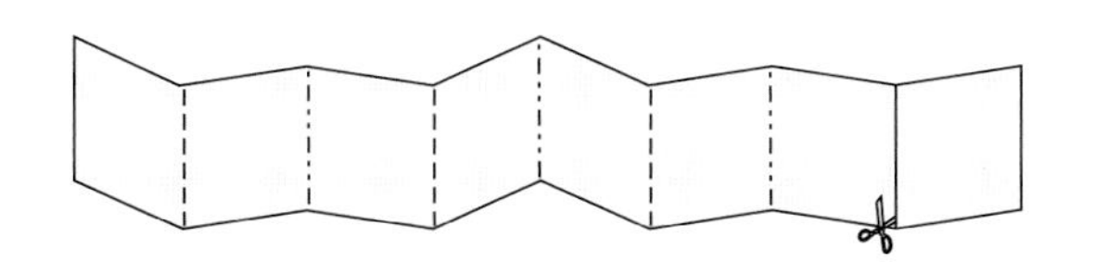

Step 6

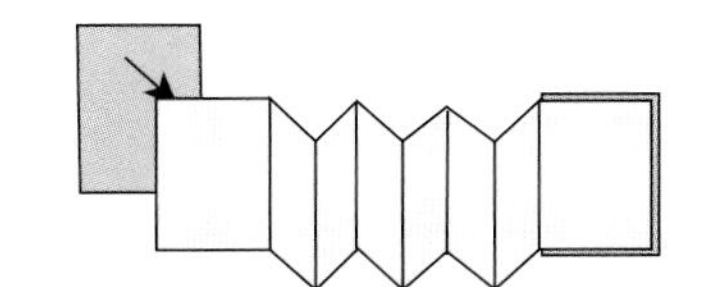

Step 7 (eight-paneled)

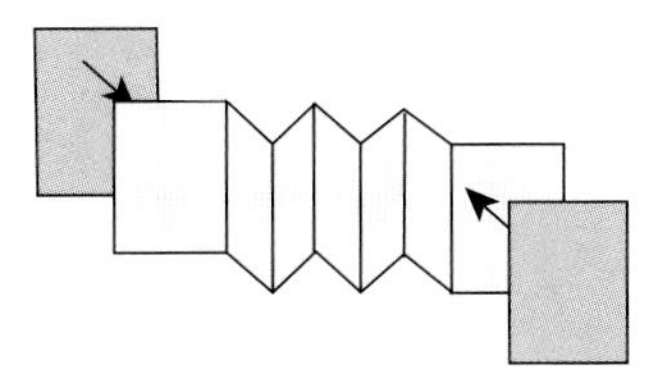

Step 7 (seven-paneled)

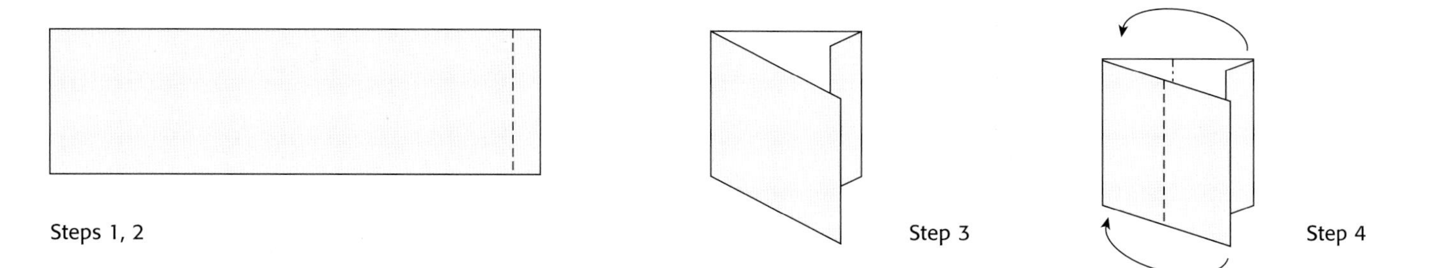

Steps 1, 2 Step 3 Step 4

Making Two Connected Accordions

These instructions are for the Larger Accordion. Use two sheets: one that is one inch longer than the other.

1. Place the longer sheet in front of you, horizontally.

2. Mark, score, and fold 1" parallel to the right short edge. You have made a tab. We will now call the longer sheet the tabbed sheet.

3. Keeping the tab folded, fold this sheet in half, matching the cut end to the fold with the tab inside.

4. Fold the ends to the center fold, one end at a time. Open and turn over. You should have valley, peak, valley, peak folds.

5. Fold the shorter sheet in half.

6. Fold the ends back to the center fold, and crease, making sure they are aligned.

7. Open. You should have valley, peak, valley folds, forming a "W." This is the non-tabbed sheet.

8. Making sure that the tabbed sheet is still valley, peak, valley, peak, (tab at the right), apply a thin layer of glue to the front of the 1" tab (the peak side).

9. Set the non-tabbed sheet on top of the tab so that the edge of the non-tabbed sheet is aligned with the peak of the tabbed sheet. Press down. (The tab will be hidden behind the second sheet).

10. Cut off one panel if you want a seven-paneled accordion.

11. Add painted hard covers or a hard cover with a spine.

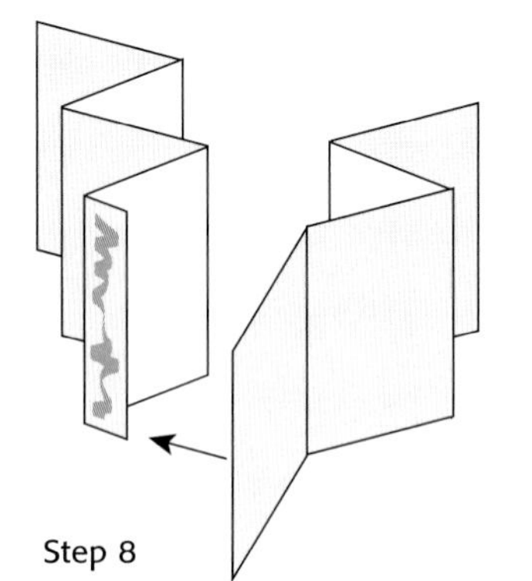

Step 8

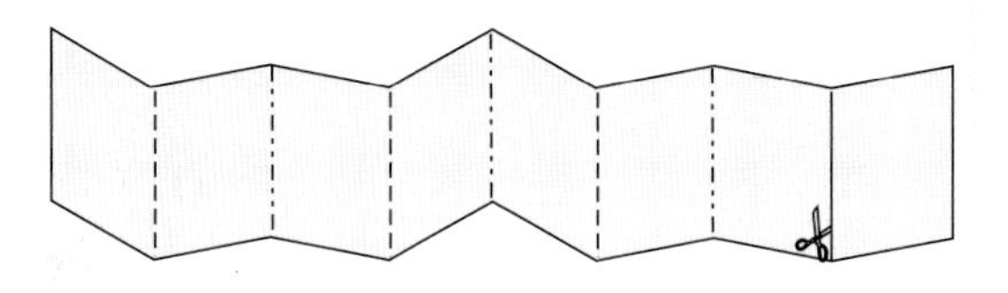

Step 10

Cover Styles

Hard Cover with Separate Boards (page 126): two 4-ply museum boards 5⅛" × 7¼" (long); two pieces of book cloth or lightweight paper 6¾" × 8¾" (long)

Case Binding (page 130): two 4-ply museum boards 5⅛" × 7¼" (long); one 4-ply museum board ¼" × 7¼" (long); one piece of book cloth or lightweight paper 12" × 8¾" (short)

Cover Ideas

- Distress the boards by hammering metal objects into the surface of the boards and then removing the objects. You can use paper clips, bolts, screws, metal type, etc. Adhere strips of board for a textural effect.
- Paint the museum boards with acrylic inks and/or gesso with or without distressing the boards. You can layer one color ink, then gesso, then a second color ink to provide more texture.
- Cover the separate boards in paper or book cloth before attaching them to the accordion. Use paper that is 3¾"–4¾" square for this 2¾" × 3" book, giving yourself a ½"– 1" margin around the boards (see page 126 for instructions).
- Wrap the separate boards in pastel paper and tuck the front and back panels into the open sides. (Note that your accordion will now have only five or six visible panels instead of seven or eight, however.) You will not need any adhesive for this. Use four pieces of pastel paper 2¾" × 4¾" (short) for the cover papers (see page 124 for detailed instructions).

Single-Flag Book

Time: 20–60 minutes

This structure turns out to be one of the most useful to know. The pages are single cards. The spine is an accordion. If you have never made a book before, make this three-page book. To make a thicker book with more pages, glue several accordions together. *She Is the Keeper* has three 16-fold

She Is the Keeper, 2003; letterpress and linoleum cuts; edition of 30; single-flag book; 2½" × 2¾" × 1½"

She Is the Keeper, 2003; open in box; 3" × 3" × 3"

accordions glued together, 22 cards, and a wraparound soft cover. The dropped-side box was inspired by Elsi Vassdal Ellis's book *Women Dream.* Since 16-fold accordions are a little tricky, for this beginning project you will make just one 8-fold accordion, like *Lost & Found.* I call *Lost & Found* an "urban-arium," because it is meant to hold things found on the streets of a city, as opposed to a conventional herbarium, which is a scrapbook of plants and where they are found.

Emily Martin used this structure in her book *Away,* about a remote vacation. She made her flags from a continuous image, then wrote her text on the back of the flags.

Lost & Found, 2003; stencils and gesso on paper; unique; single-flag book; 4¼" × 5½"

Tools: bone folder, magazines or catalogs for scrap paper, PVA, brush or piece of board for gluing
Materials: one piece of medium-weight paper 5½" × 10" (short), three cards or pieces of heavyweight paper 5½" × 4" (long)
Example: 4" × 5½" book block, 4¼" × 5½" with hard covers

Preparation: Cover the front and back of your three cards with acrylic gesso mixed with a little acrylic paint. Use as small an amount as possible on your brush, so the cards will retain a matte finish that allows you to draw on them later.

Folding the Eight-Panel Accordion

1. Fold the 5½" × 10" paper in half, widthwise. Open.
2. Fold the ends to the center fold, one end at a time.

3. Fold the ends back to the new folds, making sure they are aligned.
4. Turn the paper over, keeping everything folded.
5. Align the folded ends with the center fold; crease. You should now have an accordion with alternating peak and valley folds.

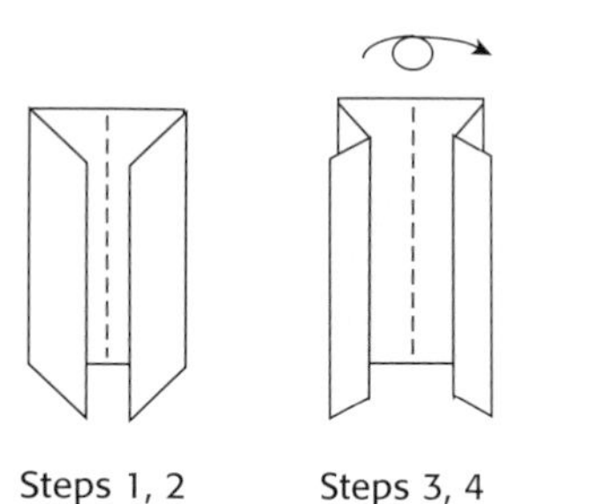
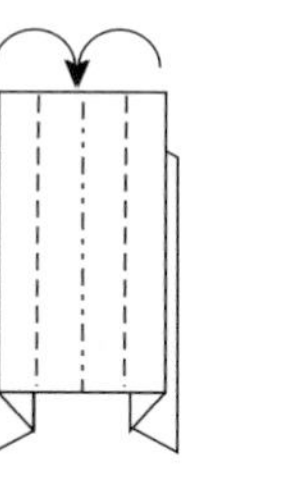
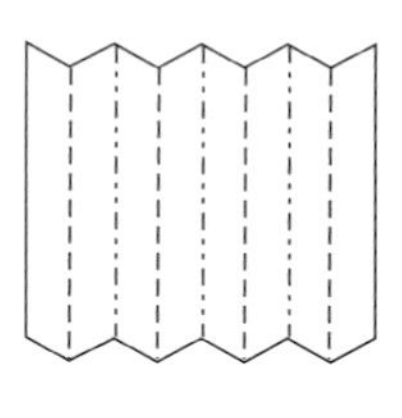

Steps 1, 2   Steps 3, 4   Step 5   Step 6

Attaching the Cards

6. Put the accordion in front of you with the valley folds at both ends.
7. Working from back to front, apply a thin line of glue to the third panel from the right
8. Take the third card and use the left edge to smooth the glue to completely cover the panel. Press the card into place. The left edge will be attached to the accordion.
9. Repeat the application of glue and attaching of the cards at the fifth and seventh panels (the cards will be at the third, fifth, and seventh panels from the right; the second, fourth, and sixth panels counting from the left).
10. Choose a cover.

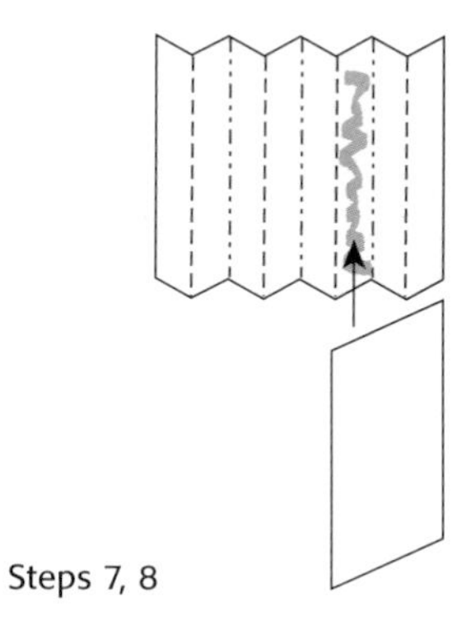

Steps 7, 8

Elsi Vassdal Ellis: *Women Dream*, 2001; letterpress on paper, museum boards, fabric; edition of 50; 6¼" cube with two concentric, smaller cubes (photo by the E.V. Ellis)

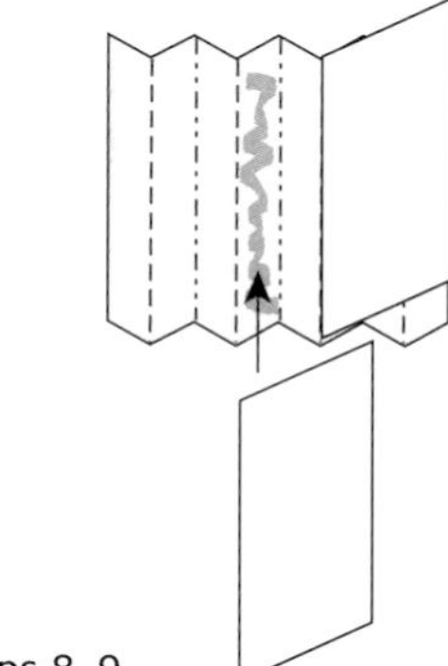

Steps 8, 9

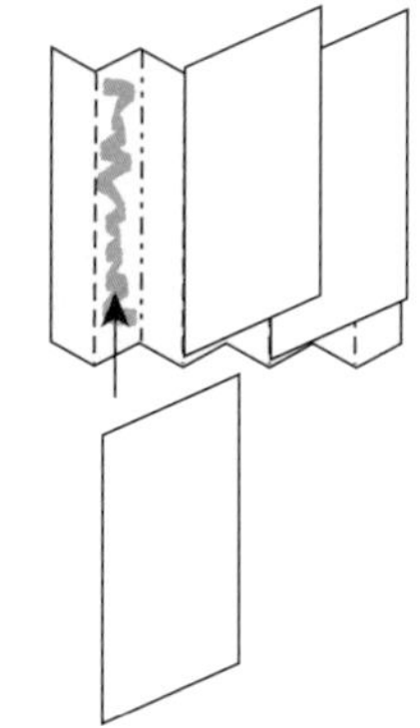

Step 9

Emily Martin: *Away*, 2002; archival inkjet on paper; flag accordion; edition of 25; 7" × 5" (photo by E. Martin)

Cover Styles

Example: 4¼" × 5½" book
The ends of your accordion spine are sandwiched between two boards or between a board and an endpaper. All of these covers are made in a similar manner, some require more pieces, some need more preparation. They are listed from basic to more complex. See also "Cover Ideas" (page 57) and instructions (pages 126 and 128).

Painted Hard Cover: Use two 4-ply museum boards 4¼" × 5½" (long). Paint one side of each board for the front and back covers. Let dry. Glue the first section of the accordion to the unpainted side of the front cover; glue the last section to the unpainted side of the back cover. Then adhere two lightweight to medium-weight endpapers 4" × 5¼" (long) on top of the accordion ends, sandwiching them.
Simple Hard Cover with Separate Boards: Use two 4-ply museum boards 4¼" × 5½" (long); two pieces of book cloth or lightweight paper 5¾" × 7" (long); two pieces of lightweight to medium-weight paper 4" × 5¼" (long)
Split-Board Cover: four 2-ply museum boards 4¼" × 5½" (long); four pieces of book cloth or lightweight paper 5¾" × 7" (long)
Split Board with Distressed Front and Back Covers: Distress the front and back covers, which are two 4-ply museum boards 4¼" × 5½" (long); then cover two 2-ply museum boards 4⅜" × 5½" (long) with two book cloth or lightweight paper 5¾" × 7" (long)

Pocket Flag Book

Time: 45–60 minutes
In this structure, the pockets fold at the fore edge, then are sealed unobtrusively at the spine. The folded edge of the diagonal pocket makes a crisp, finished edge.

Surely you have a good family story you have been telling. Perhaps you had an interesting dream about your family. Tell a different story for each member of your family, then use the pockets to hold copies of letters or photographs. You can also pick one family member and use photos of her/him at different ages, or use one photo that you alter by adding collaged paper or by painting over it. Make the three pockets or use premade envelopes instead of pieces of paper.

Tools: bone folder, pencil, 12" metal ruler, scissors or art knife and cutting mat, magazines or catalogs for scrap paper, PVA, brush or piece of board for gluing

A Black Ribbon, 2003; typewriter, color copy, copy transfer, tags; unique; 4½" × 7⅜"

Materials: two pieces of medium-weight paper 6¾" × 4" (long), three photocopies of family pictures on three sheets of medium-weight paper 8½" × 11" (long), 3–6 tags, handmade or store-bought, approximately 2" × 3¾"
Example: 4¼" × 6¾

Preparation: Photocopy, scan, or print out pictures of family members on five 8½" × 11" pages. Two will be used to cover your boards. Three will be for the pockets. You don't need to be concerned with the placement of the photos, just fill the page completely: part of the pages will be folded into the pockets. Make small collages and/or rubber stamp on three to six tags. Pick one or more of the pictures and write about it. What memory does it elicit? Pick three of the pictures and make connections between them.

Folding the Accordion Spine

1. From the 6¾" × 4" pieces, fold two eight-panel accordions, making sure that the folds are parallel to the 6¾" side, and glue them together.

2. Cut off one panel from the end so that your last two folds are both valley folds (or both peak folds, depending on which way your accordion is facing).

Folding the Pockets

3. Put one 8½" × 11" sheet in front of you, vertically, wrong-side up.

4. Fold in half, lengthwise. Open.

5. Measure, mark, and fold 4¼" from the bottom. Open.

6. Fold the right corner to touch the intersection of the two perpendicular folds.

7. Fold the left corner to touch the same intersection.

8. Fold this triangular flap up at the horizontal fold.

9. Fold the paper in half with the triangles on the outside. This will be one pocket.

10. Repeat steps 3–9 with the other two 8½" × 11" sheets.

Attaching the Pockets to the Accordion

11. Working back to front, apply a thin coat of glue to the third panel from the right.

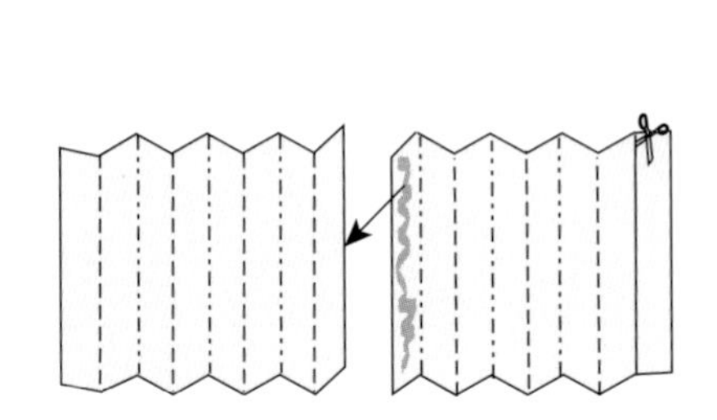

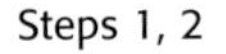

Steps 1, 2

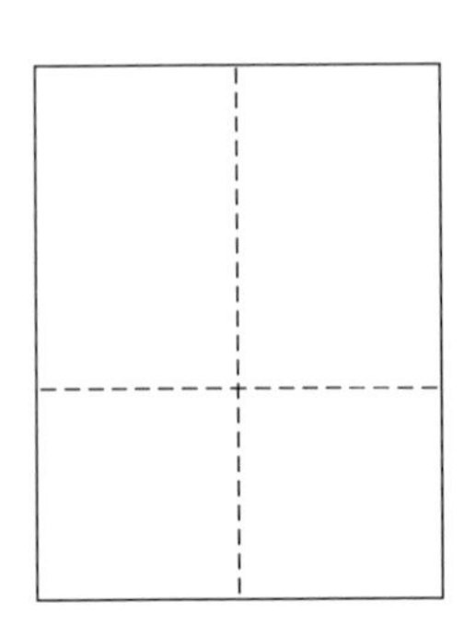

Steps 3, 4, 5

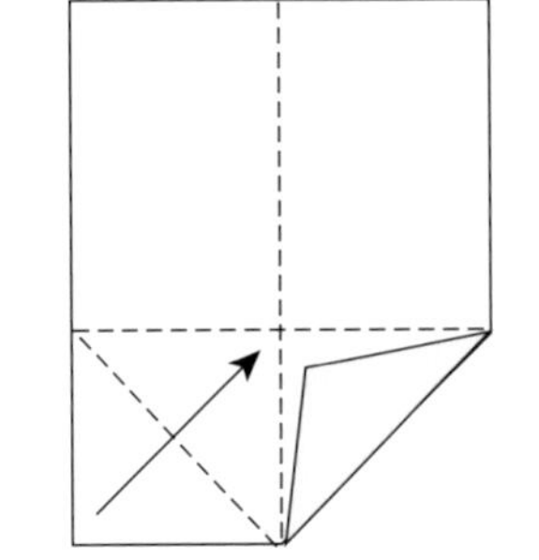

Steps 6, 7

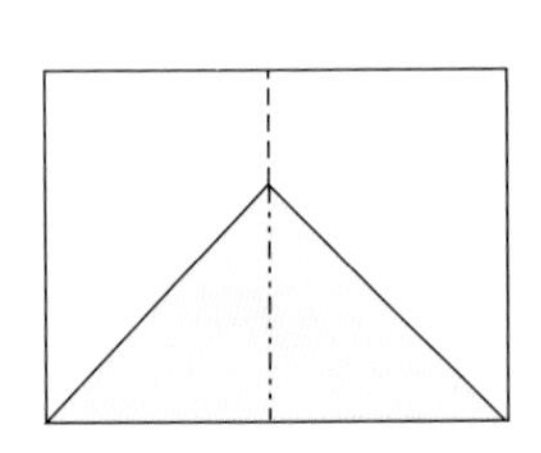

Step 8

12. Press the third pocket into place, aligning the open left edge with the valley fold. (Both of the open left edges will remain sandwiched into this valley. There is nothing fancy here. Treat those open edges as if they were connected.)
13. Apply a thin coat of glue to the panel that immediately precedes the pocket (fourth panel from the right) and press the panel on top of the pocket page, sealing the open edges.
14. Repeat the application of glue, alignment, and pressure with the remaining two pockets; be sure the two panels between each pocket do not get glued. This means that working right to left you will put glue on the third and fourth, seventh and eighth, eleventh and twelfth panels.
15. Choose a cover. *A Black Ribbon* has a split-board binding with a ribbon tie. (See Split-Board Binding, page 128).
16. If you wish to add a ribbon, you will need one that is 24" long. Glue the center of the ribbon horizontally across the back board before you attach the accordion spine.

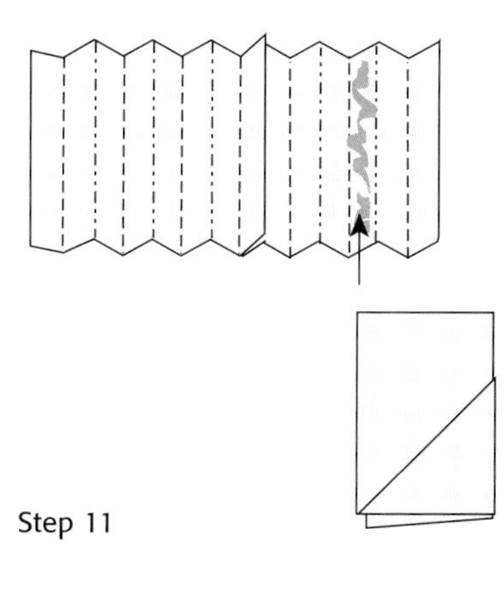

Step 11

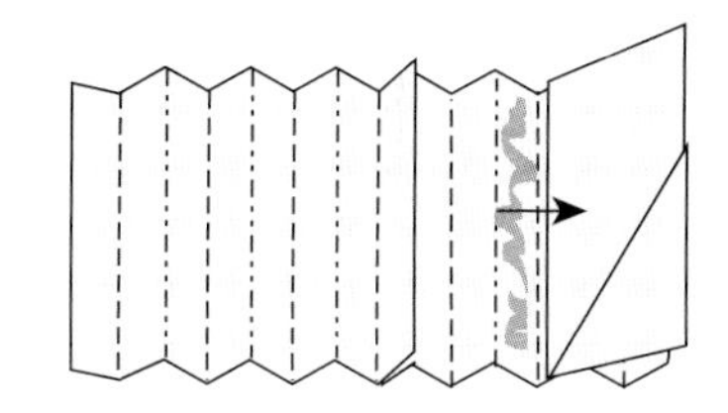

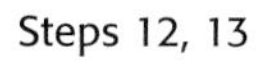

Steps 12, 13

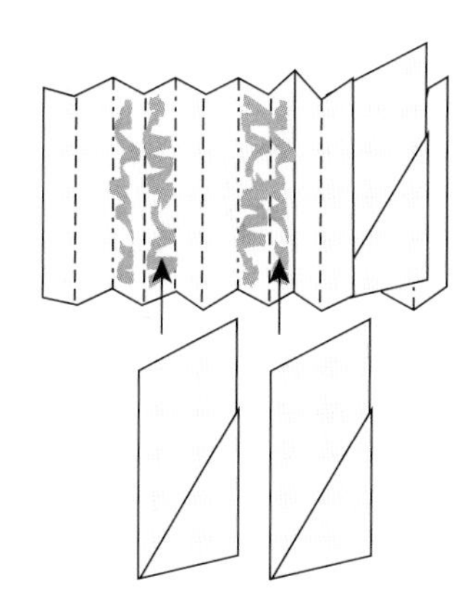

Step 14

Variation: If you have a paper with the decoration only on one side and wish to see just that decorative side, fold the paper following steps 3–5. Start with decorated side face-up.
a. Keep the paper folded along the bottom edge, right sides together.
b. Fold the edge of this new flap down to meet the bottom fold. Crease the paper.
c. The undecorated sides should be hidden inside.

Cover Styles

Choose from one of the cover styles below. Instructions are on pages 126 and 128.
Example: 4½" × 7" book
Painted Hard Cover: two 4-ply museum boards 4½" × 7" (long)
Simple Hard Cover with Separate Boards: two 4-ply museum boards 4½" × 7" (long); two pieces of book cloth or lightweight paper 7" × 8½" (long); two pieces of lightweight to medium-weight paper 4¼" × 6¾" (long)
Split-Board Cover: four 2-ply museum boards 4½" × 7" (long); four pieces of book cloth or lightweight paper 7" × 8½"
Split-Board Cover with Decorated Front and Back: two 4-ply museum boards 4½" × 7" (long); two 2-ply museum boards 4⅜" × 7" (long); two pieces book cloth or lightweight paper 7" × 8½"

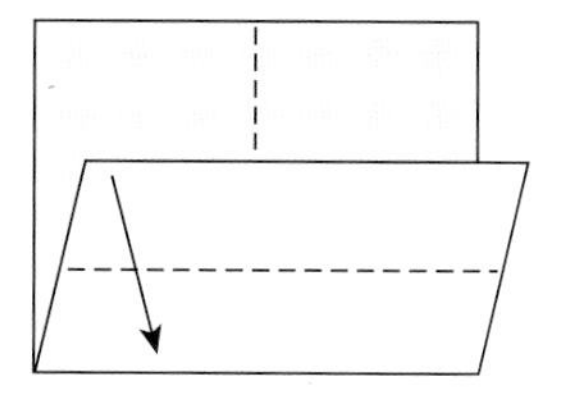

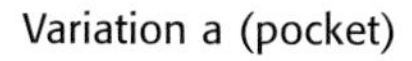

Variation a (pocket)

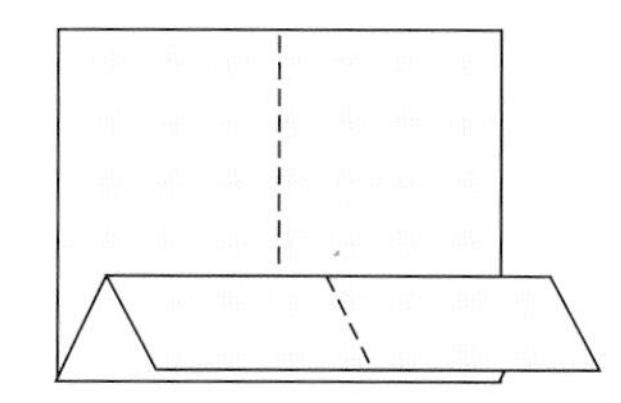

Variation b (pocket)

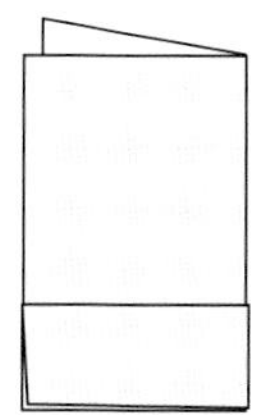

Variation c (complete)

Just Under, 2004; paste paper, stencil, acrylic inks, gesso; flag book; unique; 5" × 5⅛"

Multiple-Flag Book

Time: 45–75 minutes

While this book structure has been taught since at least the 1980s, it is still a fascinating one. It is a structure that constantly presents new opportunities; obviously, it endures. We have Hedi Kyle to thank for this one.

With this book you will have six sections to work with. Absolute beginners should start with 18 rectangular strips 1½" × 4½, grain short. For *Just Under*, I made paste paper in a wavy pattern on a text-weight paper and used it for the accordion. The cards were painted with acrylic inks on heavyweight paper. The text is hidden when the book is fully extended, showing only the sea; it is about things just under the surface.

If you are a more experienced bookmaker, try making an accordion with irregularly shaped pages. For *Where, Oh Where* I used six flames per section, totaling forty-two flames. You could use a wider shape, such as a leaf or feather, or use three, four, or five shapes, if you like.

Tools: bone folder, pencil, 12" metal ruler, scissors or art knife and cutting mat, magazines or catalogs for scrap paper, PVA, brush or piece of board for gluing

Materials: two pieces of medium-weight paper 5" × 8" (short), eighteen 1½" × 4½" strips of medium- to heavy-weight paper (short)

Example: 5" × 5¼" book

Preparation: Think of things that wave or flap in a breeze: ocean, laundry on the line, flags of many nations, your country's flag, wind chimes, kites, long hair, hands, leaves. Choose colors that support your idea. Paint or decorate one piece of medium-weight paper 8" × 10" (long), and one piece of heavyweight paper 9" × 15" (long or short). For best results, paint the backs also. Then cut the papers to the dimensions of the eighteen strips above, making sure the grain will be parallel to any folds and to the spine of the book.

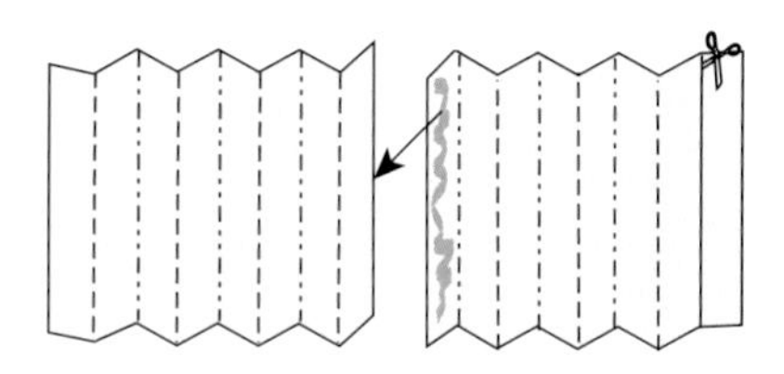

Steps 1, 2

Folding the Accordion Spine

1. From the 5" × 8" pieces, fold two eight-panel accordions, making sure that the folds are parallel to the 5" side, and glue them together. If you have decorated the strips, note that the second accordion needs to start with a peak fold, so you may have to turn it upside-down. If you are unsure how to fold an eight-panel accordion, see Seven- or Eight-Paneled Book, page 52.

2. Cut off one panel from the end so that your last two folds are both valley folds (or both peak folds, depending on which way your accordion is facing).

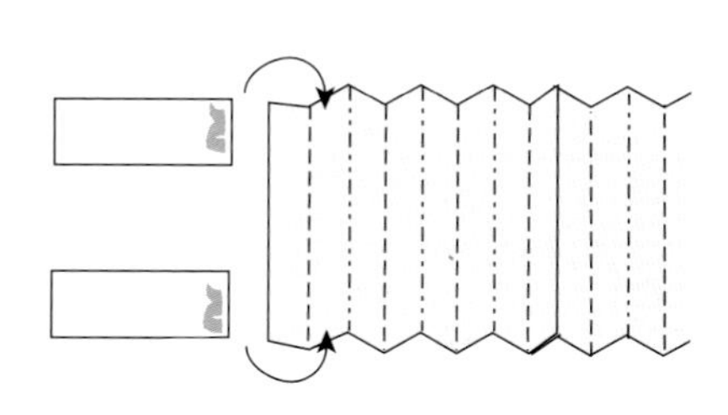

Steps 3, 4, 5

Attaching the Strips

Choose the side you want visible in the fully opened book. Apply glue on the back of the top and bottom strips at the leftmost edge. On the middle strip you will apply glue on the back at the rightmost edge. Never apply glue to the front of the strip.

3. Arrange the accordion in front of you so that the end folds are valley folds.

4. Glue two strips to the second panel. Remember that the glue goes on the rightmost edge on the back of the strip.

5. Align one strip with the top of the book (head) and align one with the bottom of the book (tail). Leave at least 1⁄16" between the valley fold of the accordion and the glued edges of these two strips. Note: It may be easier to do step 5 for all of the top and bottom strips and then add all the middle strips as per step 6.

Just Under, 2004; open

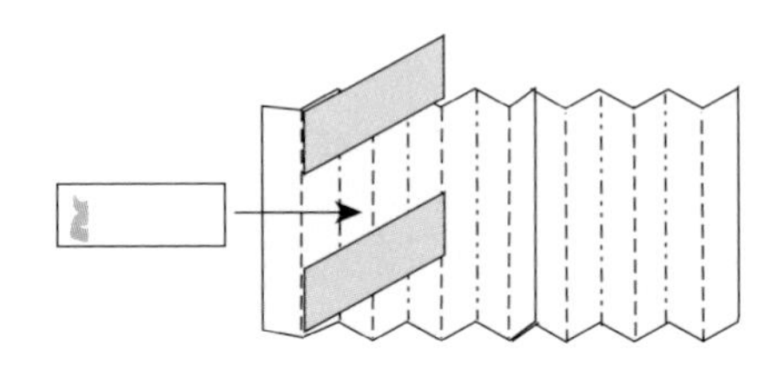

Step 6

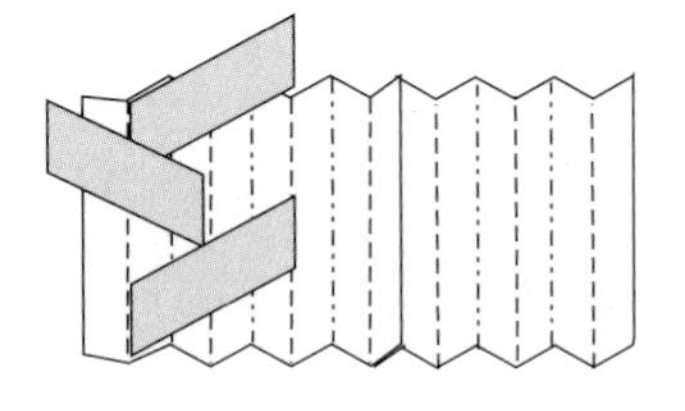

Step 6

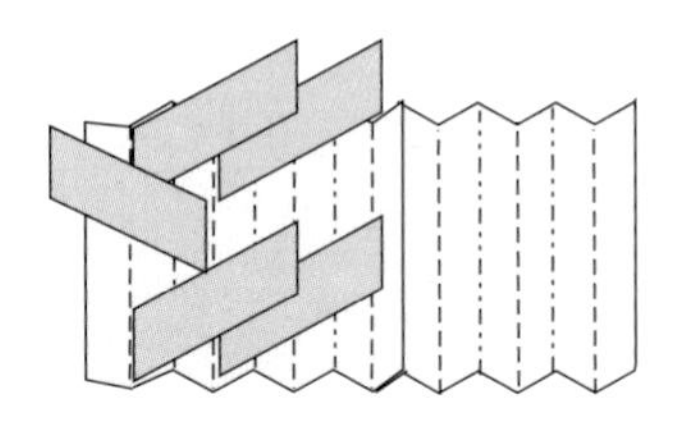

Step 7

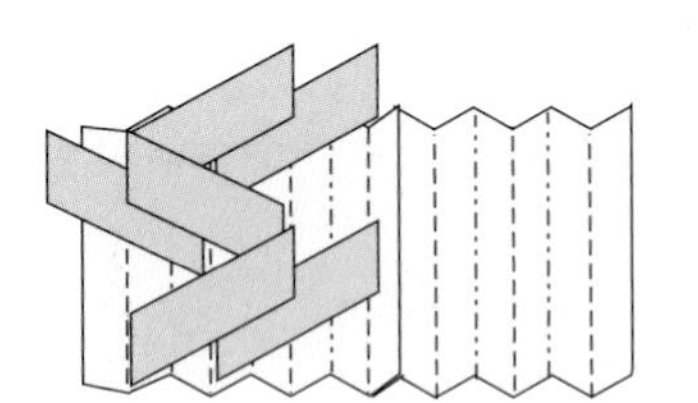

Step 7

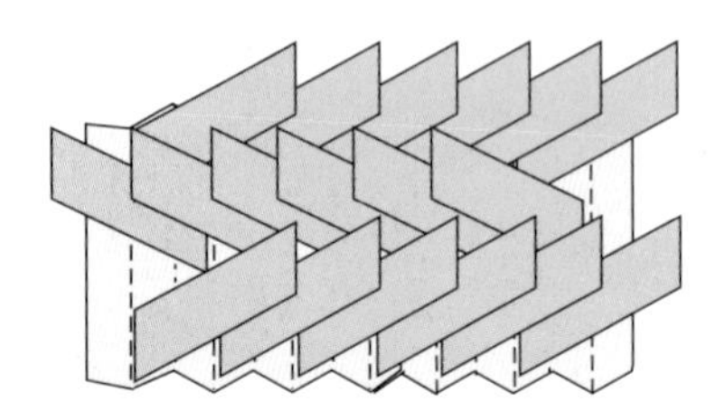

Step 7 (complete)

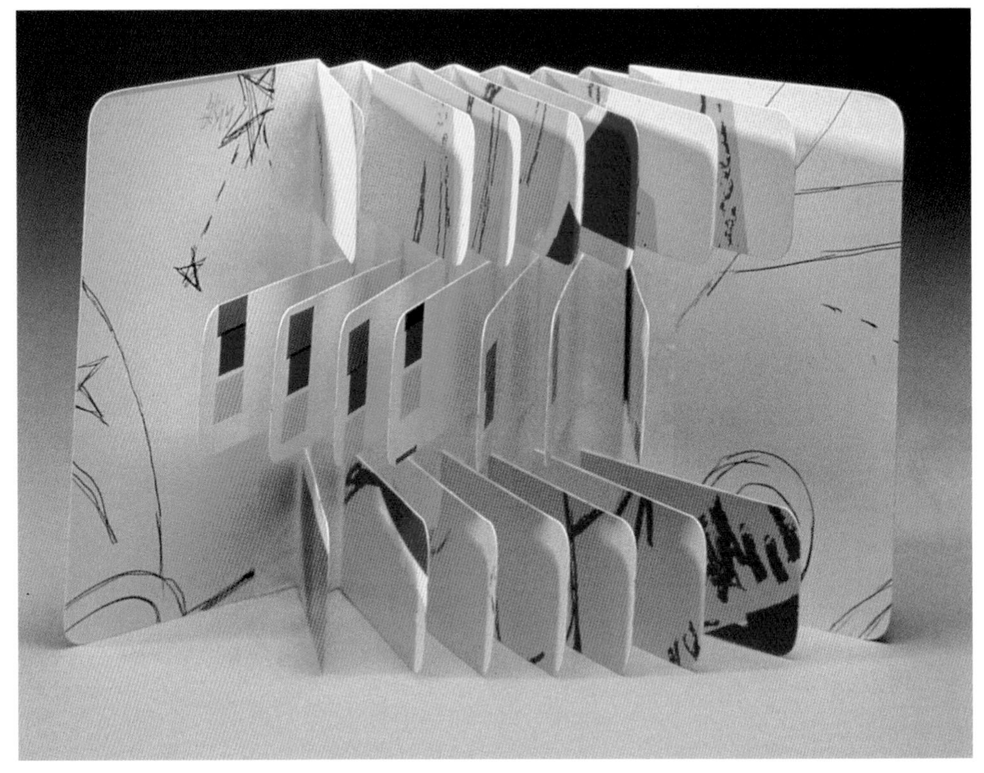

Hedi Kyle: Flag Book Model, 1997; paper; 3¼" × 5¼" (photo by Paul Warchol)

6. Turn the page. Now glue the middle strip, centered between the two strips, to the third panel. The glue goes on the back of this middle strip. When viewing the front of the strip it will be attached to the accordion to the right side of the peak fold.

7. Repeat steps 4–6 for each front and back of the accordion panels.

8. Add a cover that allows the book to stretch open (see below).

9. Add words that connect to your theme on the backs of the flags. Close the book, then open it to reveal one set of (three) cards at a time. Put a title on the first middle card.

10. Start your main text on the back of the top and bottom cards. Add the third section of text on the back of the second middle card.

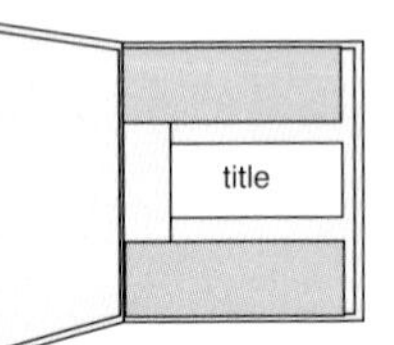

Step 9

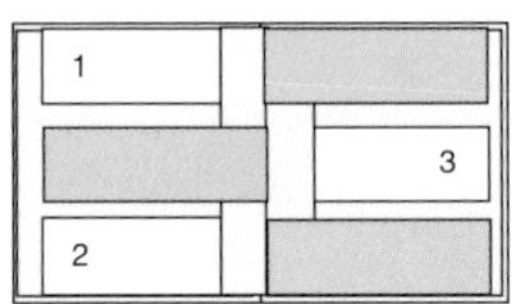

Step 10

Cover Styles

Choose from one of the cover styles below (see pages indicated for detailed instructions).

Example: 5" × 5¼" text block

Simple Hard Cover with Separate Boards (page 126): two 4-ply museum boards 5" × 5¼" (long); two pieces of book cloth or lightweight paper 6½" × 6¾" (long); two pieces of lightweight to medium-weight paper 4⅞" × 5⅛" (long)

Split-Board Cover (page 128): two 2-ply or 4-ply museum boards 5" × 5¼" (long); two 2-ply boards 4⅞" × 5¼" (long); two pieces of book cloth or lightweight paper 6½" × 6¾" (long); two pieces of lightweight paper 6½" × 6¾" (long). Wrap the boards and sandwich the ends of the accordion between each set.

Split-Board Cover with Decorated Front and Back (page 128): two 4-ply museum boards 5" × 5¼" (long); two 2-ply museum boards 4⅞" × 5¼" (long); book cloth or lightweight paper 6⅜" × 6¾" (long). Paint the 4-ply boards and cover the 2-ply boards.

Where, Oh Where, 2003; rubber stamps, acrylics, sewing, typewriter; unique; 6" × 6½"

Where, Oh Where, 2003; open

Left: *Anchor in a Tin Boat*, 2004; acrylic inks and gesso, gel pen, paper, canvas, seed pearls; file flag with ribbon loop closure; unique; 7½" × 5⅞" × 1½"
Right: *Anchor in a Tin Boat*, 2004; open

FILE FLAG BOOK

Time: 45 –60 minutes (small softcover version); 60–90 minutes (large hardcover version)
I first saw a version of this book by Robbin Ami Silverberg, called *After Midnight.* It is essentially a flag book tipped on its side: the accordion becomes the tail, and you read the book as if it were a series of file cards or folders. I made a miniature version from address file cards, called *Abstract Recipes.* Each card has a word and the ingredients for achieving the condition on the card. *House on File* has hard covers and a magnetic closure; *Anchor in a Tin Boat* also has hard covers; a single ribbon loop like a lasso can either hold the book closed or support it open for display. I recommend that beginners start with a very small, wedge-shaped book with soft covers like the model with a button and string closure.

You can use a store-bought button or make your own button closure from polymer clay. Books with the button-and-string closure will not be able to stand unassisted, because the string at the base is bumpy. Instead of a button, you can use self-adhesive magnetic strips available in some office-supply stores.

Charles Hobson made a version of this structure for his book *Degas Dancing.* Appropriately, he calls his structure an "easel accordion," for the way it displays the text and his monotypes of the painter Degas.

Tools: bone folder, pencil, 12" metal ruler; for the hard cover you will also need scissors, magazines or catalogs for scrap paper, PVA or a PVA/paste mixture, stencil brush for gluing

Materials Overview: lightweight to medium-weight paper for the spine, 7 heavy-weight cards, one piece of heavy-weight paper for the soft cover *or* 2 large boards (the same width as your book) × (the height of your cards + ⅛–½") *and* two strips of board (the width of your book) × (1–1½"). For the smaller books, I'm giving sizes for the soft covers, the larger ones will handle best with the hard covers.

Preparation: Make a list of your daydreams, the things you've desired at different ages: a pink twirly skirt, a brass compass, being a marimba player, whatever. Put one item on each of the seven cards. Write about whether you achieved your dream or not and how you feel about it now.

An alternate idea is to make a list of seven abstract concepts and your recipes for how you would achieve each one. Example: Harmony–hot chocolate, comfy chair, book by Jane Austen, telephone turned off.

Sample Sizes and Materials Needed for Each

Small example: 4" × 2¼": seven 4" × 2¼" address cards; one piece of lightweight or medium-weight paper 4" × 8" (short) for the accordion spine; one piece of heavyweight paper, 4" × 6¾" (short) for a wedge-shaped soft cover; for a closure you will need either a button, sewing thread, and thicker waxed linen thread *or* two self-adhesive magnetic strips ¼" × 3"

Large example: 6½" × 4½": seven heavyweight cards or 4" × 6" photographs (long), preferably backed with paper (see Mounting Paper, page 26); two pieces of text-weight paper 6" × 8" (short) for the spine ; one text-weight paper strip 6" × 2" (long) to connect the spine pieces; two 4-ply museum boards 6½" × 4½" (long); one 4-ply museum board 6½" × 1½" (long); one 4-ply museum board 6½" × 1¼" (long); lightweight cover paper

Abstract Recipes, 2003; brush pens, handmade polymer bead, typewriter, ink, address cards; file flag book; unique; 4" × 2½"

Left: File Flag Model, 2003; acrylic inks and gesso; unique; 4" × 2½"
Right: Charles Hobson: *Degas Dancing*, 1991; pastel/monotype; easel accordion; edition of 10; 11¾" × 15½" × 1" (photo by C. Hobson)

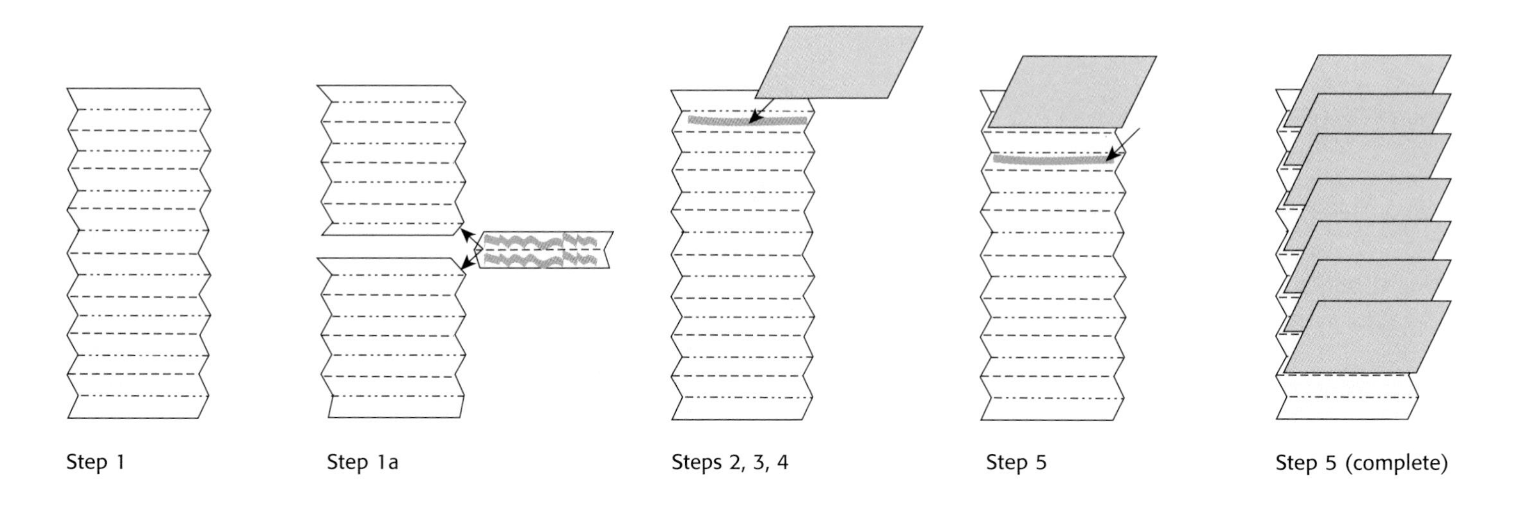

or book cloth 14¾" × 8" (short); inner lightweight paper 12¼" × 6¼" (short); for a closure you will need either two self-adhesive magnetic strips ¼" × 5" *or* about 24" of ¼–½" ribbon

Folding the Accordion Spine

All folds will be parallel to the spine, as usual.

1. For the smaller book, take the text-weight paper you will use for the accordion spine and fold an accordion with sixteen panels. This is done by first folding the paper in half, widthwise. Then fold the ends in to the center fold. Make four more valley folds by matching each folded edge and each of the two ends to its neighboring fold. Turn the paper over. Start from one end and match the end to its neighboring fold. Continue until all the paper is completely fan-folded, alternating peak and valley folds.

1a. For the larger book, take the larger, 6" × 8", text-weight paper for the accordion spine and fold two accordions with eight panels. (For instructions to make an eight-paneled accordion, see Seven- or Eight-Paneled Book, page 52.) Fold the smaller, 6" × 2", text-weight strip in half, lengthwise, and glue it to attach the accordions.

Wedge Model, 2003; acrylic inks and gesso; file flag with bead and string closure; unique; 4" × 2½" × ½"

Attaching the Cards

2. Place the accordion in front of you with the peak folds at each end.

3. Working from back to front, apply a thin line of glue to the second panel from the top.

4. Take the seventh card and use the bottom edge to smooth the glue to cover the panel completely. Press the card into place. The bottom edge will be attached to the accordion.

5. Repeat the application of glue and attaching of the cards at the even panels from the top, back to front. (If you count from the bottom or the front the cards will be on the odd panels, starting from 3.)

6. Make one of the wedge covers.

Wedge Soft Cover

You will measure, mark, and score at four parallel places on the back of the soft cover.

1. Place the cover in front of you, horizontally, wrong-side up.
2. From the left edge, measure, mark, and score ½".
3. From the first mark, measure, mark, and score ½".
4. From the second mark, measure, mark, and score a dimension that is equal to the short side of your flags plus ¼" (for example, 2½" for a little book with address cards).
5. From the third mark, measure, mark, and score the same measurement as in step 4.
6. Turn the paper over so that the two ½" scores are on your left. This is the outside of your book.
7. In the center (both horizontally and vertically) of the second ½" panel, make a mark.
8. On the first ½" panel, centered vertically, make two marks on the horizontal, approximately ⅜" apart. These should align with the mark from step 7.
9. Thread a bookbinding needle with 6" of waxed linen thread.
10. From front to back, sew into the second ½" panel at the mark, leaving a 4-5" tail of thread.
11. Poke a hole in the adjacent mark on the first ½" panel, then from back to front, sew to that hole.
12. From front to back, sew into the last mark. Turn over.
13. Knot the thread to itself on the inside by looping it through the stitch you see there. Turn over.
14. Place the cover horizontally with the two front ½" panels on the left again.
15. From the right, center your button at (but not over) the edge of the first score. Make marks on the cover to correspond to the holes in the button.
16. If your button has small holes, sew it to the cover with poly-wrapped cotton sewing thread. If it has larger holes, use matching waxed linen thread.
17. Turn the cover over. Apply glue to the flap next to where you just sewed the button. Press down the flap to cover the stitching and secure the button. Hold for 15-30 seconds or until secure.

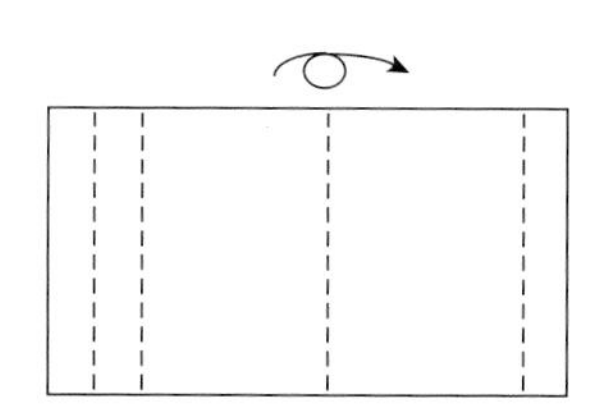
Steps 1, 2, 3, 4, 5

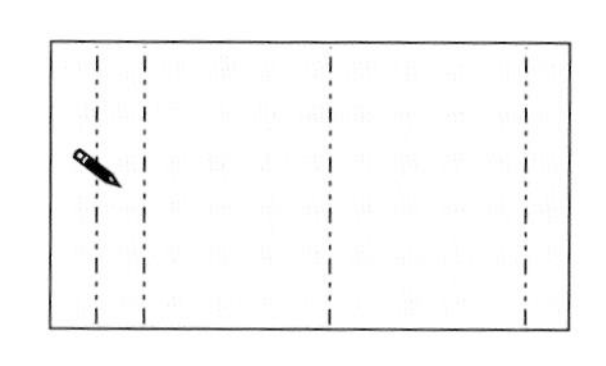
Steps 6, 7

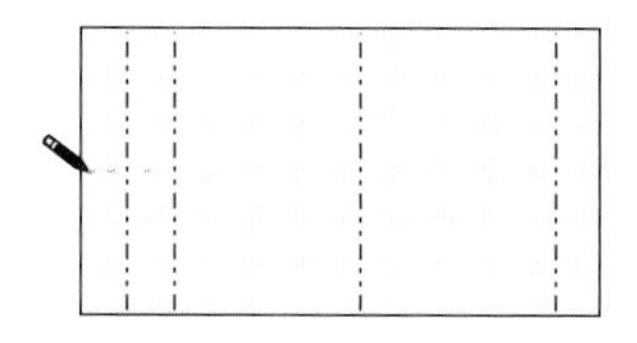
Step 8

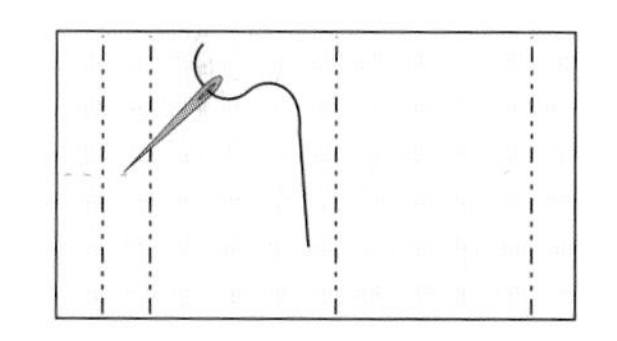
Steps 9, 10

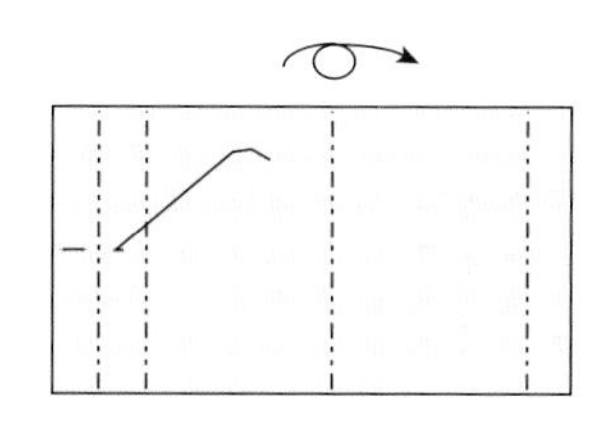
Steps 11, 12

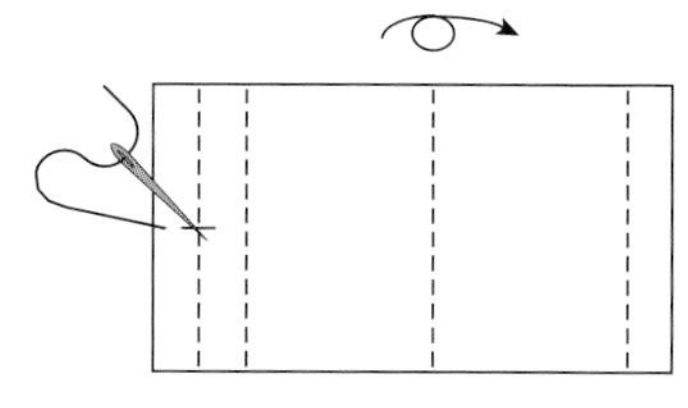
Step 13

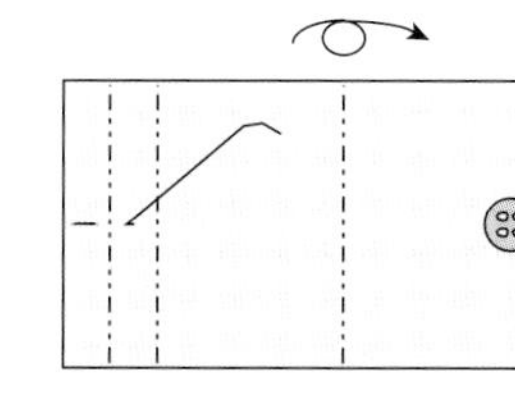
Steps 15, 16

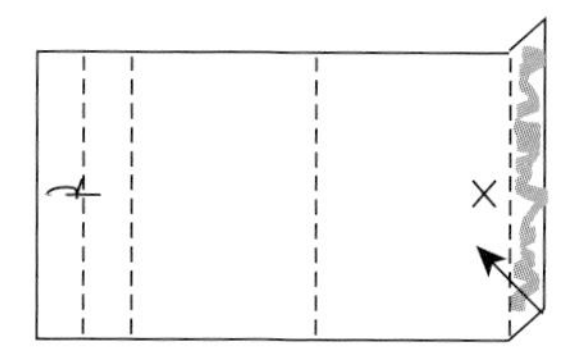
Step 17

Adhering the Accordion to the Cover

18. Spread a line of glue on the first panel of the accordion.
19. Press this panel to the front 1/2" panel of the cover, covering the stitching.
20. Spread a line of glue on the last panel of the accordion.
21. Press the last panel to the back cover, aligning the end of the accordion with the back fold.
22. Tie the book closed by folding up the cover, then winding the string around the button.

Steps 1, 2, 3, 4

Wedge Hard Cover

I made this structure for *House on File.* The techniques used to make this hard cover are similar to making any hard cover. You will need to leave 1/4" between the front board and the back board, but the usual 3/16" between the rest of the boards.

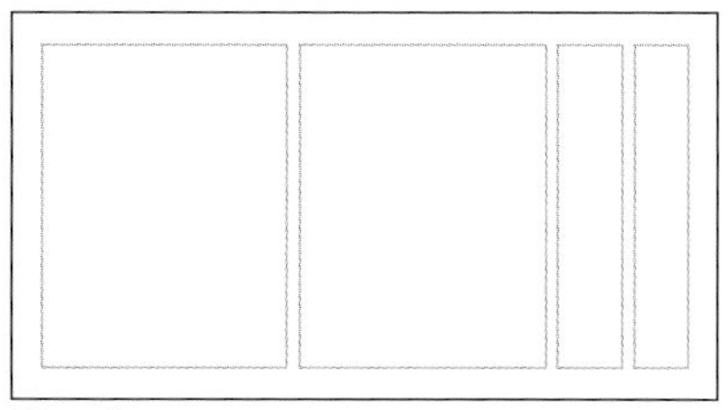

Step 5

1. Cover your work surface with layers of pages from a magazine. Discard any that you get glue on.
2. Arrange the cover paper in front of you, wrong-side up.
3. Arrange the boards on the cover paper as follows, from left to right: large front board, 1/4" gap, large back board, 3/16" gap, 1 1/2" strip, 3/16" gap, 1 1/4" strip. The 1 1/2" strip is your tail/spine. Center it top to bottom and side to side.
4. With your pencil, draw around the boards.
5. Remove the boards. Apply glue within one of the penciled boundaries and press the corresponding board in place.
6. Apply glue inside the boundaries, one at a time, and press the remaining boards in place, taking care that the gaps between the boards remain precisely as indicated. Use a spacer bar, if necessary.
7. With a scissors, cut the corners, leaving at least the thickness of the board between the board and the edge of the triangle you are cutting off.
8. Apply glue to the edges of the flaps one at a time, in any order, and fold them down. Discard scrap paper if any glue goes beyond the edges.

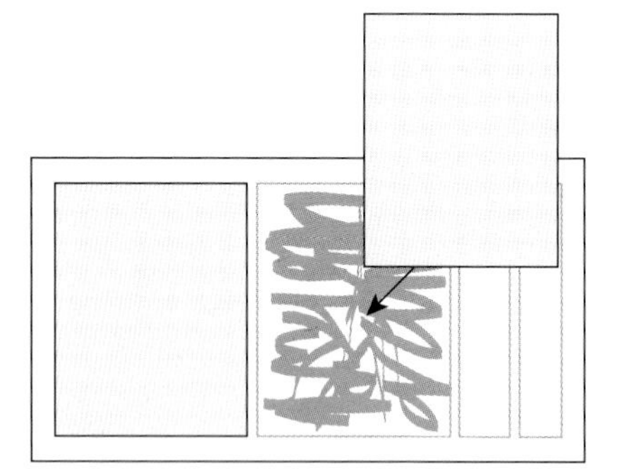

Steps 5, 6

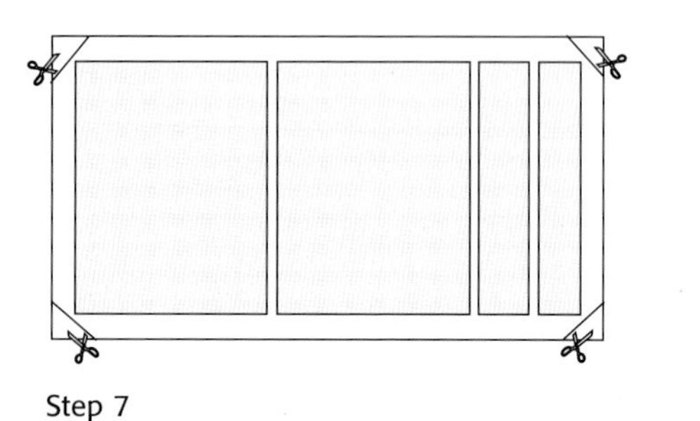

Step 7

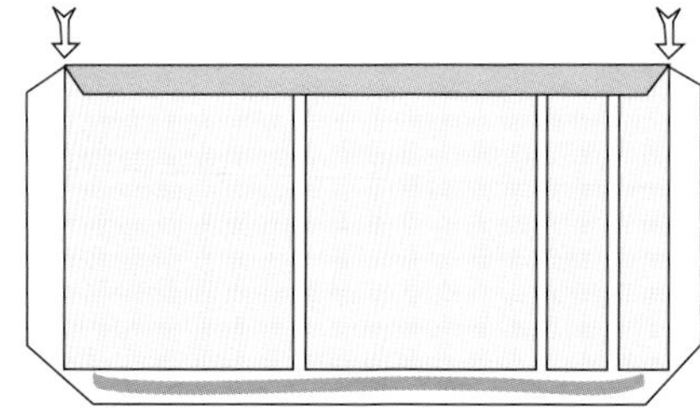

Step 8

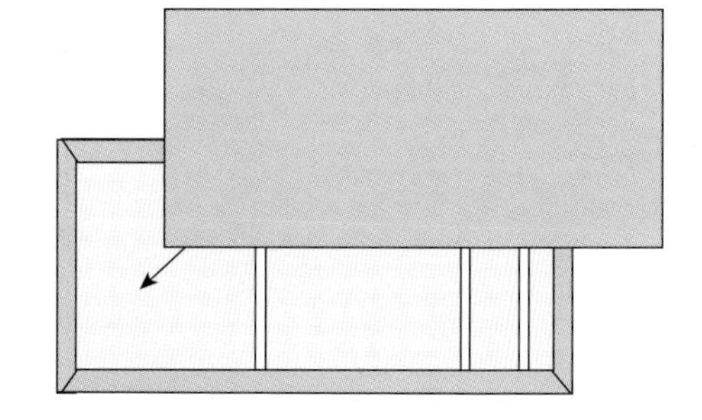

Step 12

9. Place the endpaper in front of you, wrong-side up.
10. With a stencil brush, apply glue evenly to the entire sheet, from the center outward.
11. Carefully lift the endpaper, lower it gently in a U shape onto the boards, and center it, making sure the margins are even.
12. Smooth it down gently, making sure it is completely flat.
13. Use the bone folder to press the paper into the gaps between the boards. Smooth out the front as well. Bend the boards into place, with one narrow strip at the bottom and one strip at the front.

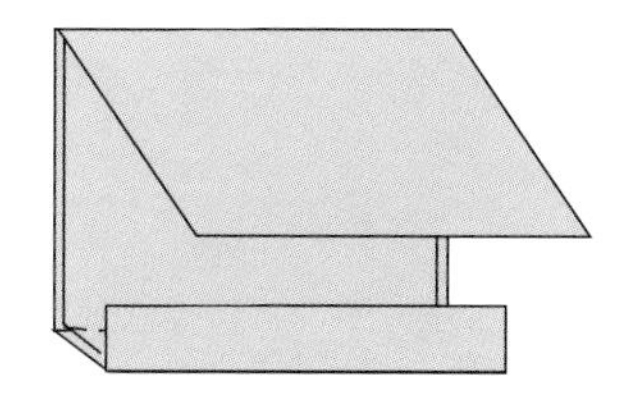

Step 13

Attaching the Accordion
14. Spread a line of glue on the first panel of the accordion (on the peak side).
15. Align the edge of the first panel with the lower edge of the 1¼" strip of board. Press down on the front panel and the board.
16. Spread a line of glue on the last panel of the accordion (on the peak side).
17. Align the edge of the last panel with the lower edge of the back board. Press down.
18. Add magnetic strips to the large front cover panel and the 1¼" flap. Detailed instructions for attaching magnetic strips are on page 139.

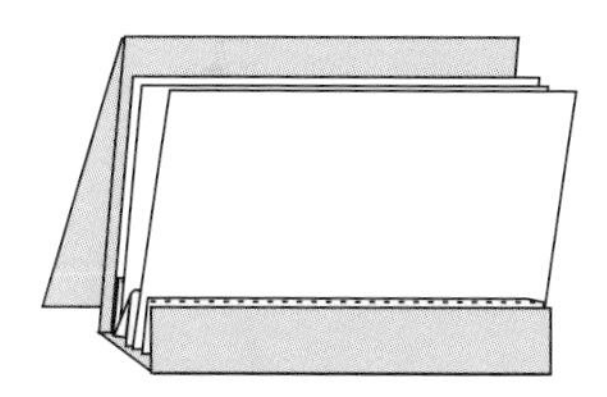

Step 17 (complete)

House on File, 2003; acrylic inks and gesso, moving stickers; file flag with magnetic closure; unique; 7" × 5¾" × 1¾"
House on File, 2003; open

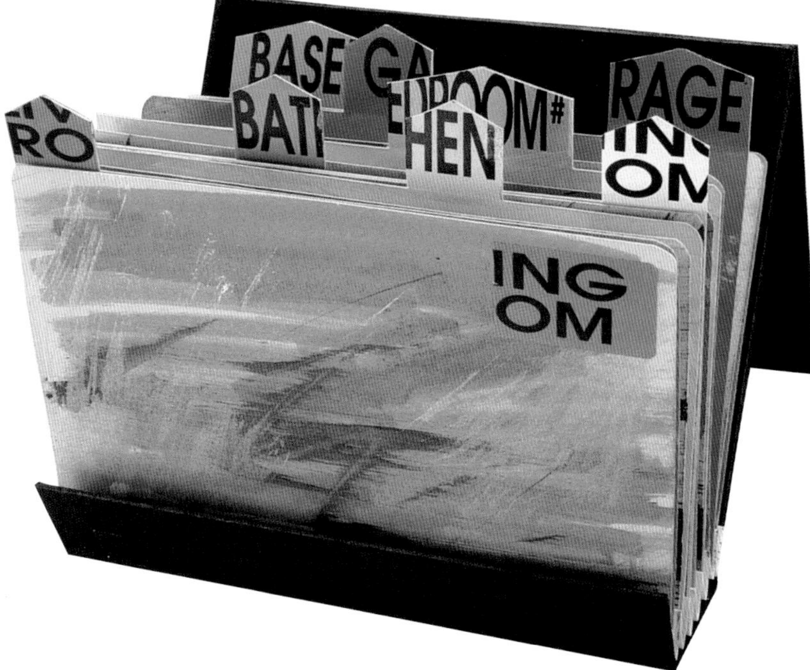

Card Book

Try writing down your dreams each morning on file cards (or 4" × 6" pieces of printmaking paper), one per card. Then look around the house and find objects or things that may have contributed to your dream. Attach articles, photographs, or photocopies of objects to the back of the dream card and write a few words about the connection and why you think you might have dreamed that scene. After a week or two you will have an impressive stack of cards and you may have cleaned your desk of ephemera: ticket stubs, library due-date notices, business cards, photographs, and cartoons. Sort by date or theme, if you like. Make a box for this collection and give it a title. Mine was simply *April Dreams*. See the Notebook Box on page 42 for box instructions.

April Dreams, 2004; gel pen, rubber stamp, collage, polymer clay cat; found objects; unique; 6½" × 4¾" tabbed cards in box, 7" × 5⅛" × 3"
April Dreams, 2004; open

SIDE BINDINGS AND SEWN SIGNATURES

Chapter Four

I had never consciously tried to make anything I considered beautiful until I started making monotypes. I became so involved with the shades of colors and shapes of objects that it really didn't matter what the subject was, I just enjoyed looking at the colors and objects. When I make a book, I am more concerned about content, but I realize that a beautiful cover may draw a reader to the message within. If you start with materials and colors that you find beautiful, you may either inspire or trap yourself. If the papers are too beautiful, you may become intimidated and worry about making a mistake. Imperfection is everywhere. Some imperfections can be seen as beautiful–the knotholes in wood, for example, or colorful layers of peeling paint. Sometimes what you think are mistakes are actually doors that can lead you to a place you might not ever have gone. Experiment and a new, better idea may eventually appear.

Sewn Structures
Back row (left to right): *Lightning Strikes a Butterfly; Invisible Berries;* Exposed Stitch Model
Middle row: *act now not why*
Front row: *Once Said a Stoic: Epictetus;* Exposed Stitch Model*;* Multiple-Signature model

Mistakes in technique, however, can be corrected only through observation and practice. If you are having trouble with something, check to see that you are following the instructions precisely. Only after you understand the technique will you be able to practice it to your advantage. Then, the more you sew, the less tangled you will become. The more knots you make, the more secure you can learn to make them.

Thread and Needles

Traditionally, linen thread is used for binding books. The thickness is similar to a heavy-duty mending thread found in fabric stores. Currently linen thread is sold at art supply and bookbinding supply stores and through catalogs.

Also purchase a small cake of beeswax to wax the thread. To wax thread, cut the length you will use and hold one end against the wax with your thumb. Take your other hand and draw the thread tightly against the wax, keeping your thumb in place. The wax will make the thread glide through the book as you sew and will help to secure any necessary knots. Waxed linen thread in a variety of colors is sold in some craft stores as a macramé thread or for basketry. It is quite a bit thicker but it is useful for almost every binding in this chapter, especially when the thread is visible from the outside of the book.

If you plan to use thread you already have, test it first. Pull it tightly. Does it stretch or break easily? If you are likely to cut yourself or cut off your circulation before the thread breaks, you have a winning thread. The thread needs to be strong enough to hold your book together securely so the pages will not shift. Choose thread accordingly.

Multiple-Signature Model with Origami Envelope Pockets, 2004; acrylic inks and gesso, ribbon; unique; 4¼" × 6"

Use a sharp needle with an eye that is small but that will hold the thread you chose. Sturdy bookbinding needles with a small eye are preferable. You can often find these in a variety pack of needles or in the type of needle "repair kit" sold in supermarkets. Bookbinding needles are sold in many art supply and bookbinding supply stores and through catalogs.

Hold your book together while you sew. Use a binder clip or bulldog clip for larger projects. Always fold a piece of paper into a pad to be sandwiched between the jaws of the clip to protect your pages. For smaller books you may use a loose paper clip.

Step 1

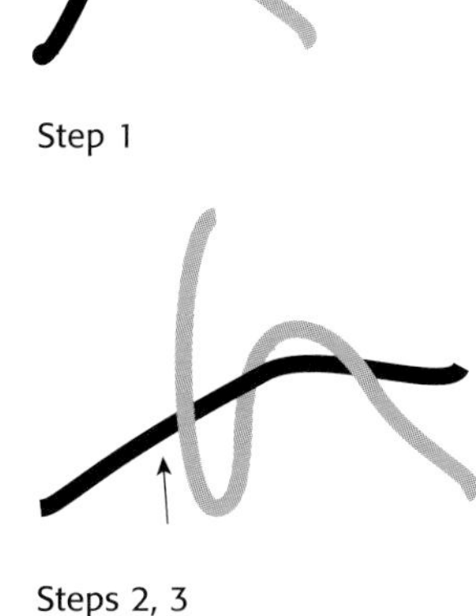

Steps 2, 3

Square Knot

You absolutely must know this knot for bookmaking. With this knot, the piece of thread held in your right hand is what I call the "working piece." The other piece, in your left hand, does not move.

1. Hold one end in your right hand, the other in your left.
2. Take the right piece over the left piece and then back under the left piece.
3. Now the piece that was originally on your right is on your left.
4. Take this (now left) piece over the right piece (formerly the left).
5. Take the (now) left piece under the right piece.
6. Pull to tighten.

Step 4

Single-Signature Book

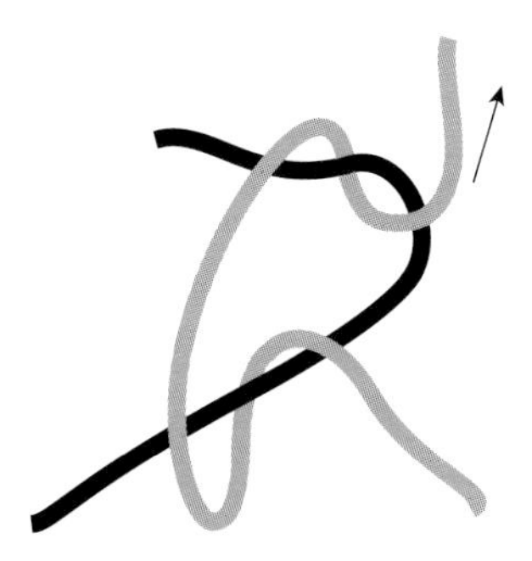

Step 5

Time: 15–20 minutes

Sometimes when you work with one theme you have individual stories that are only loosely connected, but perhaps the thoughts and style are the same throughout. Maybe each story isn't really long enough or strong enough to stand alone. If you create three simple books on the same topic, try putting them in a small portfolio for a unified collection. (See Wraparound Portfolio; page 133.)

The single signature book is generally known as a pamphlet: sheets of paper simply folded in half, nested, and sewn at the fold. Use four pieces of text-weight paper or one to two sheets of heavyweight paper per signature.

Tools: bone folder, pencil, metal ruler, needle, thread, awl, corrugated cardboard
Materials: four pieces of lightweight to medium-weight paper or vellum 8½" × 5½" (short); one piece of medium- to heavy-weight paper 8¾" × 5¾" (short) for the cover
Example: 5¾" × 8¾"

Steaming on the Stovetop: Poems from the Pantry, 2003; letterpress, linoleum cuts, collagraphs; edition of 42; 6⅛" × 8¼"

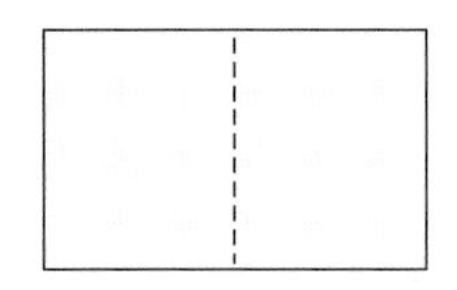

Step 1

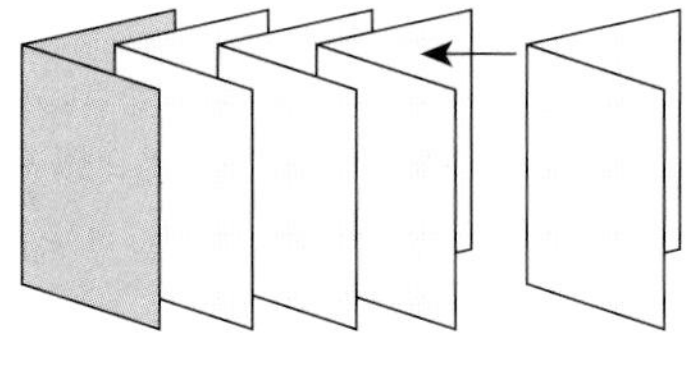

Step 2

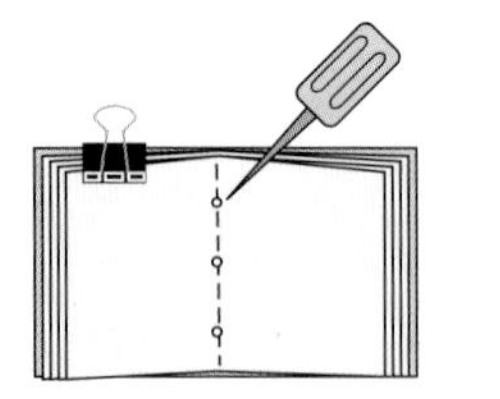

Steps 2, 3

1. Fold each sheet and the cover in half, widthwise.

2. Nest the sheets, one inside the other, with the cover paper on the outside. With the pages all the way open, use a paper clip or binder clip to clip the pages together on one side of the fold.

3. Protect your work surface with a piece of corrugated cardboard. Measure, mark, and, with the awl, poke three holes on the fold line: one in the very center and one on each side of the center hole. The outer holes can be ½"–2" from the edges of the book.

Sewing Pattern

4. Measure a length of thread that is three times the height of your book.

5. Do not knot the thread. Sew from inside to outside at the center hole. Leave about 2" of thread dangling on the inside.

6. Go in one end hole.

7. Skip the center hole and sew back out the hole on the opposite end.

8. Sew in through the center hole.

9. Make sure the loose threads are on each side of the long stitch. Tie off the ends in a square knot.

10. Trim the thread to ¼"– ½."

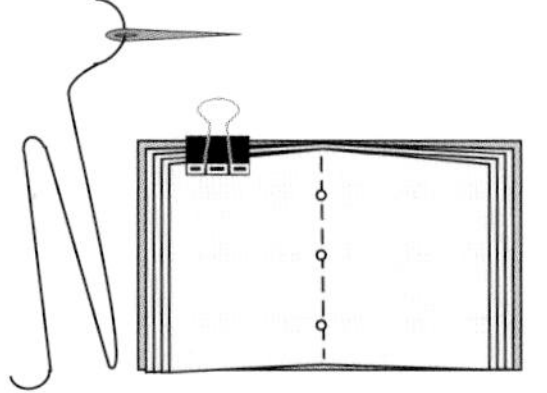

Step 4

Step 5

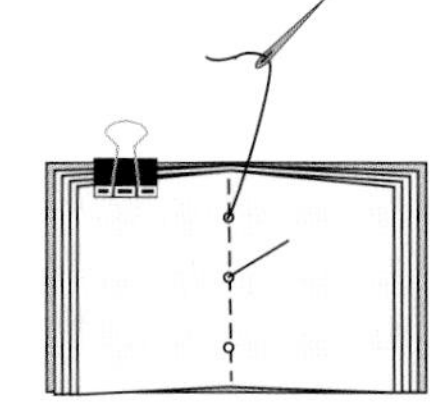

Step 6

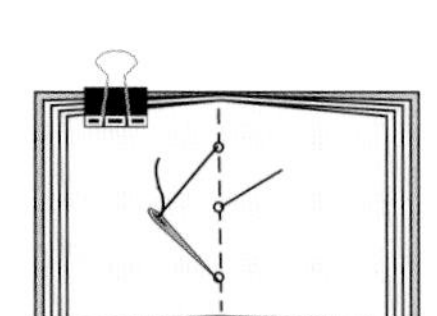

Step 7

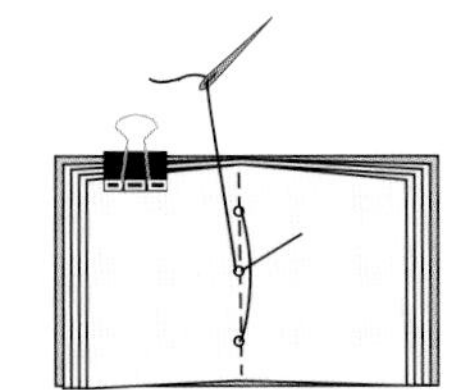

Step 8

Variation 1: If you want to see the knot on the outside of the book or you wish to tie a bead or charm to the end, reverse the ins and outs in the sewing pattern directions.

Variation 2: Make a tall, thin book of lists or poems using paper 8½" × 11", folded the long way (with the grain). Poke five holes along the fold instead of three. Go in through the center hole, but instead of making the long stitch immediately, sew a running stitch to the hole at the head of the book and back down toward the center again. When you get to the hole immediately adjacent to the center hole, skip over the center hole, then sew a running stitch to the hole at the tail and back up again Tie off the ends in the middle with a square knot.

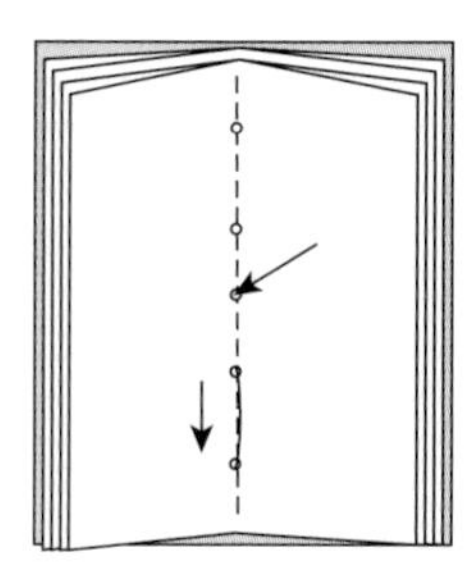

Variation 2a

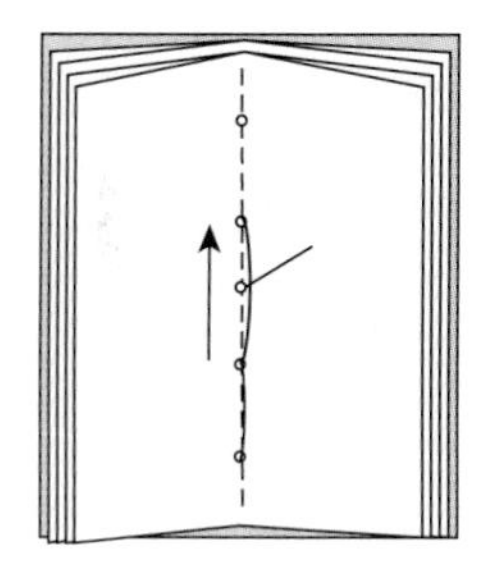

Variation 2b

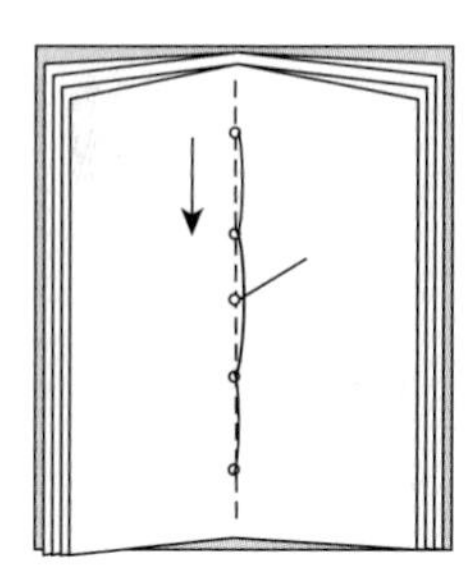

Variation 2c

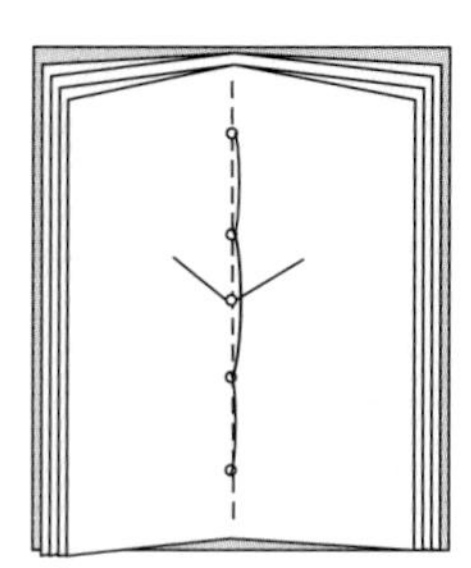

Variation 2d
(ready to tie off)

Pop-Up Accordion with Laced Edges

Time: 60 minutes

This book has two sides: one side is the pop-up; the back of each of the pop-ups provides a place for secret writing, a picture, or just an alternate idea. The Mylar cover reveals all. Because of the laces, the book does not stretch out into a flat accordion.

Invisible Berries is the story of a Hawthorne tree that had red berries one day and no berries the next. I made it in memory of Nana, my mother's mother, who died the day before the robins ate the berries. If I had not

Invisible Berries, 2003; black gesso, gel pen, graphite, photos, ink, waxed linen thread; unique; 5" × 7" × 1¼"

Dorothy Yule, illustrations by Susan Hunt Yule: *Souvenirs of Great Cities: San Francisco; London; Paris; New York*, 1996; letterpress printed from multiple polymer plates; doubled accordion with pop-ups, two removable spines, printed paper box; edition of 150: 120 boxed sets, 30 individual books; 2½" × 2½" × ⅞" (photo by Martha Blegen)

been watching, I would not have known what had happened to them: the berries would have suddenly turned invisible. I thought of things that happen that we never see.

Tools: bone folder, pencil, 24" metal ruler, art knife and cutting mat; hole punch
Materials: 4 sheets Lenox or heavyweight printmaking paper 7" × 20"; 1 sheet Mylar 7" × 21"; waxed linen thread, ribbon, raffia, or cord
Example: 5" × 7" book with 1" spine

Preparation: Think of a time in your life when you felt invisible or, alternately, vulnerable. Remember a window or a view somewhere that had meaning for you. Think of an object you hid (in childhood or now). Think of a time you felt shy or when you saw someone very shy; what happened? Was there ever a time you saw something in public that you thought should be private? A few ideas you might work with: invisible, visible, window, hidden, shy, open, obvious, privacy.

Take one anecdote or scene, vision, or memory and write it down. Then think of the outcome. Did this change your life in any way? How does it connect to the outside world? What else does it remind you of? Take it one step further; give it depth and layers by adding these connections. After you write, divide your story into either six or twelve sections, depending on how long it is and how it separates into paragraphs or lines. Make your pages and add the text to them, either on the pop-up segments or on the flat pages. If you think you will need to add more pages, consider sewing a single signature pamphlet (see page 77) at the last valley fold.

Folding the Accordions

1. Fold each sheet of paper in half, widthwise.

2. Fold the open ends back to the folded edge to make accordions with four panels.

3. Set the papers in front of you so that each begins with a valley fold and forms a "W." You now have four "W"s.

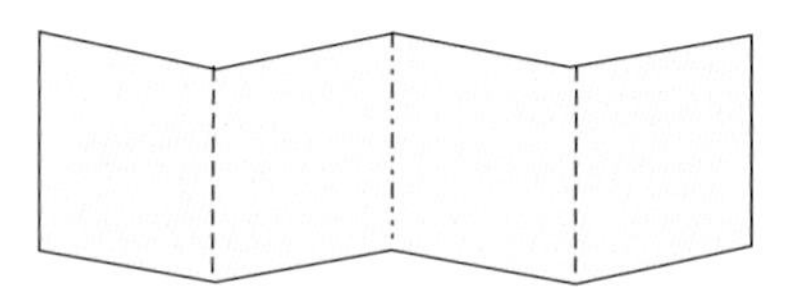

Steps 1, 2 ,3

Cutting the Pop-Ups

4. On one "W" draw a square or rectangle exactly centered in the second valley fold. The horizontal measurement should not exceed 4", meaning that you can have a square 4" × 4" or a rectangle 2" × 4" or 3" × 4", etc. This is your first accordion.

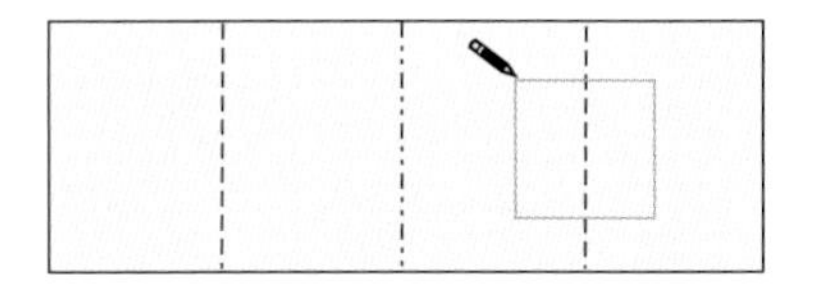

Step 4

5. On two of the "W"s draw a square or rectangle exactly centered in the two valley folds in each "W." In this case, make them identical in size to the one drawn on the first "W." These are your second and third accordions.

6. On the fourth and last "W," make this square or rectangle only in the first valley fold. This is your last accordion.

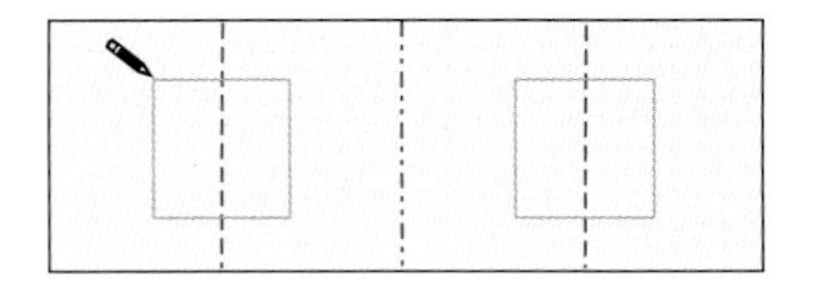

Step 5

7. With your knife against the metal ruler for a guide, cut along the top and bottom lines (horizontals) of the squares or rectangles.

8. With the bone folder or a butter knife, draw a score or indentation along the right and left (vertical) edges of the squares or rectangles. Note: To make the shapes "pop," put one hand in one of the horizontal slits and push forward at the vertical fold; refold the vertical valley fold into a peak, making valley folds at the vertical scores on each side.

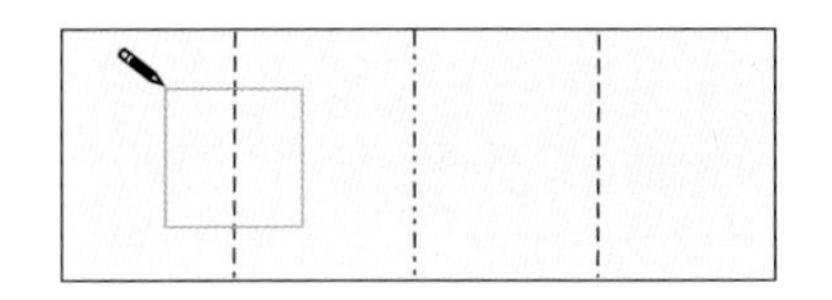

Step 6

Lacing the Book

9. Use the hole punch to punch holes along the right edge of the first accordion, about ½" from the edge. Use this punched edge as a template (stencil) and make pencil marks at the right and left edges of the next two accordions. Make marks only on the left edge of the last accordion. Punch all holes.

10. Use 1½ to 2 lengths (measure using the long side of the book) of waxed linen thread, ribbon, raffia, or cord for each pair of edges to be joined. Lace through the holes in any design you wish. You can wrap around the edge, crisscross, or do a simple running stitch (straight in and out).

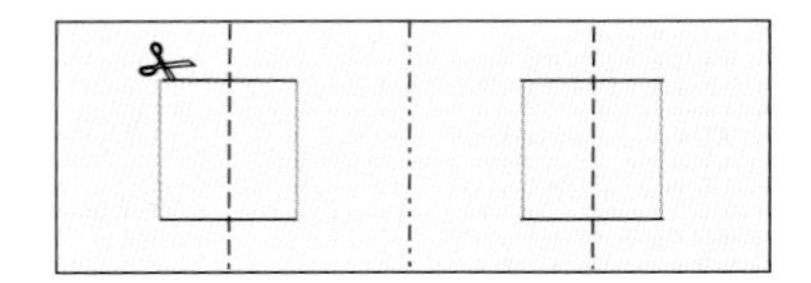

Step 7

Making the Wrapper

11. Place the Mylar in front of you horizontally, and measure 10" from each end. Mark these points by making a crease with your thumbnail, a bone folder, or a butter knife. Make two vertical scores at these marks.

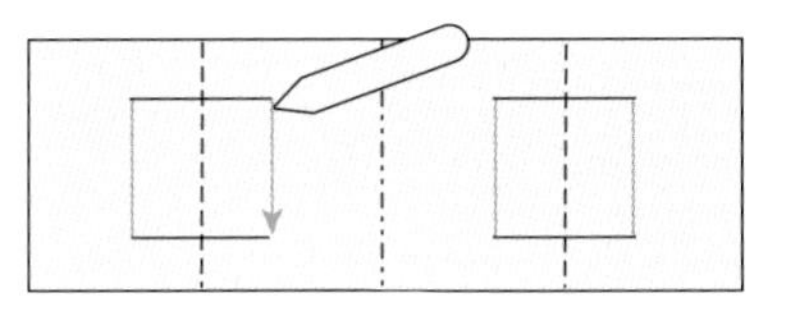

Step 8

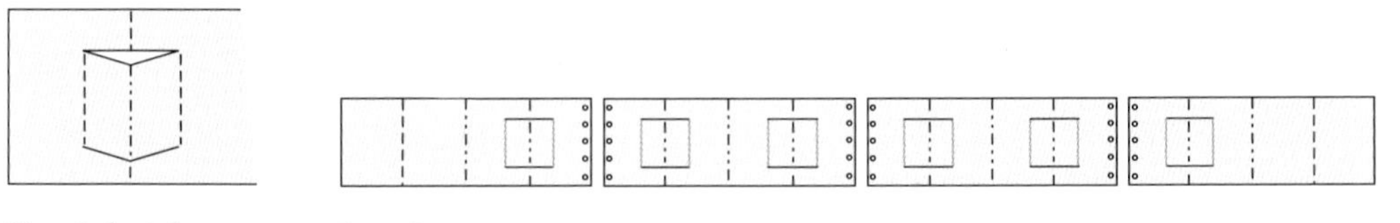

Step 8 (note)

Step 9

Dorothy Yule, illustrations by Susan Hunt Yule: *Souvenirs of Great Cities: San Francisco; London; Paris; New York*, 1996; open
(photo by Martha Blegen)

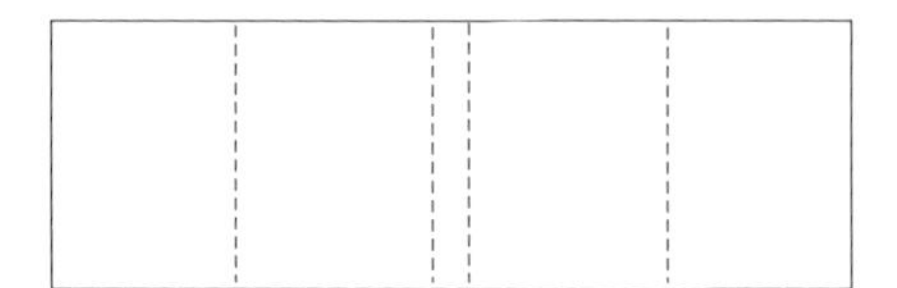

Steps 11, 12

12. Mark, crease, or score 5" from each end as well. You should now have four valley folds.
13. Wrap the Mylar around your book, tucking the first and last pages of the accordion into the cover flaps.

Variation 1: Make a square- or rectangular-shaped stencil using the sizes from step 4. Instead of drawing the shape in the valley fold, paint it with a light coat of black gesso. Or use white or gold gesso on dark paper.
Variation 2: Cut different shapes or different sizes of rectangles for the pop-ups.
Variation 3: Use a light- to medium-weight paper that is twice the height you want your book to be (14" × 20" in this example). Fold the four-panel accordions; open. Then fold the paper in half, lengthwise; open. Cut pop-ups as shown in the diagram. The lengthwise fold will be refolded to become the top of the book, so keep this in mind when cutting out your pop-up images.

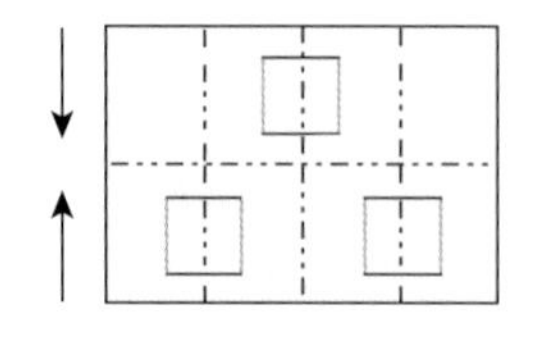

Variation 3

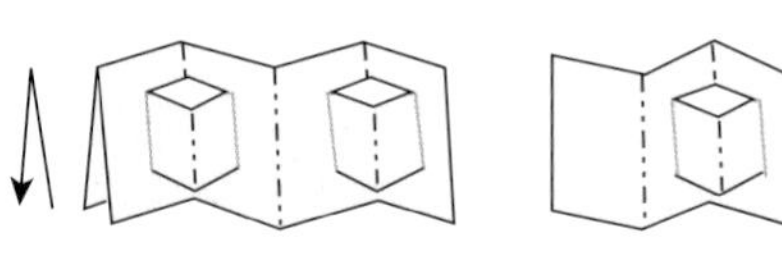

Variation 3 (front) Variation 3 (back)

Dorothy Yule used one long piece of paper (no lacing) and this technique for each of the four intricate books in her series, *Souvenirs of Great Cities*. The text is in verse and reads on both sides. An advantage of first folding the paper in half, lengthwise, was that she was able to print the whole book on one side of the paper. The non-adhesive wrapped hard covers have both a removable spine piece and removable fore edge piece; these pieces keep the book together in a neat package (see page 125).

SIDE BINDING WITH TABBED PAGES

Time: 75 minutes
Binding at the edge constricts the book so that it does not open all the way; using soft paper or a horizontal format helps the reader get inside the book. I like to work with lightweight mulberry paper, which can also be used in a vertical format. You can make these pages with or without tabs; the measurements are the same. The tabs are made like little pop-ups. Use 100% cotton stationery or résumé paper for pages with tabs. Because of the stiffness of the paper, this book with tabs calls for a horizontal format. Unlike a book with signatures, the folds of the pages will be at the fore edge, the open edges at the spine. The non-adhesive covers function exactly like the pages.

Make a small, tabbed book structure that echoes the tabbed pages in a dictionary.

The title of *act now not why* came to me before I knew what it would be about. I looked up each word in the title and thought about the definitions. Later, I wrote about my childhood memories of throwing a plastic purse out the window and my memories of things my children threw as toddlers. The book is, in essence, about cause and effect. I wrote: "Later, we experiment with words. I say this; you feel that. I can anger you or endear you to me. And I can say words that mean we will never see each other again. You can do the same. Who says we don't all have magical powers?"

act now not why, 2004; rubber stamp, gesso and acrylic inks, stencil; tabbed fore edge on side-bound book; unique; 6¼" × 3¼"

Lightning Strikes a Butterfly, 2002; letterpress, collagraphs, linoleum cuts; side bound; edition of 27; 6¼" × 8¼"

Tools: bone folder, pencil, 12" metal ruler, scissors, art knife and cutting mat, binder clip or paper clip, needle, thread, awl, corrugated cardboard
Materials: six pieces of résumé paper 3" × 8½" (short); two pieces of pastel paper or other colored paper 3" × 8½" (short)
Example: 3" × 4¼" book

Preparation: Open a dictionary and pick a word. Look at the source of the word and see how it inspires you. Write your word, piece of word, or variation, on each of the tabs. Plan to write your story within the tabbed pages. These instructions call for six tabs; instead of looking through the dictionary, just try to think of a word with six letters. If you can't think of one, use *beauty*. On a separate sheet of paper, write your thoughts or feelings about your word. How does the word connect with your past, present, or future? Do you have a memory in which this word played a key role? Write everything. Choose and revise later. If that seems too restrictive, make more pages and more tabs like the twelve-tabbed book *act now not why*.

Making the Pages

1. Fold all papers in half, widthwise, including the colored papers for the covers. Set aside the covers.

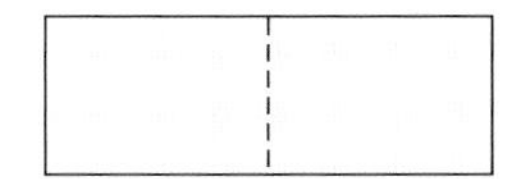

Step 1

Making the Tabs

2. Place the inner pages in front of you with the folds at the right.
3. Measure and lightly mark a vertical line ½" from the right edge of each page.
4. Measure and lightly mark horizontal lines ½" apart, between the vertical pencil line and the right (folded) edges of the pages.
5. On the first page, cut along the first (top) horizontal line to make a slit.
6. On the second page, cut a slit along the first (top) line and one along the second line.
7. On the third page, cut slits along the second and third lines.
8. On the fourth page, cut slits along the third and fourth lines.
9. On the fifth page, cut slits along the fourth and fifth lines.
10. On the sixth page, cut a slit along the fifth (last) line.
11. With the bone folder against the metal ruler for a guide, make a deep score along the vertical pencil line of each page; starting at a top or bottom edge and stopping at a slit. Do this on all of the pages. Erase the pencil lines, especially where they cross the tab.
12. One page at a time, push the fore edge into a valley fold so that it goes in toward the spine. New peak folds form along the score. Leave the ½" tab as it is. Do not refold the tab. Repeat for all pages.
13. Write, stamp, or stencil one letter on each tab.
14. Now organize the writing you did. Start by finding sentences or fragments that begin with each of the letters in the word. Put them into a sequence, rewriting if you need to. Write your text on the pages, but make sure you leave at least a 1" margin on the open edges.

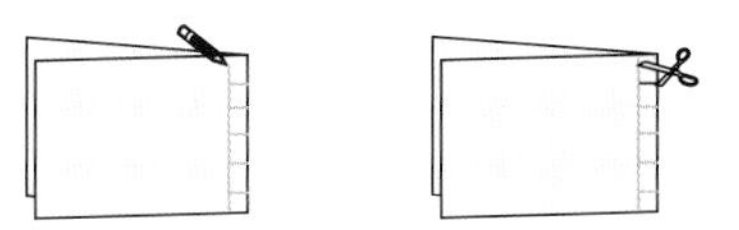

Steps 2, 3, 4 Step 5

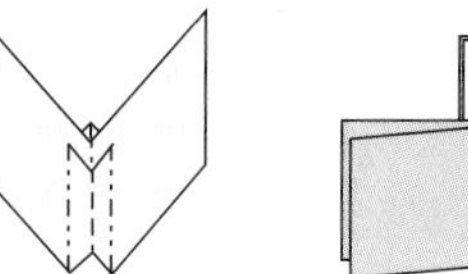

Step 12

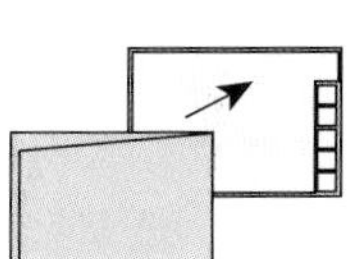

Steps 15, 16

Assembling the Book

15. Stack the pages so that the tabs are staggered, open edges aligned.
16. Add covers front and back, with the folds at the fore edge. Clip the pages together in the middle with a paper clip or binder clip.
17. Measure and mark ½" from the left edge.
18. Measure and mark 1" from the top and bottom edges.
19. Place the book on top of the corrugated cardboard. Use the awl to poke holes through the book at the intersection of the lines.

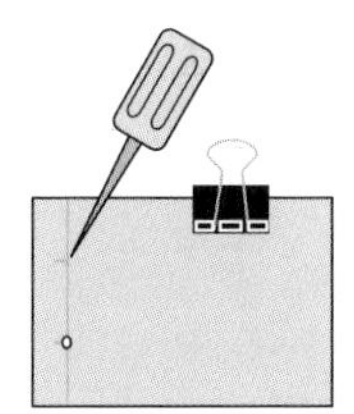

Steps 16, 17, 18, 19

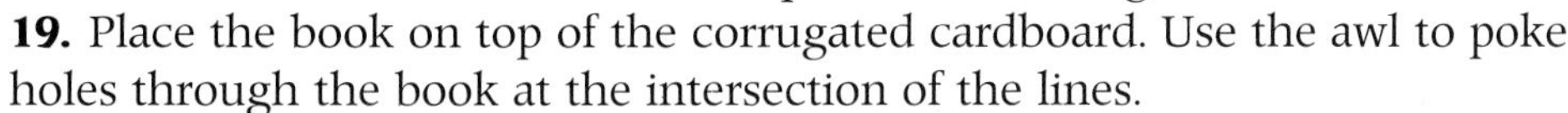

Sewing Pattern

20. Thread the needle with a piece of thread that measures about three to four times the height of your book (about 9"–12" for this example). Insert the threaded needle through the bottom hole from the back. Leave a 2" tail, or enough thread to knot later. Do not make a knot yet.
21. Wrap around the bottom of the book and sew into the bottom hole from the back.
22. Wrap around the side of the book and sew into the bottom hole from the back. (Yes, you have used the bottom hole three times.)
23. Sew into the top hole from the front.
24. Wrap the thread around the top of the book and sew into the top hole from the front.

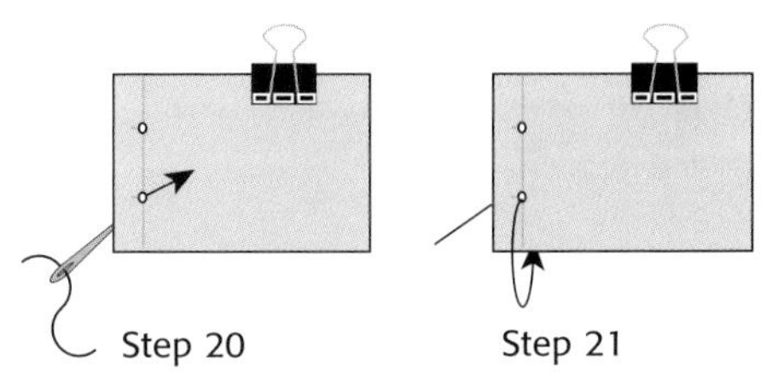

Step 20 Step 21

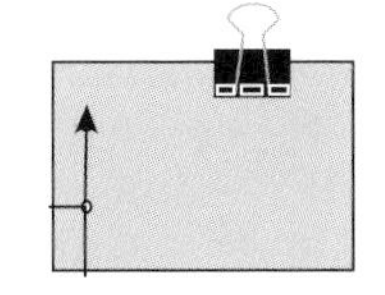

Steps 23

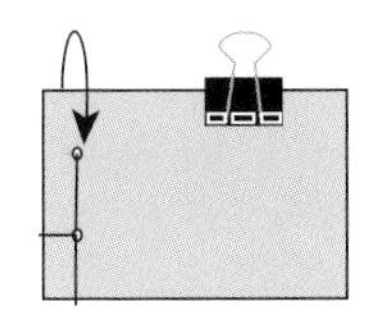

Steps 24

Left: Layered Page Models, 2003; linoleum cuts, collagraphs, wood type; 5½" × 8"
Right: Collagraphic block, linoleum block, and print from *Lightning Strikes a Butterfly*, 2002

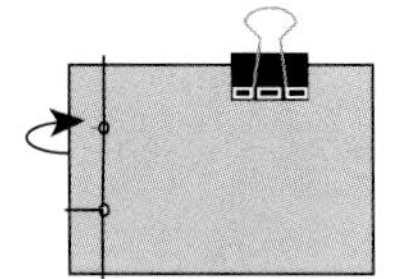

Step 25

25. Wrap the thread around the side of the book and sew into the top hole from the front.
26. Turn the book over. Tie the two ends together in a square knot, trying to center the knot over one of the holes so it will be less noticeable. Trim the ends.

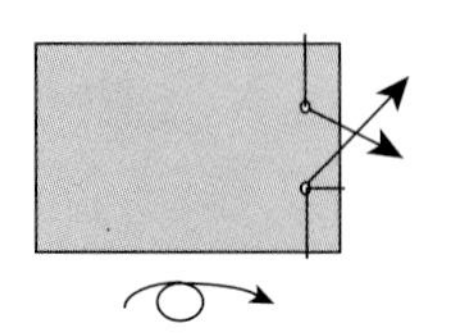

Step 26

Finishing
27. If you haven't done so already, write your word as the title of the book. Put one letter on each tab.

Variation 1: Add a hinged hard cover. Follow the instructions on page 87 to cover the boards; when the covers are dry, sew the covers with the book pages following steps 15–27 above.
Variation 2: Layered Pages and Crossed Stitching. Using soft, lightweight paper enables you to make a book in a vertical orientation; the pages turn easily. I used it for *Lightning Strikes a Butterfly*. This structure is excellent if you would like to try working with layered pages; the layers get sewn together and become a unit. This is a way to make a collage without using glue.

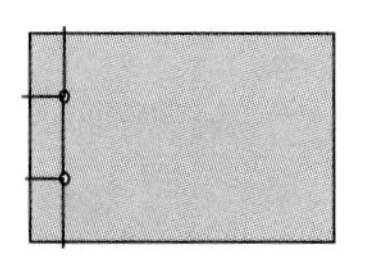

Complete

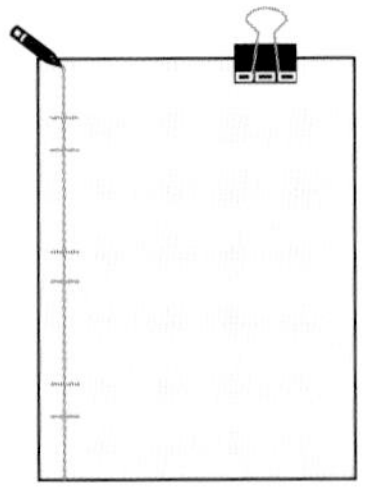

Variation 2

Hinged Hard Cover for Side Binding

This cover works well with any side binding. Just make sure the grain of your papers and boards is parallel to the spine; also, the cover paper should be 1½" larger than the boards in both directions.

For the Side Binding with Tabbed Pages (see page 83), use boards that measure 4¼" × 3¼" (short), and trim them to 3¾" × 3¼"; use a ½" strip for the spine. Or use larger boards and sew a stack of 8½" × 11" single pages for a report; the boards should be 8½" × 11¼" and trim them to 8" × 11"; use a ½" strip for the spine.

Note: For more about gluing techniques, see Adhesives, page 26, or the chapter "Covers and Closures," page 123.

Tools: bone folder, pencil, 12" metal ruler, scissors, art knife and cutting mat, magazines or catalogs for scrap paper, PVA or PVA/paste mixture, brush for gluing, 3⁄16" spacing bar, waxed paper, two Masonite boards, heavy books

Materials: two 4-ply museum boards 6" × 8" (long); two pieces of cover paper or book cloth 8" × 10" (long); two endpapers 6" × 7¾" (long)

1. Trim the boards so that you have two pieces that are 5½" × 8" and two pieces that are ½" × 8".

2. Cover the work surface with several layers of pages from a magazine. Discard any layers that get messy.

3. Arrange one outer cover paper in front of you, horizontally, wrong-side up.

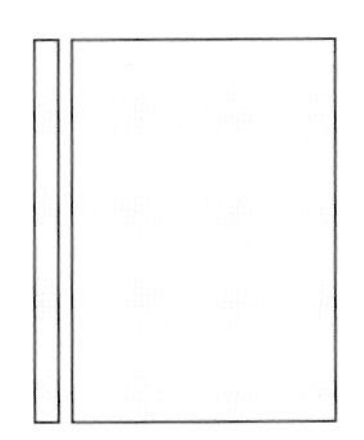

Step 1

Soup, 2004; monotype, stencil, rubber stamp, Lama Li and mulberry papers; unique book in progress; tabbed fore edge on sidebound book; 7" × 4½

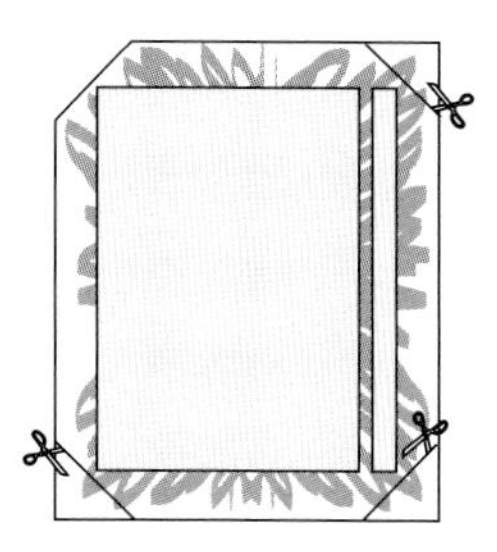

Steps 4, 5, 6, 7

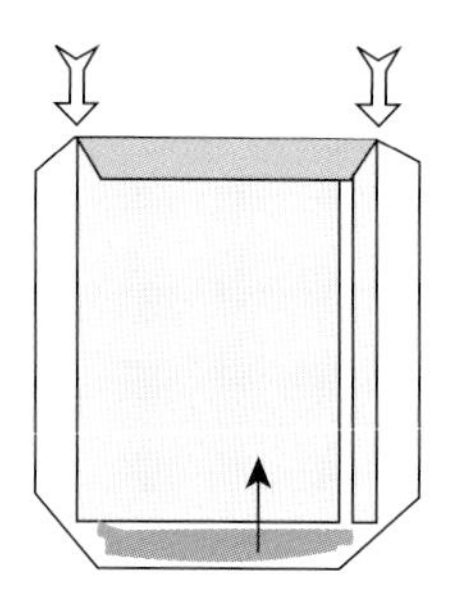

Step 8

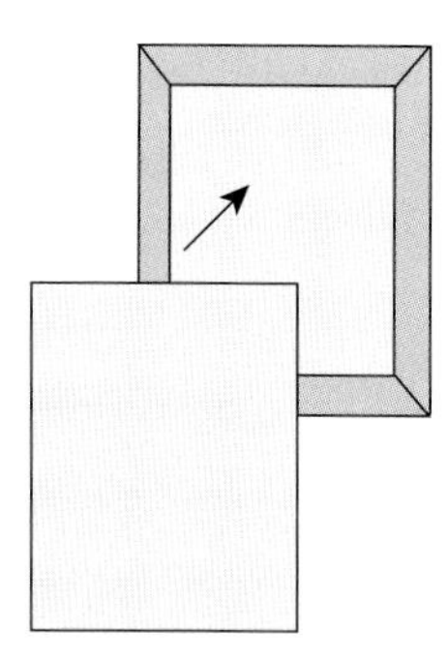

Steps 9, 10

4. Spread glue evenly on the paper with a brush or piece of board, working from the center outward. Discard one layer of scrap paper to give yourself a clean surface.

5. For the front cover, place one 1/2" spine strip approximately 1" from the right edge of the paper. Press down. (When making the back cover, place the spine strip at the left edge.)

6. Leave approximately 3/16" to the left of the spine strip (you can use a 3/16" spacing bar as a guide; take it out before wrapping the boards) and place one of the cover boards aligned with the spine strip. (When making the back cover, leave the space to the right.)

7. Cut diagonals at the corners, leaving a slight margin. Do not cut right up to the edge of the board: leave at least 1/8". Remove the corner triangles.

8. Apply more glue to each flap, if necessary. Fold the flaps over the boards, one at a time. (I like to work on the top and bottom first, then the sides). After you cover the top and bottom edges, use your fingernail to give a little push at the corners. (You want to make sure that the boards will be covered at the corners, but you also don't want the paper to bulge there). Move the project to a clean surface.

9. Place the endpaper undecorated-side up (or what seems to be the back of the paper) on a clean piece of scrap paper. Apply glue to cover completely to the edges.

10. Carefully lift this endpaper, lower it gently in a "U" shape onto the covered board, and center it, making sure the margins are even. Smooth it down gently, making sure it is completely flat.

11. Repeat steps 2–10 for the second board. Note that the back cover will have the spine strip on the left instead of on the right as indicated in step 5.

12. Place the covers between two pieces of waxed paper and put these between Masonite boards. Put books or heavy bricks on top. Let the covers press flat overnight, preferably for a few days. Continue with step 15–26 to sew the book together.

MULTIPLE-SIGNATURE BINDING

Time: 45 minutes

This is only one of many kinds of multiple-signature bindings. I find the tight binding for this particular multiple-signature book to be quite satisfying. Use a thin linen or regular sewing thread so that the gaps between the signatures are small: a thick thread will make bigger gaps. I did not make a distinctive cover for my book *Four Tea Cups* because I used heavy-weight paper for the pages. Instead, I glued a piece of strong, decorative paper in a strip around the middle, which also serves as a spine support.

If you use only text-weight paper, you might attach it to a hard cover with a hard spine (see Case Binding page 130).

Multiple-Signature Model, 2004; paste papers; unique; 3" × 2⅞"

If you want to paint the paper, use one piece of 22" × 30" medium- or heavy-weight paper and cut it into eight sheets. Use only two sheets per signature. The sewing is the same. For a book with larger dimensions, add a third set of holes and sew the same way.

Tools: bone folder, pencil, 12" metal ruler, scissors, needle, two 18" lengths of linen thread, wax, awl, corrugated cardboard, binder clip
Materials: sixteen pieces of text-weight paper, 10" × 7" (short)
Example: 5" × 7" book

Preparation: This particular project has four holes and four signatures, each with four pages. Think of things that come in fours: the elements, seasons, some families, perhaps a package of pens or other objects, corners (the Four Corners area of the United States: Utah, Colorado, Arizona, and New Mexico), the fourth month is April—can you think of something important to you that happens then? Take a piece of notebook or copy paper and divide it into quarters, either by folding it or by drawing lines. Label each quarter with one of the four things you chose, List or write in fragments everything you think and feel, dream or remember about each thing. Focus on one category at a time, moving on to the next when you can't think of anything else.

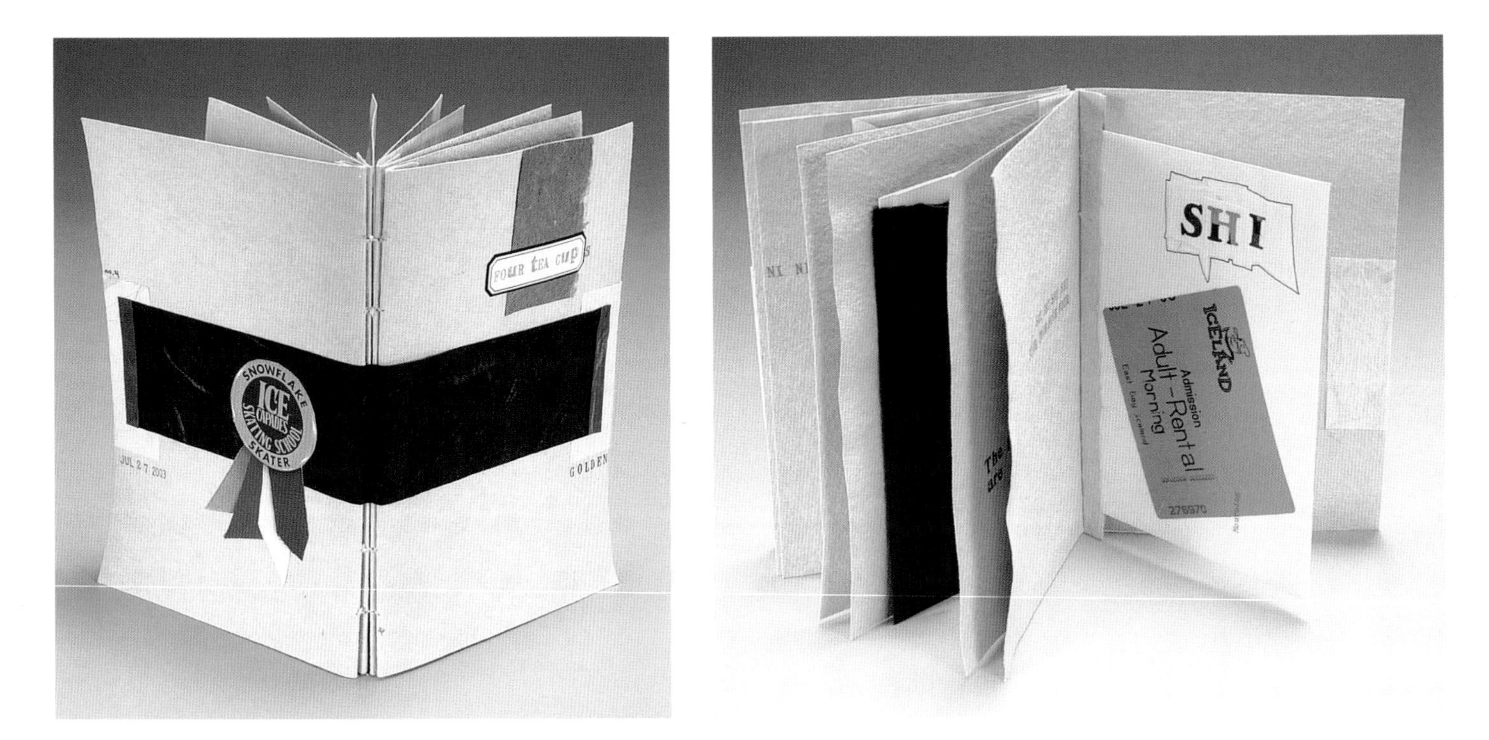

Four Tea Cups, 2003; outside
Four Tea Cups, 2003; envelope detail

When you are done, see if you can shape your thoughts into an anecdote, poem, or story. Find or create images that connect with your text. Write, stencil, stamp, or draw your content onto the pages, either after you have folded and divided the pages into signatures (step 2) or when you complete the structure, before adding any covers.

1. Fold all papers in half, widthwise.
2. Nest the papers so that you have four piles: four signatures with four sheets in each signature.
3. Take one folded sheet from the first signature and measure and mark 1" from the head and tail Now measure and mark 2" from the head and tail. You should have four marks. Place corrugated cardboard on your work surface. With the needle or awl, poke holes at the marks.
4. Take the punched paper from step 3 and put it inside the first signature to use as a template for the holes. With the needle or awl, and corrugated cardboard under the project, poke holes along the valley fold.

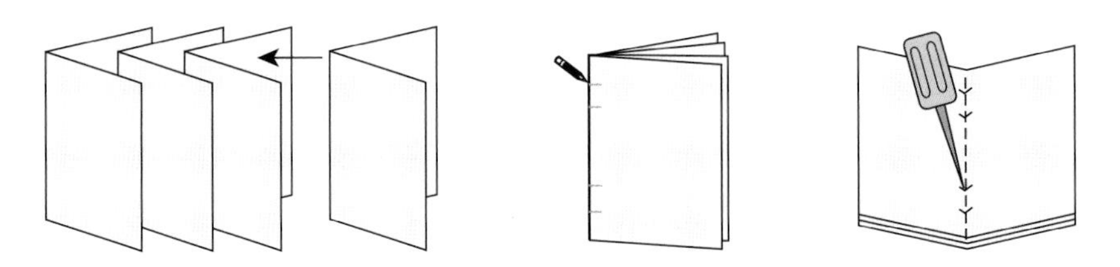

Steps 1, 2 Step 3 Steps 3, 4, 5

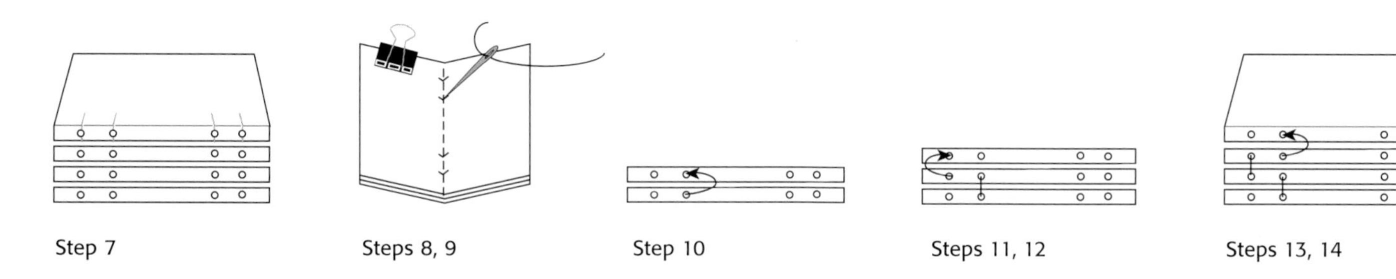

Step 7 | Steps 8, 9 | Step 10 | Steps 11, 12 | Steps 13, 14

Steps 15, 16

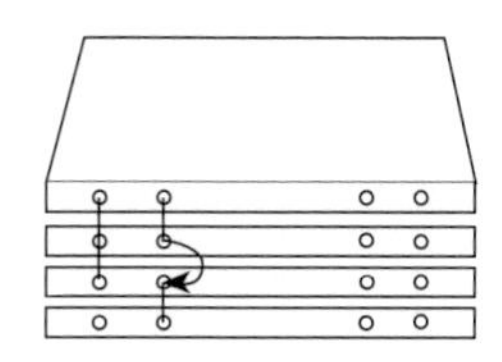

Steps 17, 18

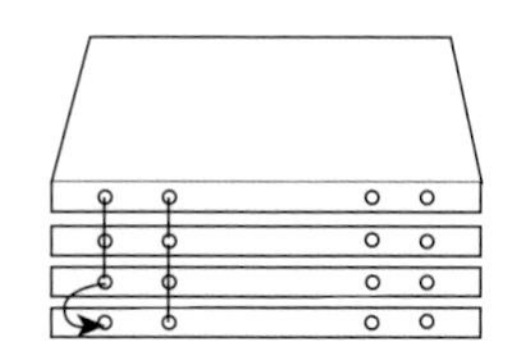

Steps 19, 20

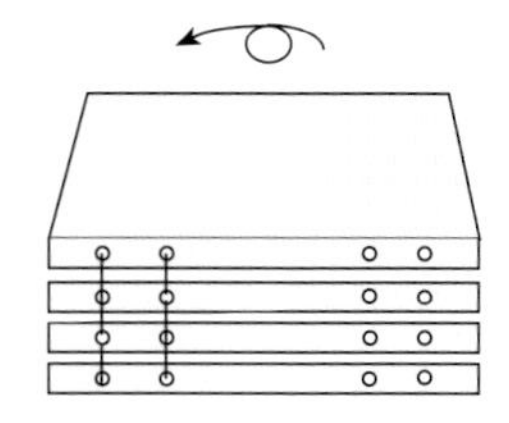

Step 22

5. Remove the template and put it inside the second signature. Poke holes along the valley fold in this signature as well. The holes should go all the way through the papers. Repeat this procedure for the remaining two signatures.
6. Take the marked-and-punched paper and put it back on the outside of the first signature.
7. Stack the signatures, one atop the other, spines aligned.

Sewing Pattern
You will need to pull the thread firmly as you sew, but not so hard that you tear the paper. It may help to keep your fingers close to the place you wish to tighten; pull gently until you feel the stitch stop, then slowly pull a tiny bit more to tighten. Thread a needle with about 18" of thread.

8. Open the bottom signature. Clip the pages on one side of the fold together to hold them in place.
9. Work with the two holes at the head of the book; sew from inside to outside of the head hole closest to the center. Leave a 3" tail of thread inside the signature.
10. Turn the signatures so that the spines are toward you. Sew into the corresponding hole of the second signature.
11. Out the head hole.
12. Into the corresponding head hole of the third signature.
13. Out the hole closest to the center of the third signature.
14. Into the corresponding hole of the fourth signature.
15. Out the head hole.
16. Into the corresponding hole on the third signature.
17. Out the hole closest to the center of the third signature (the stitch now looks doubled inside).
18. Into the corresponding hole of the second signature.
19. Out the head hole of the second signature. (Another doubled thread inside).
20. Into the head hole of the first signature.
21. Tie the ends of the two thread together in a square knot. Trim the ends.
22. Flip the book over so the tail is where the head was and repeat steps 8–21 with the second thread and the remaining set of holes.

Linked Variation: The signatures are not as tightly bound together in this variation, but it may be easier to handle while you sew. Start sewing from outside to inside at step 9 instead of inside to outside. After you finish sewing the second signature, tie the tail of your sewing thread in a square knot. Do not cut the thread. Continue sewing to the third signature. At the second hole of the third signature, take the threaded needle under the loop that connects the first and second signatures. From here sew into the fourth signature. When you come out of the fourth signature, loop under the stitch that connects the third and second signatures. Then tie off the two ends in a square knot. Repeat for the other set of holes.

Hard Cover
With the following tools and materials, make the Case Binding on page 130.
Tools: bone folder, pencil, 12" metal ruler, scissors, PVA/paste mixture, brush for gluing, magazines or catalogs for scrap paper, 3/16" metal spacing bar, waxed paper,
Materials: two 4-ply museum boards 5⅛" × 7¼" (long); one 4-ply museum board 7¼" x ½" (or the depth of the text block; long); one lightweight cover paper 12½" × 8¾" (short) ; one lightweight inner spine paper 5" × 2" (long)

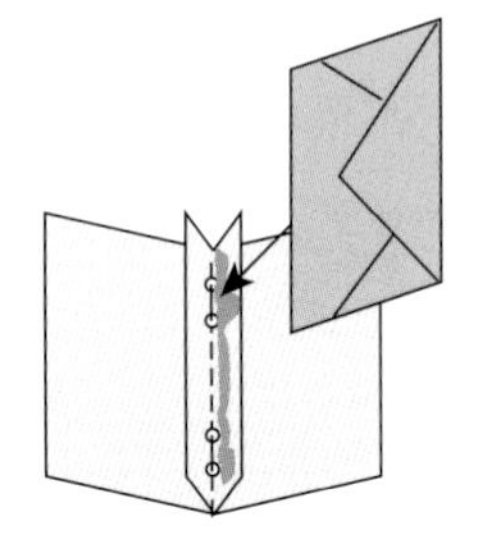

Attaching Envelopes A

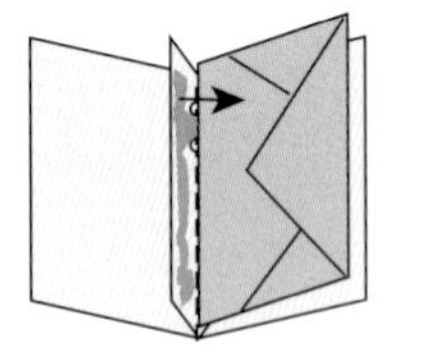

Attaching Envelopes B

Attaching Envelopes

In the center of any signature you can sew a folded strip to which a card or envelope can then be glued. I realized after I made the book *Four Tea Cups* that I would have liked to cut the strips to the same length as the envelopes. You may also use this technique to attach a handmade origami pocket to the center of the Shorts Book (see page 104) or to any other book that has a valley fold. Putting envelopes inside books provides a place to store personal material.

Consider making a collaborative book for a friend. Have each person write or create an image on a piece of paper, one per envelope. In addition to the inner material, have each person write his/her return address on the envelope. For an accordion-fold book you may sew a strip at each of the valley folds for the envelopes to swing free or you may glue the envelopes to the pages with the flap visible.

Altered Text

During the week I was making *Four Tea Cups* I took a walk and found a stray page from a novel that related to my theme of motherhood, love, loss, and grief. In order to use it in the book, I decided to transform it by changing the words around. Because I like puzzles, I wanted to use only the words that were actually on both sides of the paper. To keep the text to one side of one page, I would need to glue words from one side onto the other side. Eventually I knew I wanted to fold it and put it into an envelope, but was worried that the glued-on bits would fall off. Making a color copy of the finished text solved the problem. Here is a way to play with altered text without destroying a book.

Tools: copy machine or scanner, knife and cutting mat or small, sharp scissors, PVA and tiny brush or piece of board for gluing, archival pens
Materials: a book with text that you like; two pieces of 8½" × 11" 100% cotton résumé paper

1. Photocopy two different pages onto the sheets of cotton paper.
2. Cut out the words from one paper.
3. Rearrange these words and glue them on top of some of the words on the second paper, creating new sentences.
4. Use archival pens to cross out any words you don't need.
5. If this page will be handled, such as being folded and put into an envelope, consider color copying or scanning the finished page and folding the copy instead. Copying the original will ensure that the word bits don't fall off the paper.

Four Tea Cups, 2003; altered text

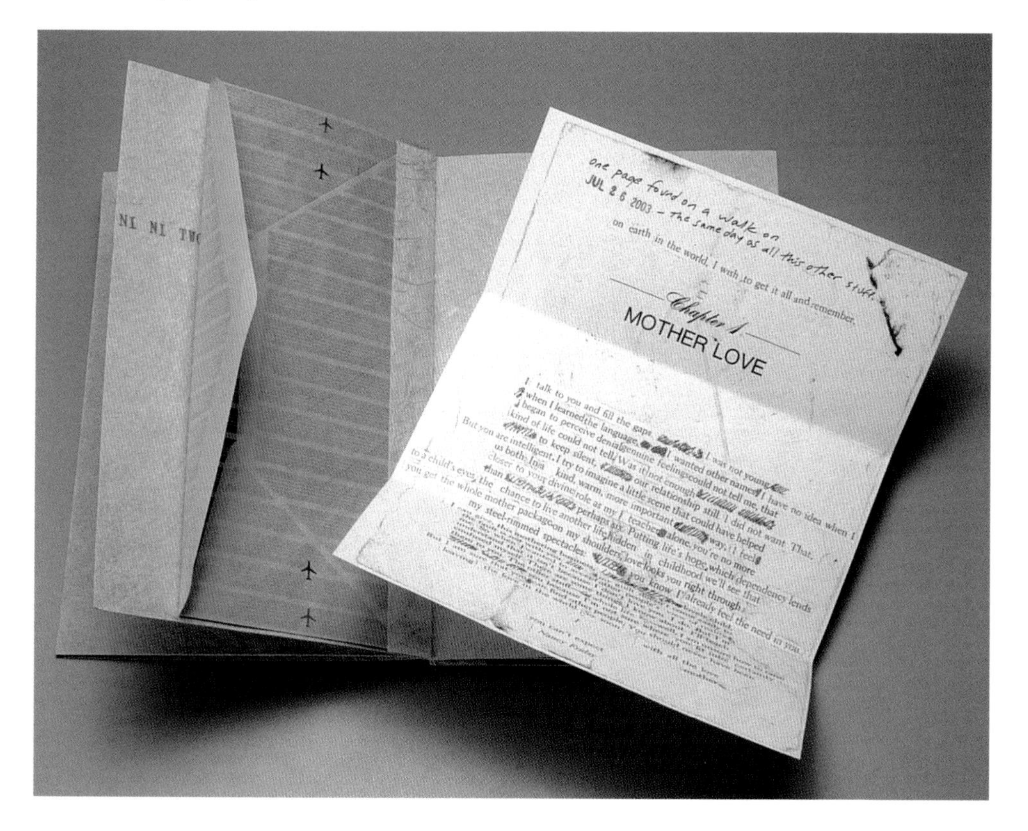

EXPOSED STITCHING OVER PAPER STRIPS

Time: 45–75 minutes

Everything about this book is exposed, so you have plenty of color possibilities. I painted big sheets of paper with bright colors, then figured out the book *Sun Melon Aversion,* which has poems about the colors themselves, the sun, melons, migraines, and girls' bright dresses at the ice skating rink. For the three books in progress I drew some images, then cut stencils from them; they are full of visuals and colors, but have no words yet.

I started working with the exposed-stitching-over-paper-strips structure after being inspired by the binding used on Jody Alexander's *Crossed-Structure Journal,* which was developed by an Italian bookbinder/conservator named Carmencho Arregui. Although Jody mostly uses the structure to make herself a date book every year, she occasionally makes one into an artist's book; *Lost Whispers III* is one of a series of artist's books that contains several samples of lost languages as well as verse written by Jody.

Three Books in Progress, 2004; gesso, stencils, acrylic inks; exposed stitching over paper strips; 5" × 7" × 3/8", 5" × 7" × 3/8", and 5" × 7" × 1"

Left: *Sun Melon Aversion*, 2003; acrylic inks, graphite, ink, waxed linen thread; unique; 5" × 6" × 5/8"
Right: Jody Alexander: *Crossed Structure Journal* and *Lost Whispers III*, 1999; handmade and various papers, threads; unique; 4 3/8" × 5 5/8" × 1/2" and 7" × 8 1/2" × 3/4"
(photo by J. Alexander)

Tools: bone folder, pencil, white plastic eraser, 12" metal ruler, art knife and cutting mat, needle, awl, corrugated cardboard, macramé thread, acrylic ink and brushes, container of water
Materials: one sheet of 22" × 30" heavyweight paper
Example: 5" × 7" x 1/2" book

Preparation: With a pencil, draw random abstract shapes all over the large paper. Draw on the back also. Select three colors of acrylic ink that you think look exciting together. Dip your brush in the water, then apply the inks to the paper. Try using one color per closed shape and leave some shapes white. After you finish the first side, let it dry, then paint the reverse.

While the ink is drying, choose a theme for your book based on the shapes and colors. Start thinking about things you've noticed in the world that connect to that theme. Keep the theme in mind as you continue working on the book.

Assembling the Book

1. Cut the paper into eight pages, each 10" × 7" (short). Save the scraps.
2. Cut three strips from the scraps, each 3/8" × 8" (long).
3. Fold the pages in half, widthwise.
4. Choose one to be the front cover and one to be the back. Decide on the order of all the pages. As you decide, look at the colors of the spines. Also notice how the back of one page flows into the front of the next page. Stack the pages. For this structure, each one is its own signature.
5. From the head of the book (top edge, with the spine on the left), measure and mark along the folded spine at 1/2", 1 1/2", 2", 3 1/4", 3 3/4", 5", 5 1/2", and 6 1/2" and at the fore edges of the front and back covers.
6. Draw vertical lines across the spines. Use the knife and lightly cut into the spines at these marks, making tiny punctures. If they do not go all the

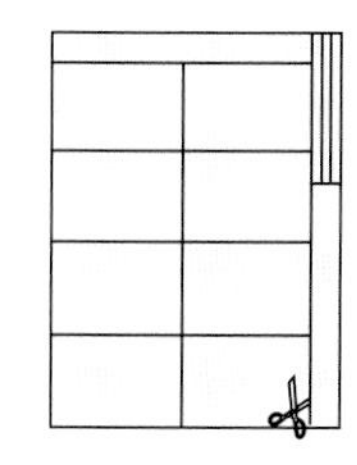

Steps 1, 2

Steps 4, 5, 6

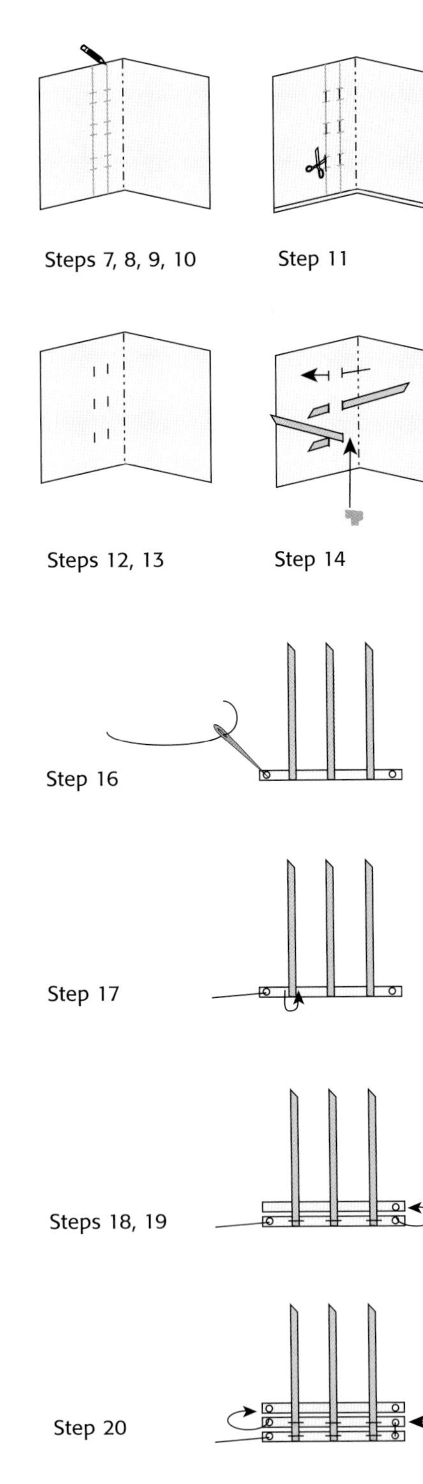

Steps 7, 8, 9, 10

Step 11

Steps 12, 13

Step 14

Step 16

Step 17

Steps 18, 19

Step 20

way through to the center open up these slits by poking them with a needle or awl. (Use corrugated cardboard under your paper).

7. Separate and open the page that will be your back cover. Place it in front of you, cover-side up.

8. Working from the peak fold to the left, measure and mark at 1" and 2" at both head and tail.

9. Lightly draw two vertical lines connecting the marks.

10. Along each vertical line, mark at 1½", 2", 3¼", 3¾", 5", 5½". Make sure these marks line up with the cuts at the spine.

11. Put the back cover inside the front cover so you can cut the slits at the same time without having to measure again. Make sure that you will be cutting through the desired side of the front cover. With the knife against the ruler for a guide, make six ½" vertical slits between each pair of marks that are ½" apart.

12. Remove the back cover from the front cover.

13. Erase the pencil lines.

14. Take each of the three strips and weave one end through the back cover. You may want to trim the end to a pointed diagonal to make it easier to slip through the slit. Two-and-a-half inches of the strip should show on the back cover. Use a little PVA to glue the strip in place near the spine.

15. Place the rest of the signatures on top of the back cover, including the front cover.

Sewing Pattern

Turn the book so it is resting on its back cover, spines facing you, the three strips perpendicular to the resting book.

16. Slide the back cover out from the bottom. Start from the outside of the back cover (first signature, counting from the bottom to the top). Use 4–5 lengths of thread, a length being the height of your book. Sew in through the first hole at the head and leave a 4" tail of thread. Do not knot.

17. Sew out through the second hole, over the strip, and into the third hole.

18. Sew out and in, over the strips, until you come out the last hole (at the tail).

19. Sew into first hole at the tail of the second signature; sew out and in along the spine until you get to the head.

20. Sew into first hole at the head of the third signature; sew out and in along the spine until you get to the tail.

21. This time, before you sew into the fourth signature, insert your needle under the stitch that holds the second and third signatures together. (This will link the third stitch with the previous two signatures.)

You need to link the end stitches from now on. Sew into the first hole at the tail of the fourth signature.

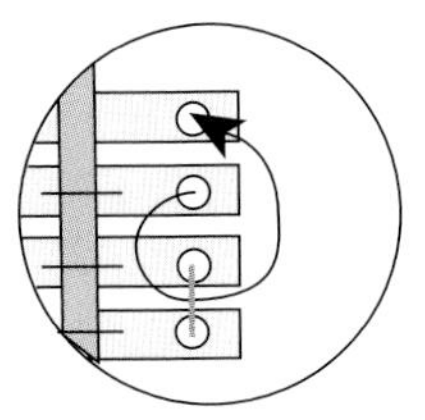

Step 21

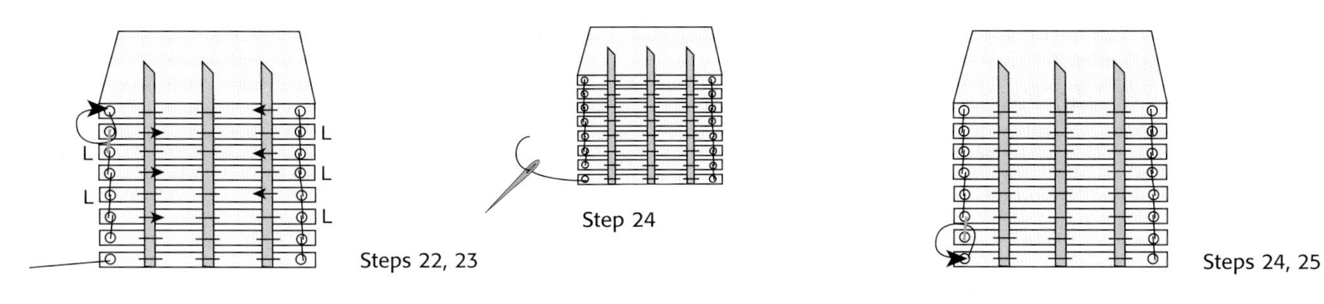

Steps 22, 23

Step 24

Steps 24, 25

22. Continue sewing over the strips and linking the end stitches.
23. When you get to the last stitch of the last signature (the front cover) link the end stitch, then go back into the same hole. Tie the thread to itself on the inside. Remove the needle.
24. Now you will need to link the thread left over from the first signature. Thread the needle with the tail of thread that is still visible from your very first stitch. Take the needle between the end stitches of the second and third signatures.
25. Go back into that first hole. Tie the thread to itself on the inside. Remove the needle.

Finishing
26. Take each of the three strips and weave the ends through the front cover. Two-and-a-half inches of the strip should show on the front cover. Trim, if necessary. Before you weave, use a little PVA and glue the strip in place near the spine, if you like.
27. Use a drop of PVA and glue down the ends of the strips on the front and back covers, or stitch them in place instead.
28. Add a title. Write your text by hand; use rubber stamps, stencils, or a combination.

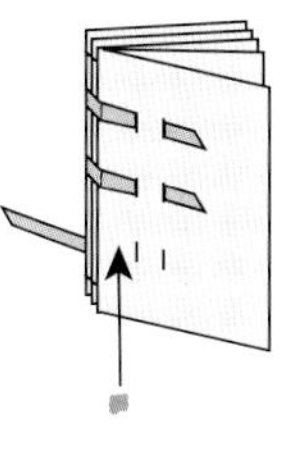
Step 26

Coptic Binding with Accordion

Time: 60–75 minutes
The lovely thing about making a Coptic binding with an accordion is that the pages are doubled so they are thicker, which means you need fewer of them, which means you can complete the book sooner, which means not exactly instant gratification but very close. On the other hand, an accordion makes the pages spring open, so you need to have a closure for this book. *Once Said a Stoic: Epictetus* utilizes a flap tucked into a strip of paper. *A Dime Date* simply has ribbons.

You can take any random idea or element, usually something you are interested in, then connect it to something about you. Layer it. Weave it together. Sometimes you can take two things that seem to have absolutely

Once Said a Stoic: Epictetus, 2003; letterpress from wood and metal type; accordion with Coptic stitch; edition of 41; 2½" × 3"

no connection and then make one up. Take *potato* and *chair*, for example. The only obvious connection may be that they are both brown. But what about "hot potato" and "sitting in the hot seat"? Now *hot* is the connector. The unifying emotion can be things to avoid or that cause discomfort. As a quick exercise, pick two random objects and try the same connection practice. Use your idea for your book.

Tools: pencil, 12" metal ruler, scissors, art knife and cutting mat, needle, waxed linen thread, awl, corrugated cardboard, magazines or catalogs for scrap paper, PVA, paste (optional), brush or piece of board for gluing, paper plate to decant PVA or paste, waxed paper, heavy book
Materials: two 4-ply museum boards 2½" × 3" (long); 1 medium- to heavy-weight cover strip 1½" × 4" (short is preferable, but long will work); three pieces of heavyweight paper 3" × 10" (short) ; one piece of heavyweight paper (same kind as previous) 3" × 12¼" (short); three strips of light- or medium-weight paper 1" × 4" (long); two pieces of book cloth or light-weight paper 3½" × 4" (long)
Example: 2½" × 3" x ½" book

Wrapping the Boards

1. Put layers of magazine pages down as scrap paper. If you feel fast and confident, use PVA. If not, use paste or a PVA/paste mixture. Place a piece of book cloth with the paper-side up in front of you vertically. Center one of the boards on the book cloth. Draw around it lightly with a pencil.

2. Remove the board. Apply glue to the center of the rectangle you just drew. Press the board into place.

Step 1 Step 2

3. Cut off the corners of the book cloth with scissors, leaving at least ⅛" between the diagonal cut and the board.

4. Apply glue to one book-cloth flap. Fold it over the board. Tip: At the corners give the book cloth a little push toward the board with your thumbnail before you glue a perpendicular side so that the corners will turn in neatly.

5. Repeat the remaining flaps.

6. Repeat steps 1–5 with the second board and book cloth.

7. Center the cover strip on the covered side of one of the wrapped boards. Fold over the excess at the top and bottom.

8. Apply PVA to the folded-over flaps, one at a time, and press them into place on the back of the wrapped board. Hold them firmly for at least 20 seconds so the PVA has time to bond.

9. Wrap both boards in waxed paper and set them flat under a heavy book.

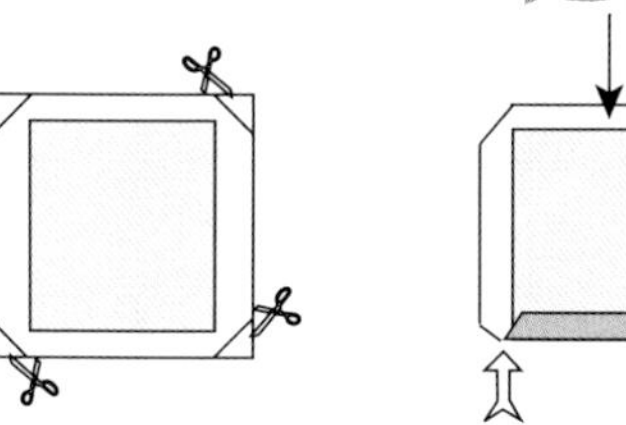

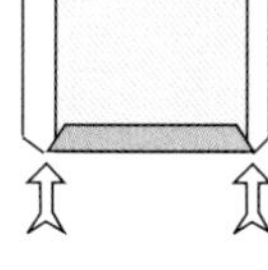

Step 3

Steps 4, 5

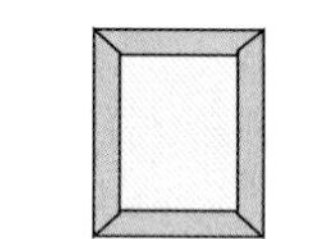

Step 6

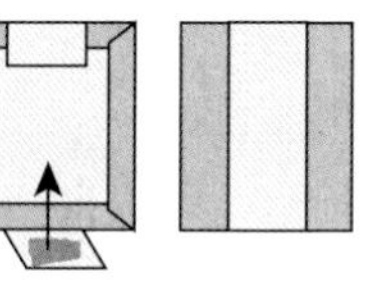

Steps 7, 8

Folding the Accordions

10. Fold the three shorter pieces of heavyweight paper (undecorated sides together, if applicable) in half, widthwise.

11. Fold each open end back to the folded edge. When looking at it from the front you should see the folds as valley, peak, valley.

12. Place the 3" × 12¼" piece of heavyweight paper in front of you, horizontally, wrong-side up. Measure, mark, and score a line 10" from the left edge.

13. Fold the right edge at the scored 10" mark.

14. Keeping the right edge folded, take the left edge and align and crease it with the right (now folded) edge.

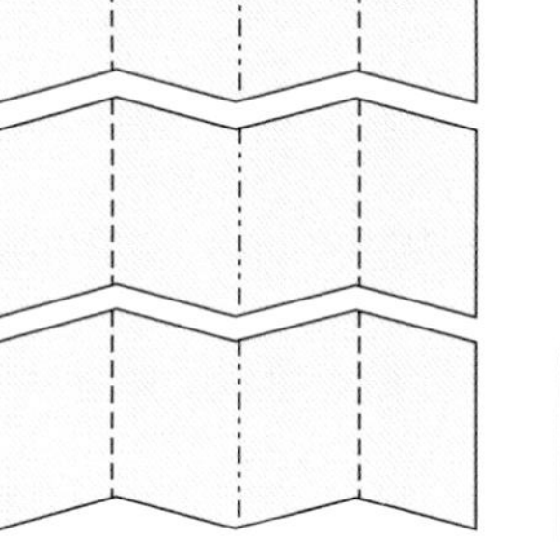

Steps 10, 11

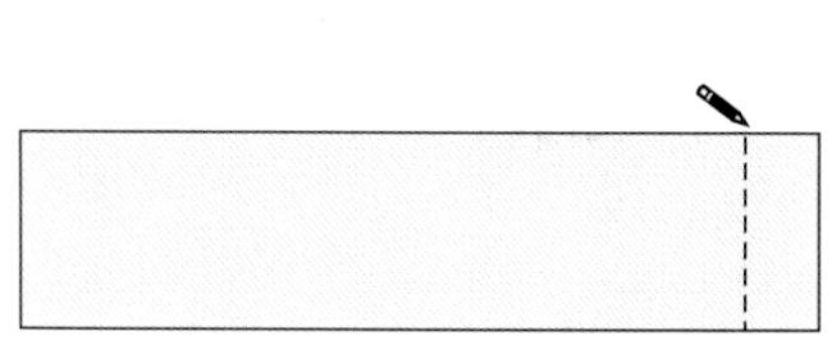

Step 12

15. Fold the ends back to what now looks like the center fold, pretending the folded flap is not there. You should have an accordion with four equal panels and a fifth smaller panel. The latter will be your wraparound flap.

16. Open the accordion. Measure, mark, and score ½" to the right of the 10" mark. The ½" panel will be the fore edge.

17. From the top and bottom of the right edge of the paper, measure and mark 1".

18. Using a knife against a metal ruler, make two diagonal cuts from these marks to the top and bottom of the first fold on the left, cutting off the corners completely.

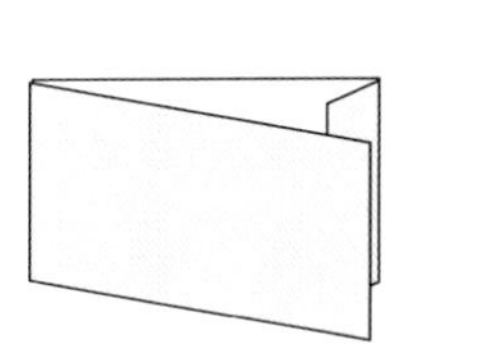

Step 13

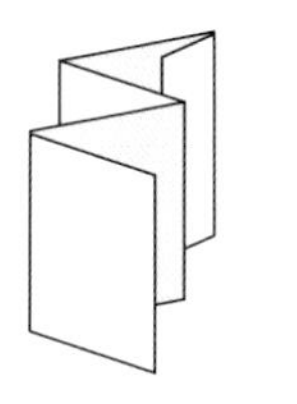

Steps 14, 15

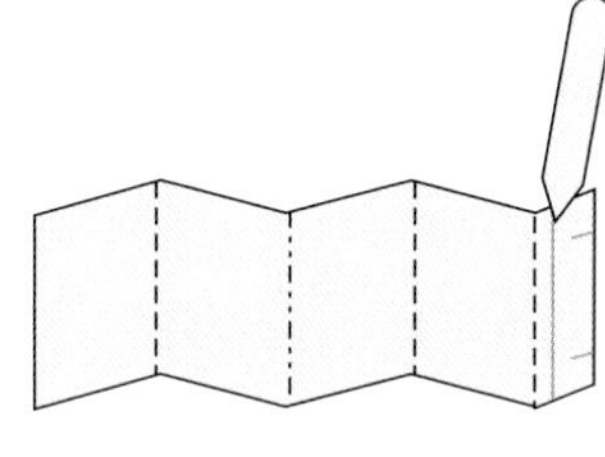

Steps 16, 17

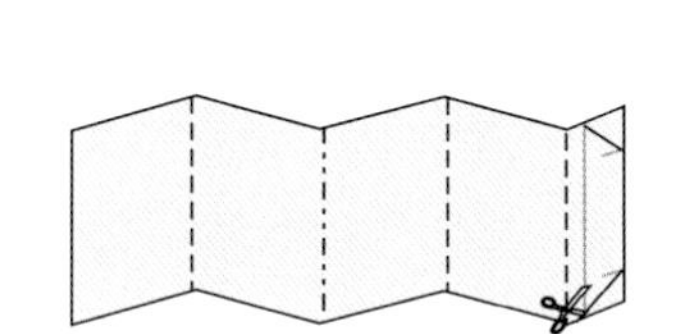

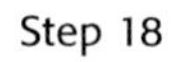

Step 18

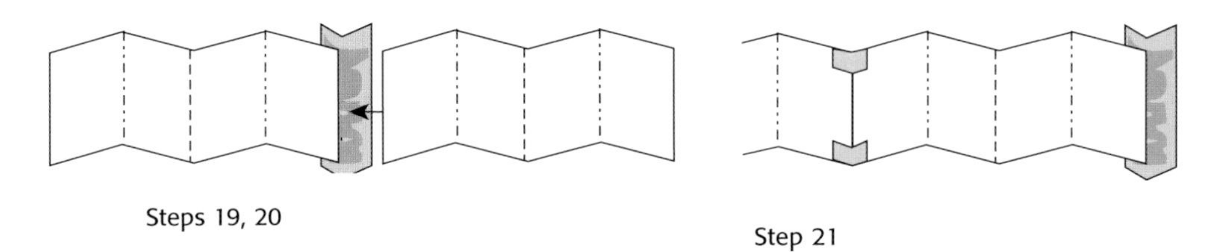

Steps 19, 20

Step 21

Attaching the Accordions to Each Other with Tabs

19. Fold the three 1" × 4" strips in half lengthwise.

20. I like to work with the back of the accordions: this way the glued edge is facing me and I can see it. Then I can allow a tiny bit of space between the accordions. Completely apply glue to one strip and press one half to the end of one accordion and one half to the beginning of the next one. The accordion with the diagonal cuts is the last. Fold the top and bottom of the strip over the edges of the accordions and smooth down.

21. Apply glue to each strip, one at a time, and attach the remaining accordions in the same way.

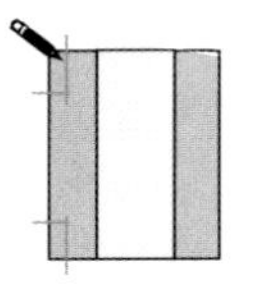

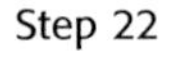

Step 22

Preparing the Covers and Accordion for Sewing

22. Retrieve the covers from under the heavy book. On the front cover measure and mark ½" down from the head and up from the tail, ¼" from the spine, or left edge.

23. Put down some corrugated cardboard to protect your work surface. Use an awl to poke two holes at each penciled intersection.

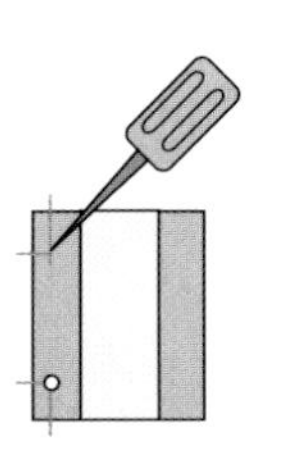

Step 23

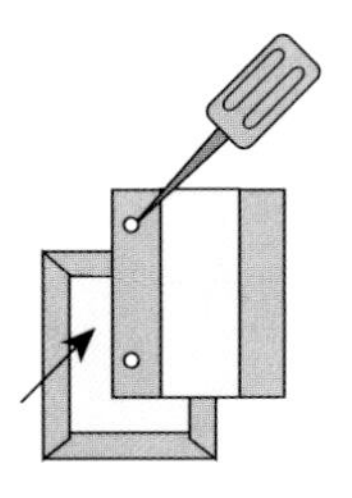

Step 24

24. Align the back cover with the front cover, wrong sides together. The back cover will have its exposed board facing up, the cloth facedown. Using the front cover as a template, poke two holes in the back cover as well.

25. Place the accordion with the spine toward you, the strips and flap away from you. Measure and mark ½" from the head and tail. These marks should be aligned with the holes in the covers.

26. With your knife lightly cut a shallow vertical slit in each of the folds of the accordion. Use a needle to poke through and open up the holes, if necessary.

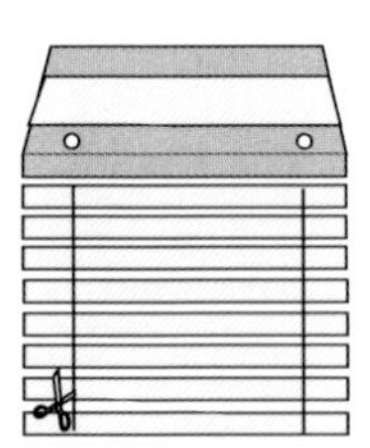

Steps 25, 26

Sewing Pattern

What makes this easier to sew than some multiple-signature bindings is that the pages are connected already, eliminating the need for clips.

27. Cut a 30" length of thread. Pull the thread through the needle to make it a manageable length (about 18"). You will still use a single strand, however.

28. From the inside of the first fold sew out one hole, go through the corresponding hole in the cover, and leave a 2" tail of thread inside the folded paper of the book.

29. From the cover hole, go back into the same hole in the folded paper. Tie a square knot with the tail that was left inside.

30. Repeat steps 28 and 29 with the other hole in the folded paper and the cover; this time tie the knot around the inside stitch.

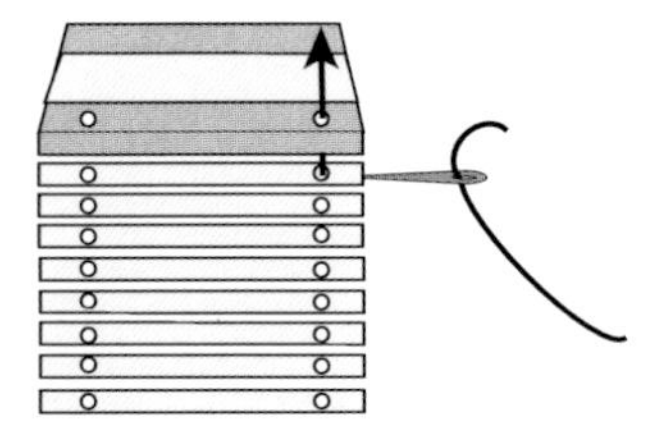

Steps 27, 28

A Dime Date, 2004; ink-written text, rubber stamps, stamps made from Model Magic™, dimes; accordion with Coptic stitch; edition of two; 3¼" × 3¼" × ⅞"

31. Go back out the same hole.
32. Sew into the corresponding hole on the second folded edge and come out the hole on the other end.
33. Take your needle under the stitch above it and sew into the first hole of the third folded edge.
34. When you come out the hole in each section (with the exception of the final hole), keep looping under the previous stitch until you have linked all eight folded edges.
35. Come out the last hole and loop under the previous stitch.
36. Go through the corresponding hole in the back cover and back into the hole in the last folded page of the book.

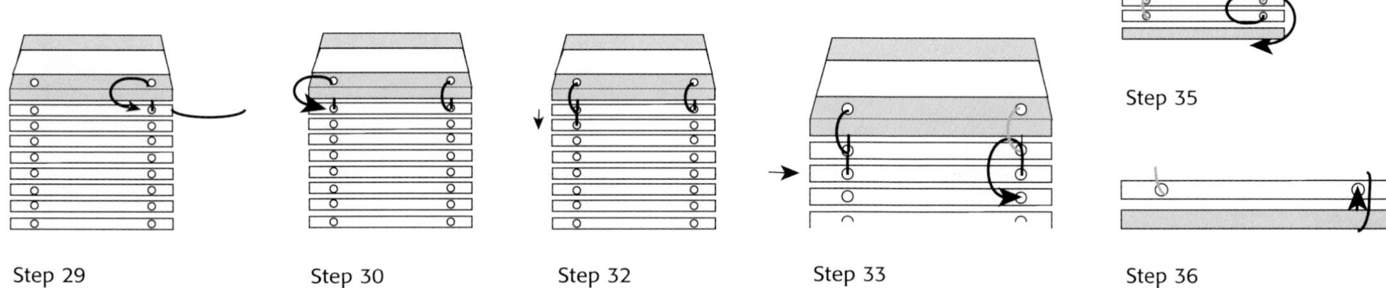

37. Double back to the next-to-last hole, come out, loop around.
38. Go through the hole in the back cover and back into that next-to-last hole.
39. Tie off the ends inside the book into a square knot. Note: You will notice that the last section has one knot and two strings inside. The first section has two knots and one string.

Gluing the Ends to the Boards
40. Place a sheet of scrap paper between the first and second pages (the cover does not count as a page).
41. Apply glue completely to the back of the first page.
42. Align the page with the front cover and press it into place, Move it a little, if you need to, to make sure it is truly aligned. Let dry.
43. Repeat steps 40–42 for the back cover.
44. When the book is dry you should be able to tuck the diagonal flap into the cover strip to hold the book securely closed.
45. Add a title to the front cover strip and to the fore edge panel on the flap if you haven't done so yet. Note: If tearing occurs at the fore edge panel folds, you may reinforce this section by gluing down a 1" × 3½" strip of decorative paper aligned with the height of the book and centered over the folds (see photograph on page 98).

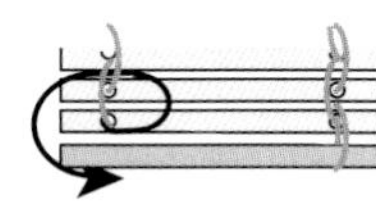
Step 37

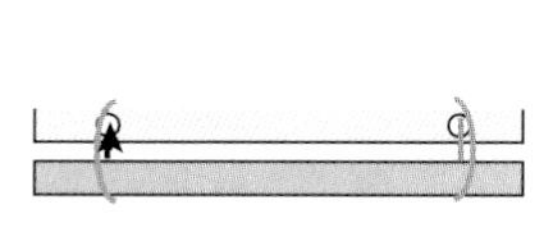
Step 38

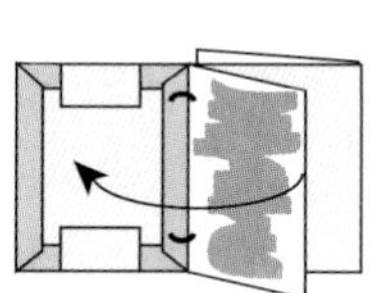
Steps 41, 42

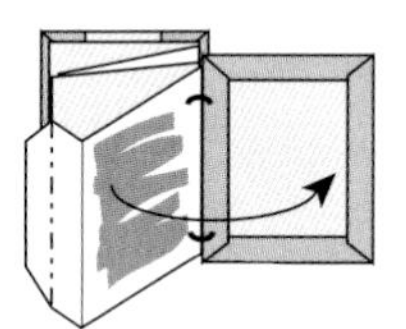
Step 43

Step 44

Complete

Chapter Five

Folds and Twists: Books with Multiple Paths

The process of reading a book doesn't have to start at the beginning and end on the last page. It can be more like reading the newspaper or surfing the Web: skimming for an interesting word or article, following it, then starting again, going forward and back. Certain book structures and stories reinforce this style of nonlinear reading, which makes reading a book more like playing a game or wandering in a garden. When you create a book of this type you can alter the reading by including multiple stories with a line from each story on every page, multiple page openings, pockets, or a book inside a book.

Origami, the art of Japanese paper folding, is a very playful art. It works perfectly for making informal books and for teaching in classrooms, where sharp, pointy objects like awls, knives, and needles are discouraged. These books often set up alternative reading situations; the reader gets to choose

Folds and Twists
Back row (left to right): *Who Says Home Has Four Walls and a Roof?; Confused Living: a Jumble Book; Beyond Pluto*
Middle row: *A Few Dollars; Blue Leash for a Black Dog*
Front row: *Paper Petals, Pocket Resource Guide, Snapshots of Sea Glass*; Square Flexagon Model; Triangle Pocket Model

how to read the book. The content is there, but how to read it is the game. Some readers object to doing this kind of work, others enjoy the puzzle.

For this section, many books may be made with standard 8½" × 11" copy paper. After making the individual pages for some of these books, you will join them to make each final product. A bone folder is helpful for making tight folds and creases. While you may use a glue stick to join the pages, a light application of PVA is recommended for a more reliable hold.

Shorts Book

Time: 15–30 minutes
I like making this square booklet and putting it into the origami pocket envelope. In classes I have heard pocket stories about worry stones, dog biscuits, falling stars, spare change, seashells, and beach-glass treasures. One student told me of her favorite pair of childhood shorts with seven pockets. In *Mints by the Pool* I explore my feelings about life and death and about an elderly man who sat by the pool at my grandparents' apartment. He always had peppermints in his shirt pocket for the neighborhood children.

Pockets are often used in stories as turning points. In chapter five, "Riddles in the Dark," of *The Hobbit* by J.R.R. Tolkien, the question for the entire chapter is about what is in a pocket. *Alice's Adventures in Wonderland* by Lewis Carroll also employs a pocket in chapter three, "A Caucus-Race and a Long Tale."

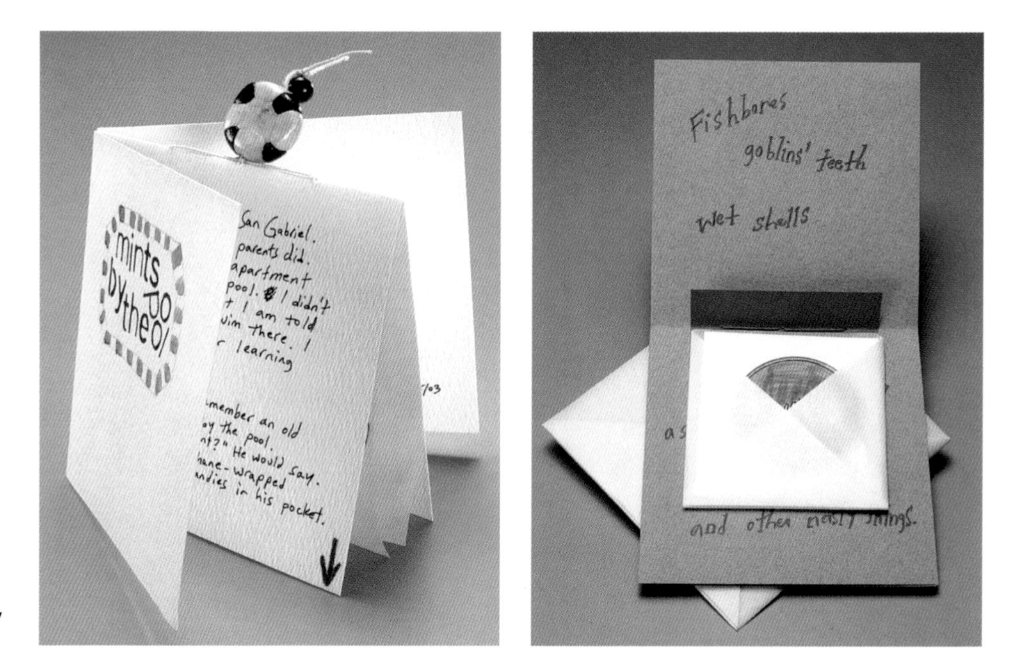

Left: *Mints by the Pool*, 2003; stencil, ink, watercolor, handmade polymer bead; unique; square shorts book, 3¾", in square origami envelope, 4"
Right: *Pocketses* (text by J.R.R. Tolkien), 2003; stencil, ink, rubber stamp, graphite; unique square shorts book, 4¼", in square origami envelope, 4½"

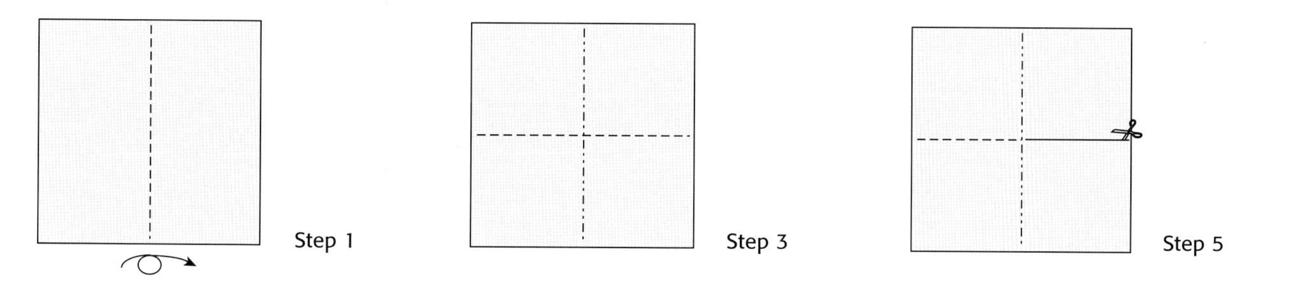

When Katherine Ng teaches art in the Los Angeles public schools, she calls the larger version of this pamphlet the "pants" book because the paper, before it is folded into a book, does look like a pair of pants. Extrapolating from that, we can happily call this the "shorts" book. The idea of a pants or shorts book works well with the pocket theme.

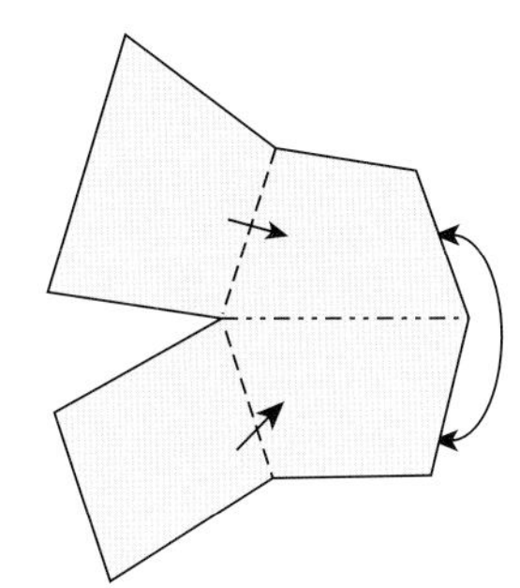

Step 6

Tools: bone folder, pencil, 12" metal ruler, scissors or knife and cutting mat
Materials: one piece medium- to heavy-weight paper 8½" × 8½"
Example: 4¼" × 4¼" book

Preparation: Think about pockets for a moment. Do you have something special that you carry with you in your pocket? Do you know someone who carries something special? What is something you wish you had? Do you have a favorite article of clothing that has pockets? How do you feel about pockets in general? Pick one of these questions and write down your story. It may be an anecdote you may have told someone on the phone or saved to tell a friend.

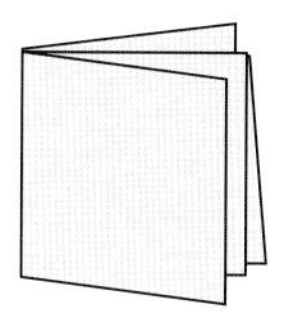

Step 6 (folded up)

1. Fold the paper in half (either way, the paper is square). Open.
2. Turn it over.
3. Fold the paper in half the other way. Open.
4. You now have two folds, one is a peak, one is a valley.
5. With your knife against the metal ruler for a guide, cut from the intersection of the two folds to the edge. You may make this cut along either the peak or the valley fold. The diagram shows it along the valley fold, but in this case it will not matter which. Note: Do not cut the paper completely in half. Do not cut a square out of the paper. You are making one long slit only.
6. Fold the pamphlet according to the peak and valley folds. Arrange it so that the first page has open edges on the right, top, and bottom; the second and third pages have a folded edge at the top; the fourth has open edges on the right, top, and bottom again.
7. Put your name or the date on the back of the book, centered at the bottom, so you will understand the orientation of it when adding text and images.

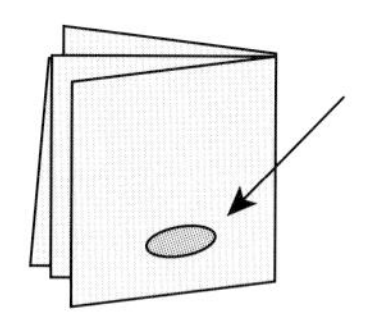

Step 7

Variation: Single Signature. Sew a single signature into the valley fold in the center of the book. See instructions for single signature on p. 77 and 78. Start sewing from the outside.

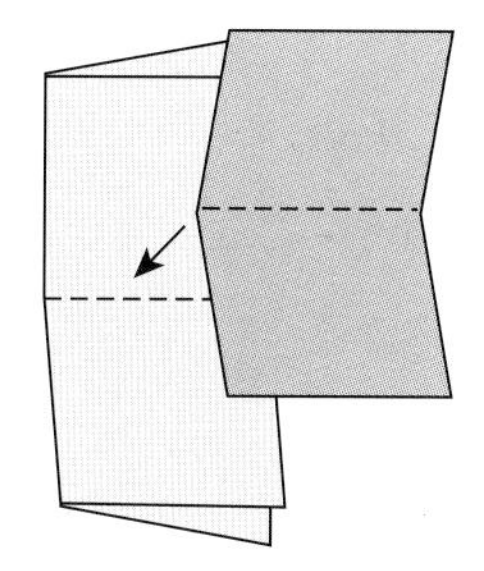

Variation

Pocket Envelope Models, 2004; acrylic inks and gesso

ORIGAMI POCKET ENVELOPE

Time: 10–20 minutes
This pocket makes a nice slipcase for the Shorts Book or the Origami Pocket Pamphlet. If you use different dimensions, make sure that the pocket is ¼" larger than the book it will hold.

Tools: bone folder
Materials: one piece of medium- to heavy-weight paper (short). The length of the paper = 4 × height
Example: 4½" × 18" paper to make a 4½" pocket or envelope to fit Shorts Book, page 104.

1. Place paper horizontally on your work surface.
2. Fold paper in half, widthwise. Keep closed.
3. Take a single layer and fold it back to the first fold. Open.

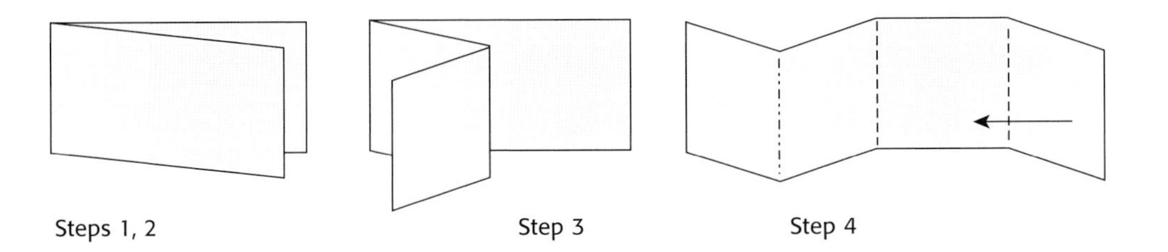

Steps 1, 2 Step 3 Step 4

4. Bring the other end to the center fold (gate fold). Open completely.
5. On the right square, fold down the top edge to form a triangle by aligning the top edge of the paper with the rightmost fold.
6. On the second square from the left, fold down another diagonal, making the total shape resemble the peaked roof of a house with a flat top. Do this by aligning the top edge of the paper with the center fold. This diagonal will have a square attached to it.
7. Fold up the square, covering the new diagonal.
8. Valley-fold the section on the left toward the triangle on the right. Make sure that the open right edge of the folded section does not extend over the valley fold of

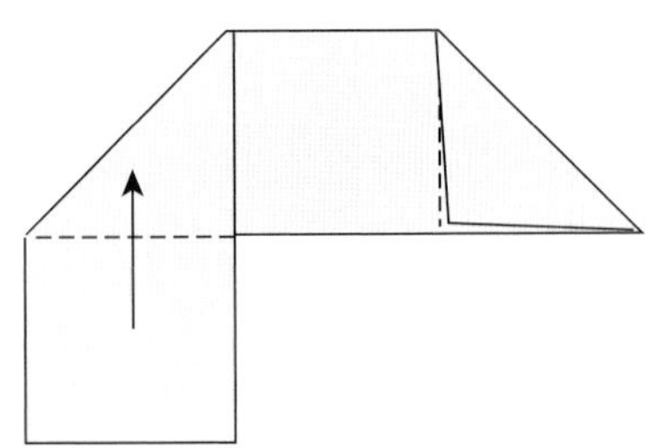

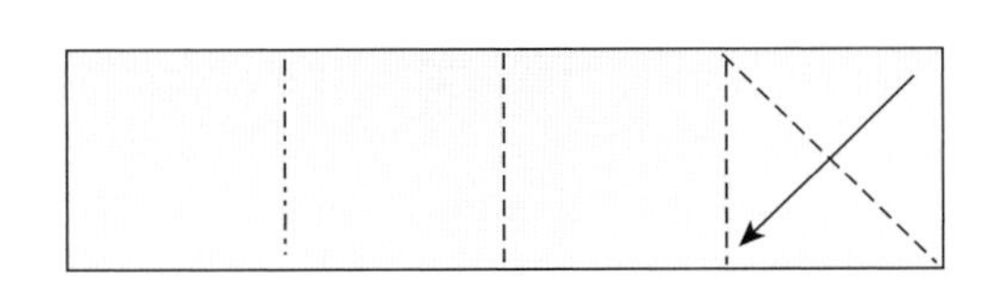

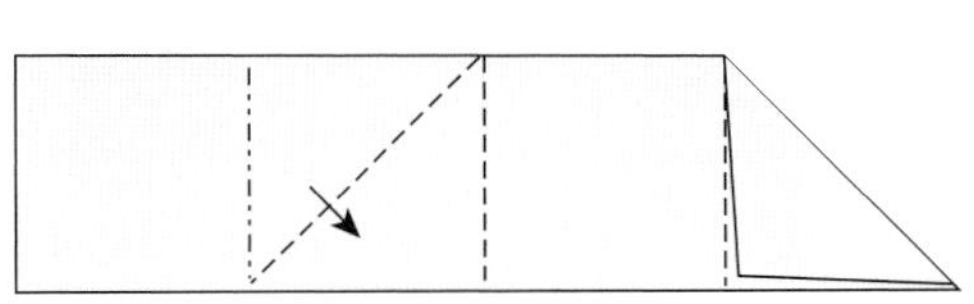

Step 5 Step 6 Step 7

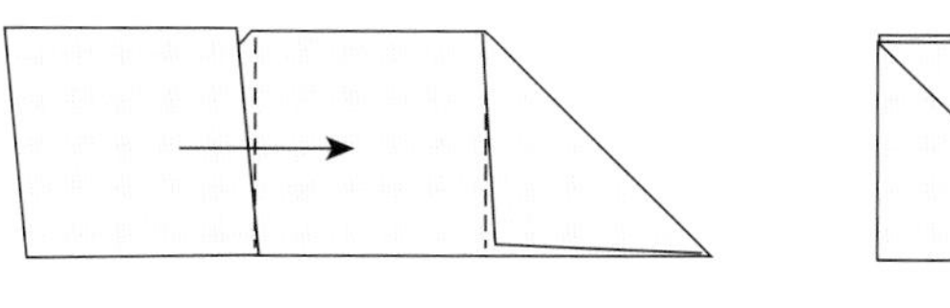

Step 8

Step 9

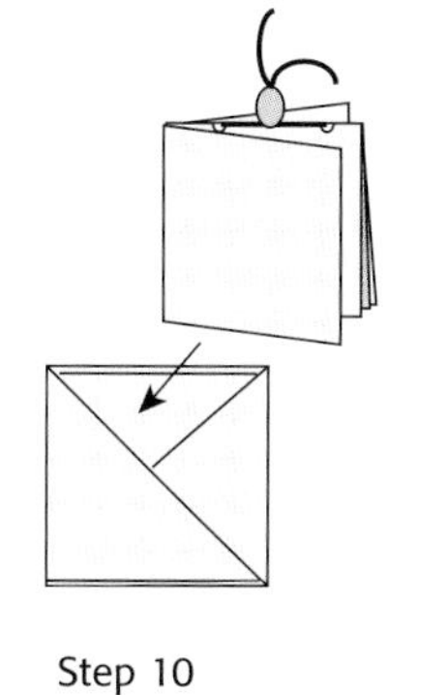

Step 10

Complete

the flat section. If the folded section protrudes, you may need to nudge the folded section back toward the left and re-crease it. In all cases, when this section folds over, a triangle will be visible on the left.

9. Tuck the right triangle into the triangle on the left. If the triangle doesn't fit neatly, open the project and adjust the folds so they are aligned. If it still doesn't fit neatly, trim the right edge of the square flap. Tuck it back together.

10. Slide a book or note into the pocket.

Origami Pocket Pamphlet

Time: 10–20 minutes

This square booklet may be used in place of the Shorts Book and tucked into the Origami Pocket Envelope. It is a variation of an origami structure by Hedi Kyle. In pure origami form, it employs neither glue nor scissors. If you use paper that is a different color on each side, the pockets will be one color and the endpapers another.

Pocket Pamphlet and Pocket Book Models, 2004; acrylic inks and gesso

You can make this booklet any size by using the ratio of three units by four units. You can figure out the size paper you need by first choosing the size book you want and multiplying it first by three, then by four. A five-inch book means you need paper that is 15" (5x3) × 20" (5x4).

Tools: bone folder
Materials: one sheet of any weight paper, 8¼" × 11" (short)
Example: 2¾" × 2¾"
Paper dimensions for a matching Origami Pocket Envelope: 3" × 12"

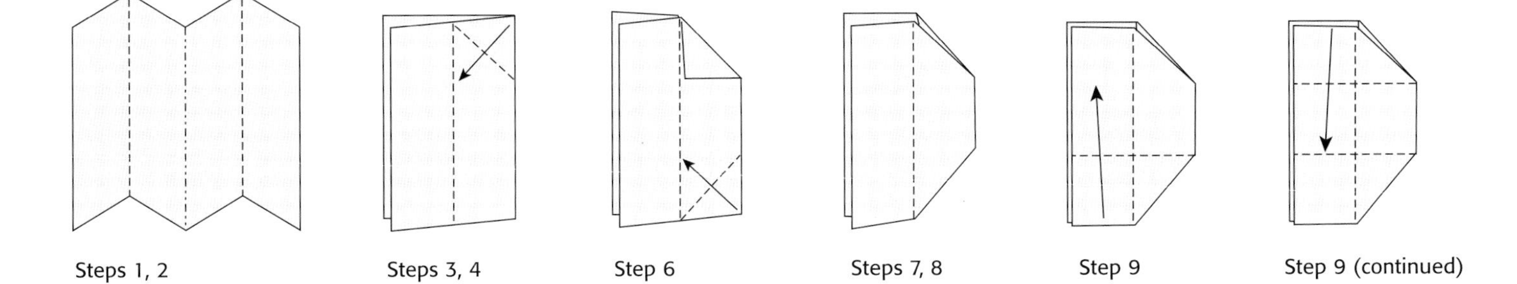

Steps 1, 2 | Steps 3, 4 | Step 6 | Steps 7, 8 | Step 9 | Step 9 (continued)

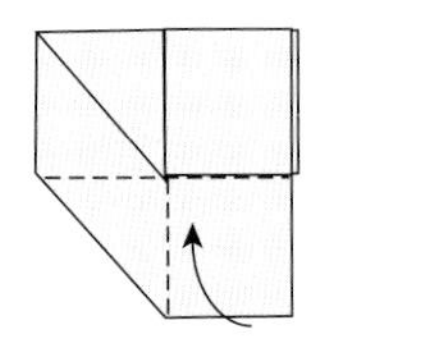

Step 10

Steps 11, 12

1. Fold paper in half, widthwise. Keep closed.
2. Fold each open end back to the fold from step 1, creating an accordion.
3. Open the ends, leaving the paper folded in half.
4. Fold the closed, top corner down into a triangle.
5. Fold it back in the opposite direction, so the diagonal crease can go in either direction.
6. Repeat steps 4 and 5 with the bottom folded corner.
7. Open the corner triangle folds. Pinch the point where the diagonals meet at the top and push the straight peak fold of one corner triangle inside, turning it into a valley fold.
8. Repeat step 7 with the bottom corner triangle. The diagonal folds of the large triangle are now both peak folds.
9. Orient the paper with the diagonal folds on the right. Fold up the bottom flap. Fold down the top flap. Turn the page.
10. Fold down the top section. Fold up the bottom section.
11. The pamphlet will naturally divide into two sections. Fold one open end over the diagonal pocket page. Crease it tightly. Turn the pamphlet over.
12. Fold the remaining section over the pocket page on this side. Crease.

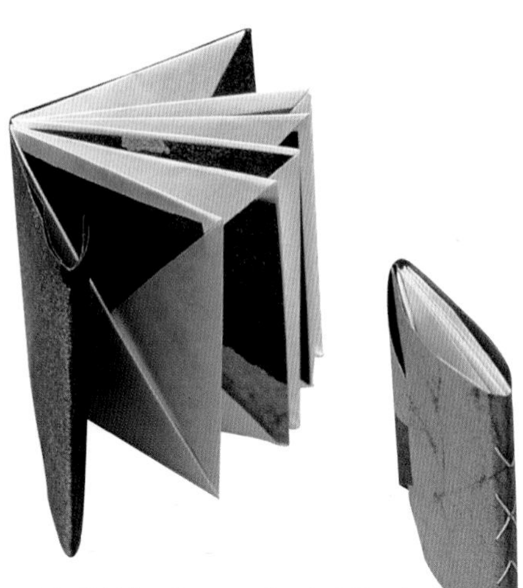

Hedi Kyle: Square Pocket Book Model, 1997; handmade paper; 4½" × 4½" (photo by Paul Warchol)

Variation 1: To make a 3"-square book with three double-sided pockets, similar to the many-paged books that Hedi Kyle makes, use a longer piece of lightweight to medium-weight paper, 9" × 24" (short), and fold it into an accordion with eight panels. Fold down the corners in the same manner as steps 3–10 above. This is also known as one of the Blizzard Books.

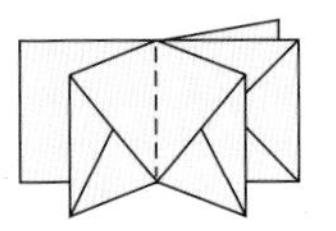

Variation 1

Variation 2: To make this book more suitable for a hardcover binding: (a) fold down the loose corners at the outside front and back of the book before (b) you fold over the edges at step 9. This gives you two extra pockets, one on the inside front and one on the inside back, which become the endpapers.

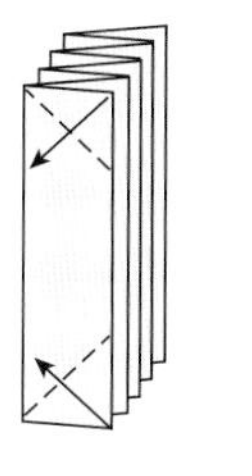

Variation 2a

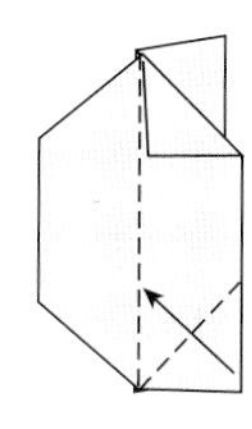

Variation 2b

Double Binding

Time: 20–40 minutes

The double binding has no special physical fold or twist: it has a mental one, making it another book with multiple paths. Susan King used this idea for a book that was both about dealing with breast cancer and traveling through Europe, *Treading the Maze*. To view her book, you open all the blue pages to the right and all the white pages to the left. Once the book is completely open, you alternately read the blue and white pages, weaving the book together as you go. She incorporates multiple texts–her own writing and relevant quotations–and a variety of images.

I used a double binding for *Blue Leash for a Black Dog* about a dream I had and the illuminating discussion with my daughter after relating the dream to her. Because my black paper was so thick, I made a paper clasp loop to hold the book closed.

Susan's book was bound with a wire spiral binding and has a sturdy back board and a thick front sheet. Mine was sewn with a single-signature

Left: *Blue Leash for a Black Dog*, 2004; gesso and acrylic inks, cutouts, stencil; double binding with paper loop closure; unique; 4$\frac{3}{8}$" × 5$\frac{1}{2}$"
Right: *Blue Leash for a Black Dog*, 2004; open

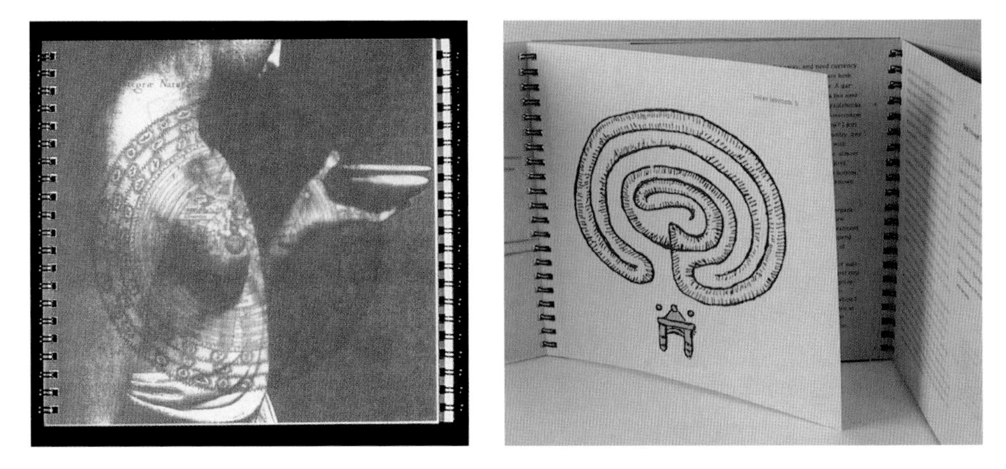

Susan King: *Treading the Maze*, 1993; offset printed with photocopiess; double wire spiral binding; edition of 800; 8" × 7¼" (photos: left by John Kiffe, right by A. Golden)

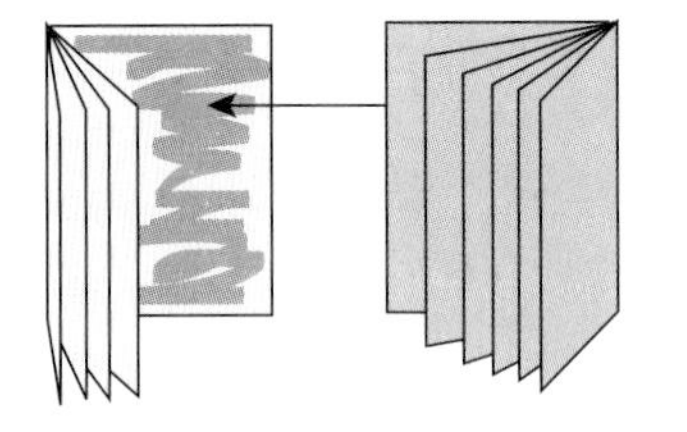

Soft Cover

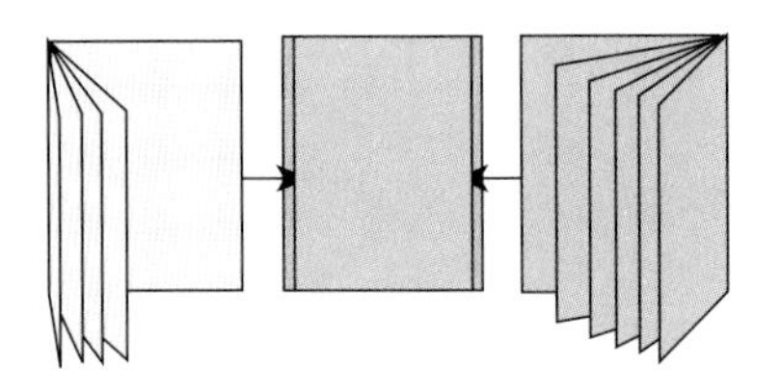

Tucked into Wrapped Hard Cover

stitch, one on each side and tucked into a wrapped hard cover. See Single Signature on page 77 for the instructions on sewing. Make two pamphlets. Then face them toward each other and glue them to a covered board or tuck them into a wrapped board. Instructions for wrapping the boards are on pages 124–125.

CHECK BOOK

Time: 45–60 minutes
A friend brought back some hexagonal pressed-paper coasters from Spain, which inadvertently contributed to my designing this book; I had wanted to make a book shaped like a hexagon. When the pages are joined, the hexagon is not visible. The size of the book is exactly the same as a bank check, hence the name. Checks or rectangular pieces of paper the same size will fit in the diagonal pockets. Like traditional origami, the pages start with a square. Unlike traditional origami, they need to be glued together. This structure works well as a travel book with color-copied maps for the main pages and ticket stubs, small photographs, and receipts tucked into the pockets.

Tools: bone folder, pencil, magazines or catalogs for scrap paper, PVA, brush for gluing
Materials: five sheets of medium-weight paper 8½" × 8½"
Example: 3" × 6" book (3⅛" × 6¼" with added hard covers)

Preparation: Assemble materials for a travel book as described above, or glance through your bank checkbook and see if any of the checks you have already written spark a strong emotion. Pick out five to ten checks and

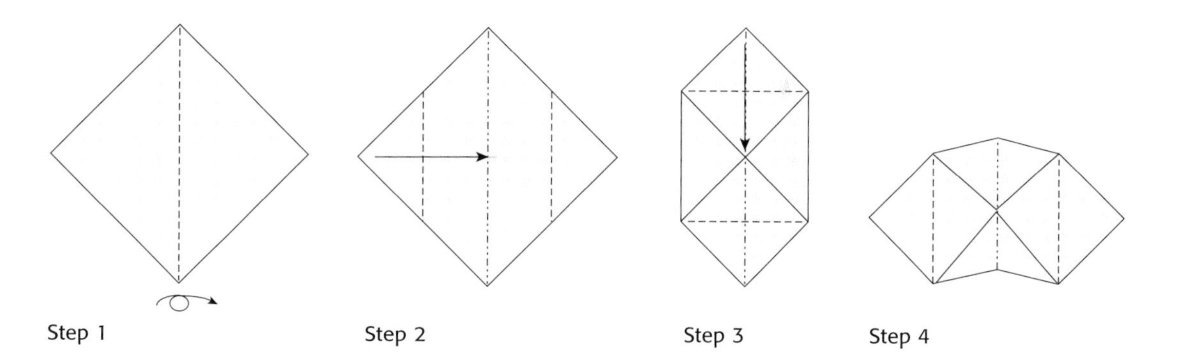

describe the circumstances of them, or write a related story. Stencil or draw the numbers of the checks onto the triangular flaps of the pages after you complete the structure. Write your stories on separate check-sized cards and tuck them into the pockets.

Folding the Pages

1. Put the paper in front of you like a diamond. Fold it in half, vertically, from corner to corner. Open. Turn the paper over.
2. Find the exact center and make a light mark with a pencil. Fold the left and right corners so they touch this center mark. All your folds are now parallel.
3. Fold the top and bottom corners in toward the center mark.
4. Open the side triangles. These will be the flaps that will attach to neighboring segments, holding the book together.
5. Repeat steps 1–4 with the remaining sheets of paper.

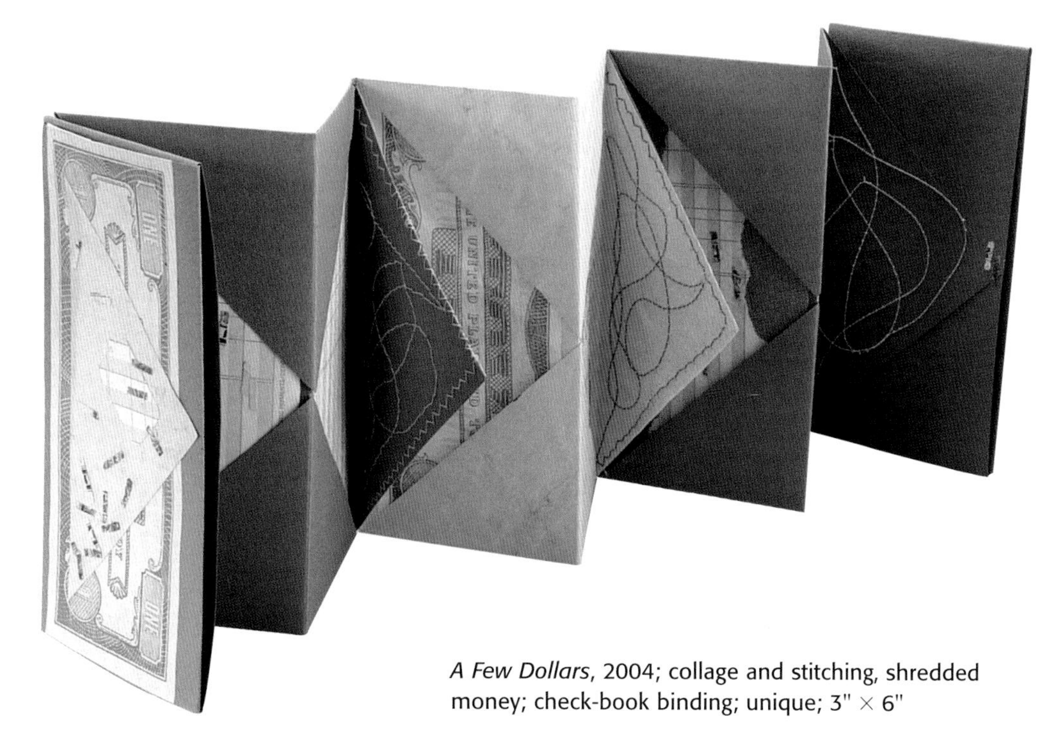

A Few Dollars, 2004; collage and stitching, shredded money; check-book binding; unique; 3" × 6"

Steps 6, 7

Assembling the Book

Work from back to front. Place the pages in a row in front of you.

6. Start with the last page. Put scrap paper from a magazine between the left triangle and the rest of the folded sheet. Apply a thin, even coat of glue to the back of the triangle. Remove the scrap paper.

7. Align the back of the right triangle from the preceding page with the sticky left triangle. Press down.

8. Repeat steps 6 and 7 until the pages are joined in a line. You should have one loose flap at the front and one at the end.

9. Make one of the following optional covers, if desired.

Optional Covers

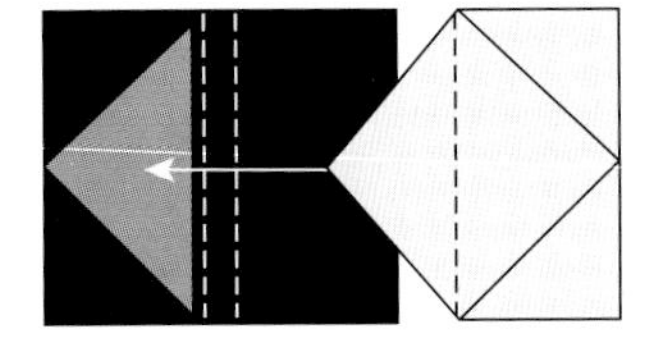

Soft Cover

Soft cover: Use one piece of heavyweight paper $6\frac{1}{2}$" × $6\frac{1}{4}$" (short). Measure, score, and fold a $\frac{1}{4}$" spine in the center that is parallel with the short side (and the paper grain). Align the valley fold of the first page of the text block with the valley fold of the front cover. Do likewise for the back page and back cover. Glue or stitch the end triangles to the front and back covers in these places.

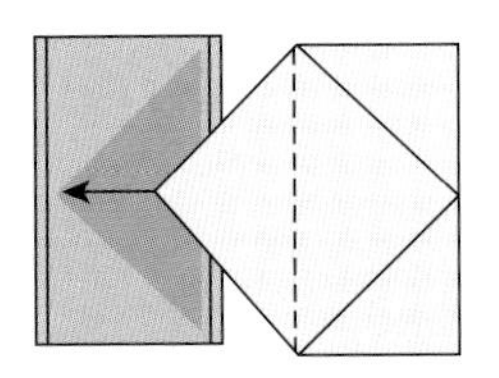

Wrapped Hard Cover

Wrapped hard cover: Use two 2-ply museum boards 3" × 6" (long); two pieces of medium-weight paper 3" × 8" (short); two pieces of medium-weight paper 6" × 6" (make the folds parallel to the grain). See page 124 for detailed instructions. Center and sew or glue the end triangles to the 3" × 8" sheets; these are the inner endpapers.

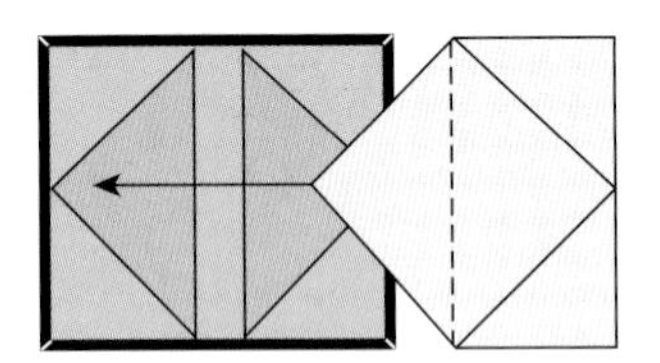

Adhesive Hard Cover

Adhesive hard cover: You will need two 4-ply museum boards $3\frac{1}{8}$" × $6\frac{1}{8}$" (long); two pieces of book cloth or lightweight paper $8\frac{1}{2}$" × 8 (short); one lightweight endpaper $6\frac{3}{8}$" × $6\frac{1}{4}$" (short). You may glue boards front and back like sandwiches (see Covering Separate Boards, page 126). This will enable your book to extend to its full length. Add a triangular recess in the inner front and back covers for more integrated look (see photograph on page 149). Alternatively, if you use fewer pages or want your book to be more contained and not pull out into a long accordion, you can make a connected hard cover that has a $\frac{3}{8}$" gap at the spine.

House Book

Time: 40–60 minutes

During my quest to make a hexagonal book I folded the house shape. More than four folded pages joined together give the feel of a neighborhood. Start with a horizontal rectangle for this one.

Tools: bone folder, pencil, 12" metal ruler, scissors or art knife and cutting mat, magazines or catalogs for scrap paper, PVA and brush for gluing (or glue stick)

Who Says Home Has Four Walls and a Roof?, 2004; acrylic inks and gesso; house origami book; unique; 3" × 6¾"

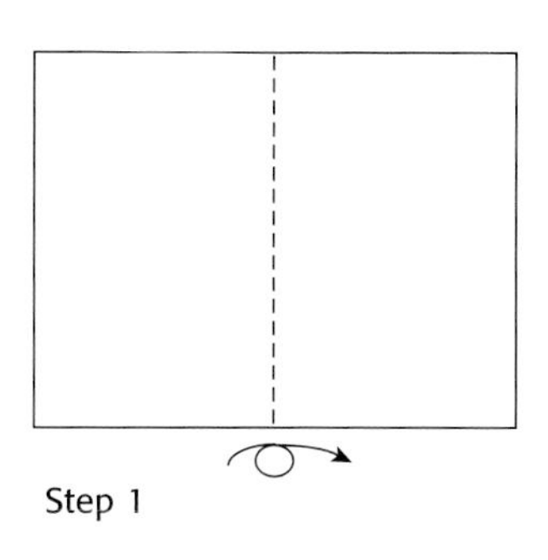

Step 1

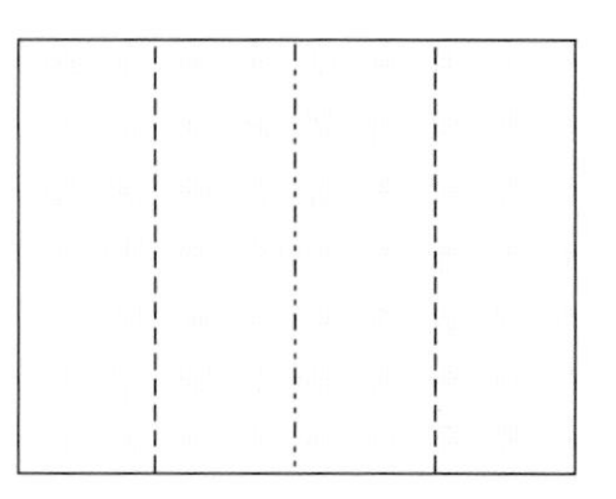

Step 2

Materials: four sheets of medium-weight paper 8½" × 11" (long), one piece of heavyweight cover paper 6¼" × 6¾" (long)

Preparation: Take eight vertical photographs of houses, stores, or apartments on your street. Enlarge them, then scan them or color-copy them, two per horizontal page. Fold your book from these sheets, making sure that all the flaps fold toward the white (unprinted) side, leaving the color side for the front. Use a permanent pen to write about something characteristic of this street, your memories or feelings, or an anecdote about something that happened here.

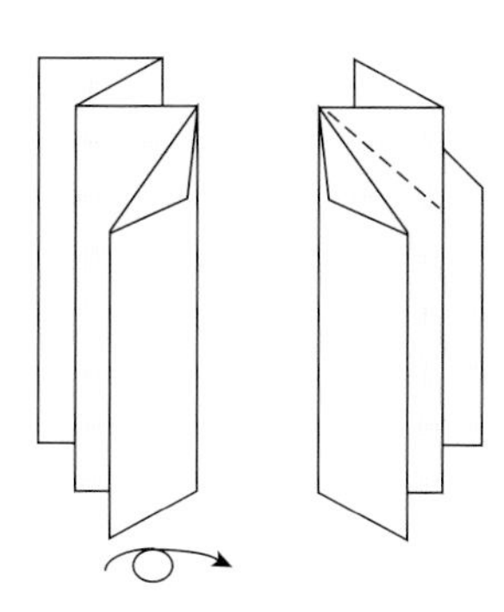

Step 3

Step 4

Folding the Segments

1. Arrange one sheet of 8½" × 11" paper in front of you, horizontally, picture-side down. Fold it in half, widthwise. Open. Turn the paper over.

2. Fold the ends to the center peak fold (this is a gate fold, also known as the cupboard in origami). You may keep them folded.

3. From the top, fold one loose corner down in a triangle so that the point touches the fold. Turn over.

4. Fold the other loose corner down in the same manner. Then take the center two sections and fold them over the diagonal fold you just made. Then fold them back the other way, over the previous diagonal fold.

5. Open the paper. Turn it so that the folded flaps are facing away from you; the diagonals are peak folds. Refold the center triangles so these diagonals are also peak folds, and the vertical fold between them is a valley fold. All diagonals should be peak folds on this side. Refold by pushing down on the center fold and aligning the diagonals. Crease. Turn the paper over so that you see the right and left diagonal flaps. They may be folded down.

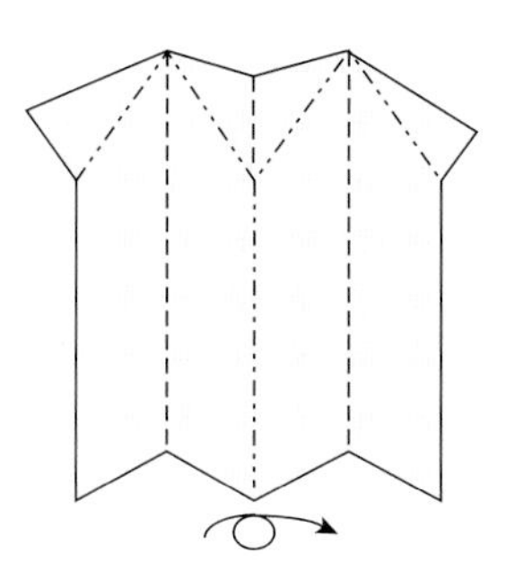

Step 5

6. Measure, mark, and fold 2" up from the bottom. Refold the vertical folds on the 2" flap to match the longer folds that are already there.

7. Repeat steps 1–6 with the remaining pages.

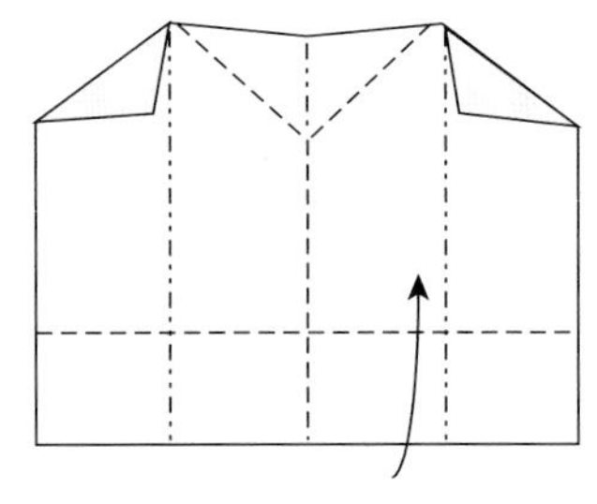

Step 6

Assembling the Book

Notice that one side of the folded paper has flaps, the other side is smooth. You will be applying glue only to the side with the flaps. The smooth side will be the front of the book.

8. On one segment , put a smooth, very spare line of PVA (or use a glue stick) on the diagonal edge, continuing down the side and across the bottom. You do not need to apply PVA to the whole back side. You may use glue stick on it, though. Align a second segment with the sticky one and press down.

9. Repeat step 8 until all the segments are joined as an accordion, with the very first and very last ends free.

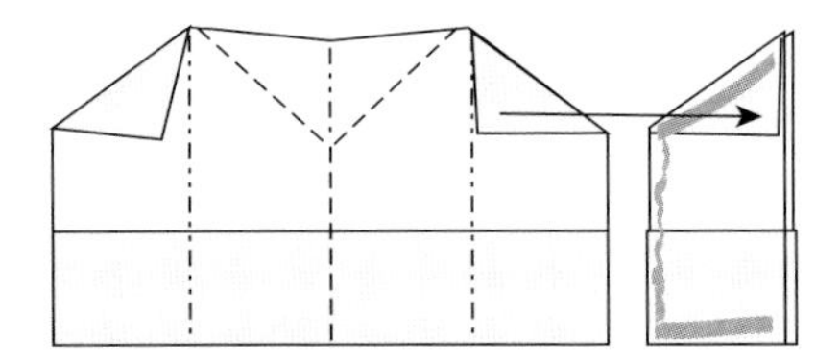

Step 8

Making the Soft Cover

10. Arrange the cover paper in front of you, horizontally. Find and mark the center at the top and bottom. Measure 1/8" on either side of the center line at the top and bottom. Use the pencil and ruler to connect one set of top and bottom marks, then score the cover vertically. Repeat to connect the other set of top and bottom marks. Fold along the scores.

11. Measure 3" down from the top, along the left edge. Or nestle your text block into the cover and use it as a template to draw around the diagonal. Remove the text block.

12. With the knife against the metal ruler for a guide, make a diagonal cut from the closest score to this mark or across the diagonal you drew.

13. Repeat steps 11 and 12 for the right edge.

14. Put a piece of scrap paper between the first two pages of the text block. Apply a smooth, even line of glue to the diagonal of the text block, continuing down the edge and across the bottom. Remove the scrap paper. Nestle and center the text block in the cover and press down.

15. Repeat step 14 for the other flap and opposite end of the cover.

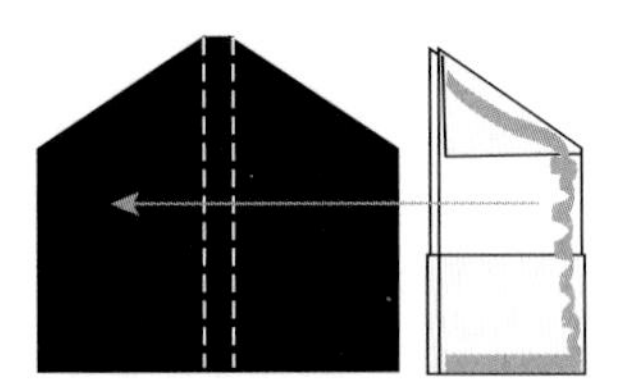

Steps 10, 11, 12, 13, 14

Variation: Hard Cover. After step 9, cover separate boards (see page 126) or make a case binding. Shape the boards into the half-house shape first, if you like, by placing the text block on the boards with the spine aligned with one edge of the board and drawing the diagonal. Or measure and draw. Remove the text block and use the knife against the metal ruler to cut the diagonal to make a margin that is equal to the other sides. For separate boards, use two 4-ply museum boards that are just slightly larger than your text block. **For the hard cover with hard spine, use the following:** two 4-ply museum boards 3" × 6¾" (long); one 4-ply museum board 1/8"–1/4" × 6¾" (long); one piece of book cloth or lightweight- or medium-weight paper 8⅛" × 6¾" (short); one lightweight inner cover paper 6⅛" × 6½" (long)

Rocket Book

Time: 40 minutes
The house shape I was working with reminded me of an old-style rocket ship, but it needed the fins. After some reworking, the Rocket Book was born. When folded flat it also resembles an airplane. Unlike the House Book, however, the rocket starts with a vertical piece of rectangular paper. *Beyond Pluto* tells of my indifference, as a child, to Neil Armstrong's walk on the moon, and my delight in playing with a glow-in-the-dark pen at a planetarium show.

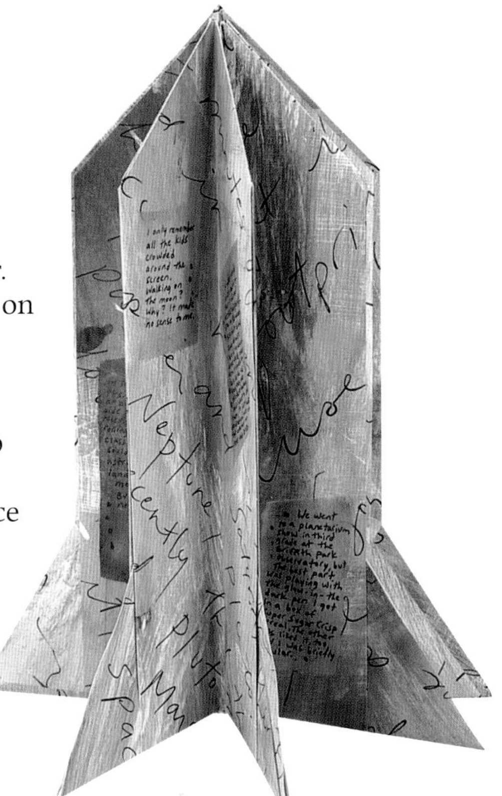

Beyond Pluto, 2004; acrylic inks and gesso; rocket origami book; unique; 4" × 10"

Tools: bone folder, pencil, 12" metal ruler, magazines or catalogs for scrap paper, PVA, and brush for gluing (or glue stick)
Materials: five sheets of medium-weight paper 8½" × 11" (long), one piece of heavyweight paper or two 2-ply or 4-ply museum boards 4" × 10" (long)
Example: 4" × 10"

Preparation: Think of flight, journeys, space. Write about a place to which you have traveled or a place you would like to go. It can be an imaginative place or a metaphysical place, not just a country or a planet.

Folding the Rockets

1. Place one sheet of paper in front of you, vertically. Fold in half, lengthwise. Open. Turn paper over.
2. Fold the top corners down to meet the center (peak) fold. Keep folded.
3. Fold the right and left edges to meet the center fold. Keep folded. (Stop here to make a book about the Washington Monument or continue to make the rocket.)
4. Fold up the open corner at the bottom to form a valley fold that bisects the folded corner and ends at the lower corner of the diamond shape formed in step 3. This is one of the rocket's fins. You may score a light line here, but it may show through to the other side.
5. Repeat step 4 with the other bottom corner.

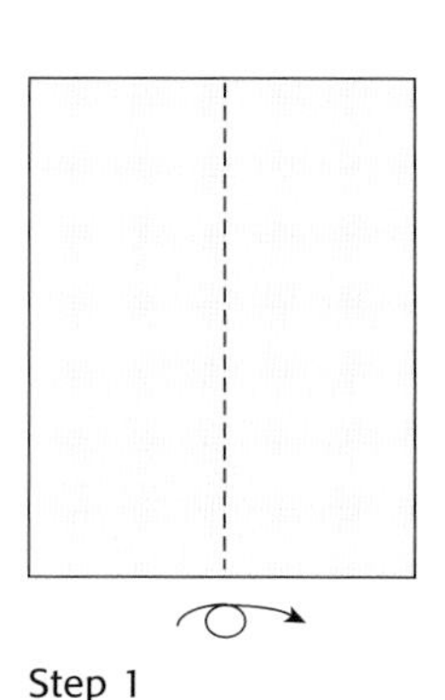

Step 1

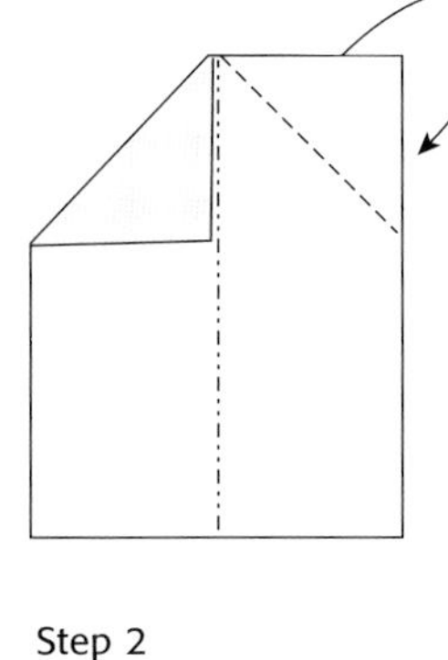

Step 2

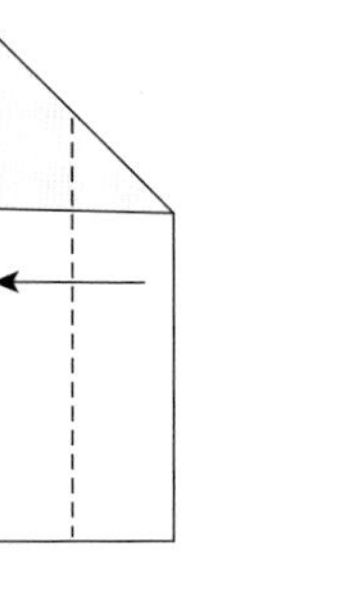

Step 3

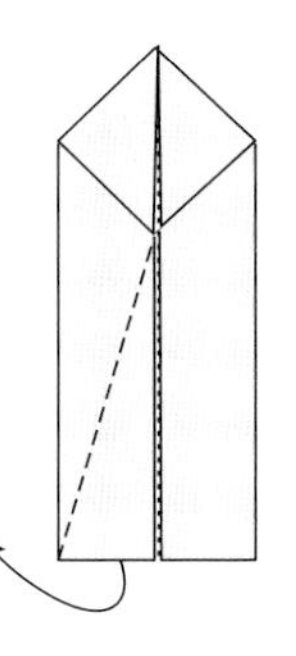

Step 4

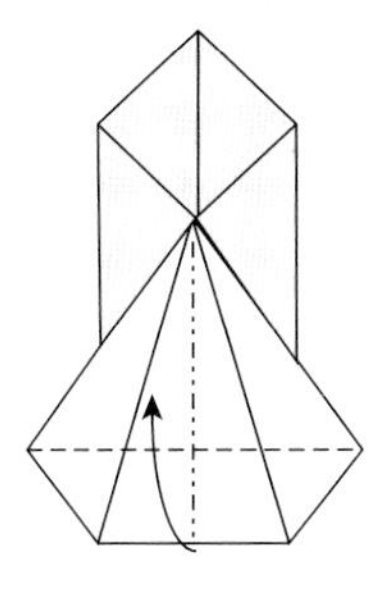

Steps 5, 6

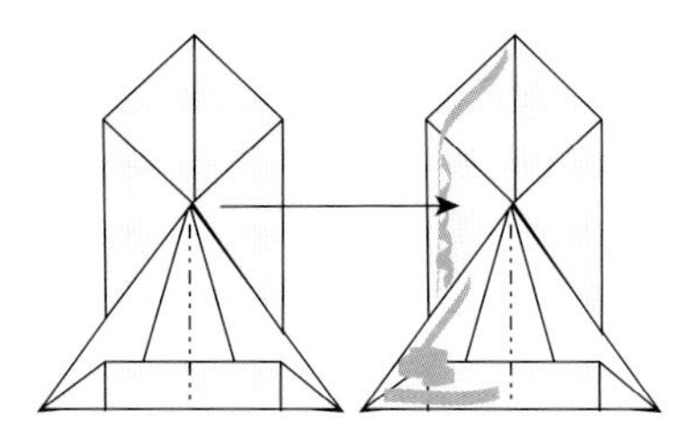

Step 8

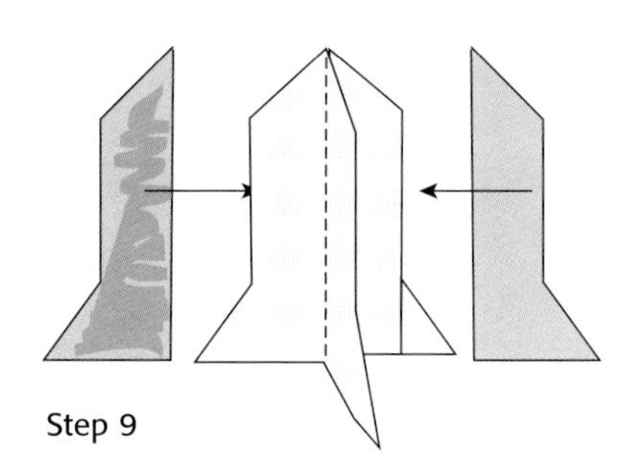

Step 9

6. Fold the paper up from the bottom to make a bottom edge that is completely straight. The fold should run through the point of the rocket fins.

7. Repeat steps 1–6 with all of the remaining pages.

8. Apply PVA (or use a glue stick) to the edges of one-half of the rocket. Align a second rocket and press down.

9. Use the text block as a template and trace around the rocket shape with a pencil onto the heavyweight paper or boards. Remove the text block and cut out the shape. Attach the shaped soft covers or boards by gluing at the front and back. Note: You may cover the boards with decorative paper first, before you attach the text block. (See Covering Separate Boards, page 126.)

TETRA-TETRA-FLEXAGON

Time: 30 minutes

Technically, most flexagons don't qualify as origami, since they use scissors and a little bit of adhesive. They also didn't originate in Japan. It is generally agreed that, in 1939, Arthur H. Stone, then a mathematics student, created a type of this structure, which launched an interest, or perhaps renewed interest, in it years later; Martin Gardner wrote about flexagons in a variety of puzzle books in the 1960s. American Heritage Dictionary defines a flexagon as "a folded paper construction that can be flexed along its folds to reveal and conceal its sides alternately."

Edward Hutchins, a book artist and teacher in New York, has been interested in this structure for many years and introduced me to it. He views the flexagon as "the book equivalent of the dissolve shot in movies:

Confused Living: A Jumble Book, 2003; watercolor, ink; tetra-tetra flexagon, 5⅜" × 8¼", in portfolio, 6" × 8¾"; unique

Pieces from *Confused Living*, 2003

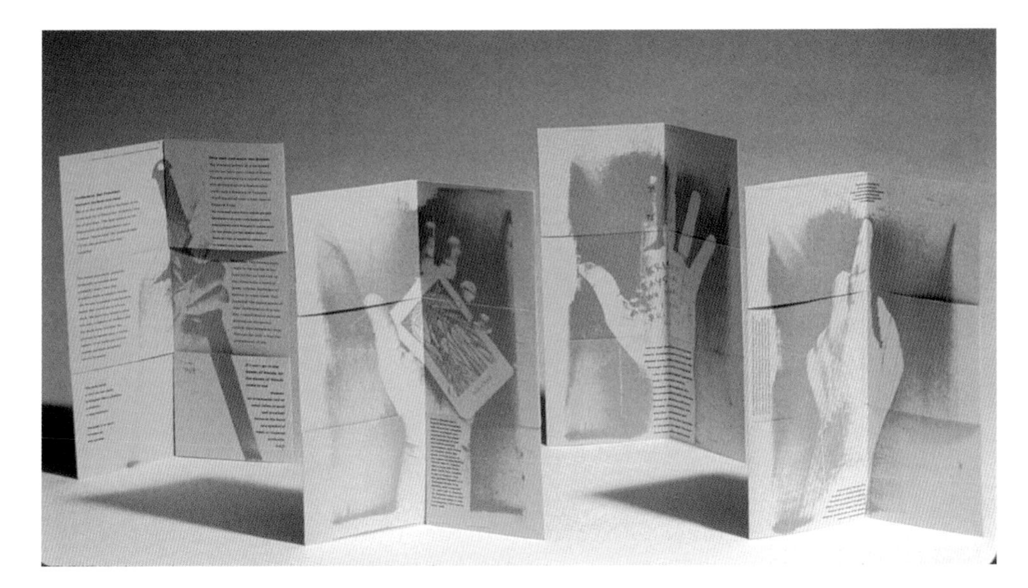

Susan King: *Queen of Wands*, 1993; offset printed from Haloid photocopy original, gold-foil stamping; tetra-tetra flexagon; edition of 800; 7 1/16" × 12 1/16" (photo by John Kiffe)

powerful at showing how one image melds into another. " Ed discovered flexagons in the 1966 book *The Mysterious Flexagons* by Madeline Jones, and made his first one as a book list for his show, called "Playing with Pages," at the Small Press Center in Manhattan in 1992, a time when few people were familiar with flexagons.

Choose snippets of text, related anecdotes, or images that can be seen in a variety of orders or choose images that are obviously sequential (baby to adult, seasons of a tree). Check the diagrams carefully. This is a tricky one. It appears to be like a Jacob's ladder or like woven paper. It is much easier to assemble the book first, then add text or imagery. The only drawback to making an all-white flexagon is that it is more confusing to find the first side. Label the sides with light pencil marks to aid you in using the layout

Susan King, a book artist in Kentucky, made a good-looking book, *Queen of Wands,* that works well because you don't have to read it in one correct sequence. I made my flexagon *Confused Living* with four scenes of places that are meaningful to me.

This particular flexagon is divided into squares. The height of the three sections can vary; the widths must be equal for the book to flex properly. You can see in Ed Hutchins's *Album* how he used a narrower height for the text segment.

Edward Hutchins: *Album*, 1997; offset printing and collage; tetra-tetra flexagon; edition of 350; 5" × 4 13/16"

Tools: bone folder, pencil, 12" metal ruler, scissors or art knife and cutting mat

Materials: one sheet 8½" × 11" medium-weight paper (printmaking or very lightweight watercolor paper will work), self-adhesive linen tape *or* a strip of paper ¼"–½" wide × 1¼" and PVA (if you are working with a child you may use a glue stick)
Example: 5½" × 8¼"

Preparation: Choose four related images, anecdotes, poems, or a combination of them. Put them in a sequence, even if they do not appear to have a natural order. Some simple subjects are:

Growth: How something changes; four pictures of the same child at different ages; four views of an animal; two people separately, then together as a couple.

Things that come in fours: the elements (earth, air, fire, and water); the directions (north, south, east, and west); a musical quartet (you choose the instruments)

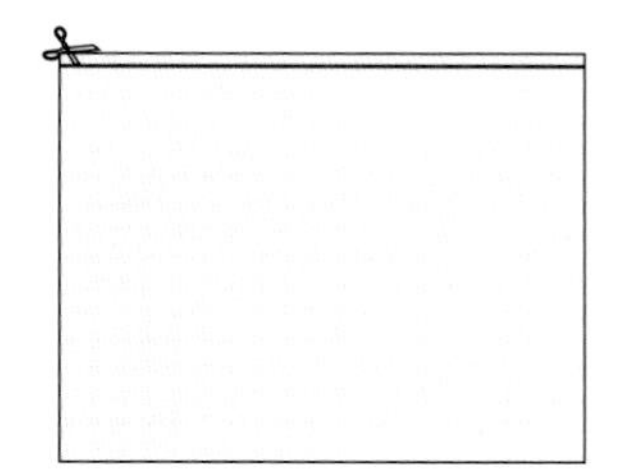

Step 1

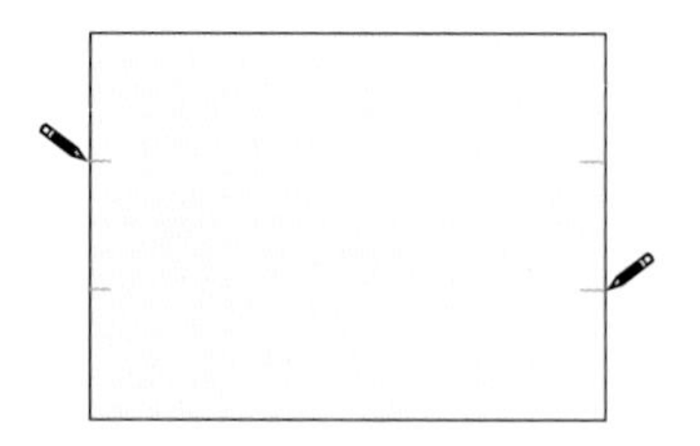

Step 3

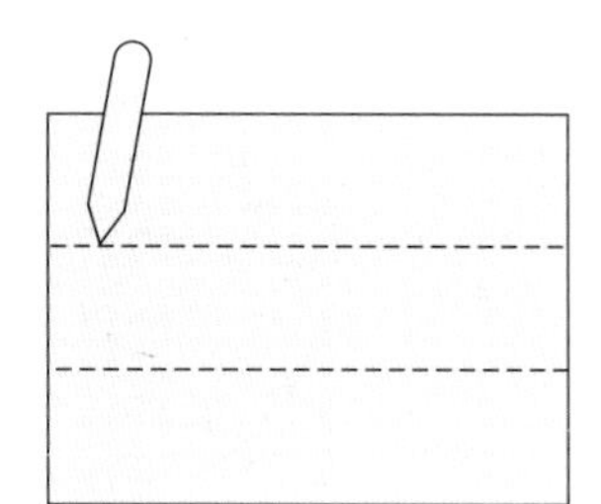

Step 4

1. With your scissors or knife against the metal ruler for a guide, trim the paper to 8¼" × 11".
2. Place the paper in front of you, horizontally.
3. Divide the paper into three equal horizontal sections as follows: measure and mark 2¾" from the head (top) and tail (bottom) along the right and left sides.
4. Score two horizontal lines with a bone folder or your thumbnail.
5. Fold the paper in half, widthwise.
6. Fold the open ends back to the folded edge to make a four-page accordion fold with three square sections on each vertical page.
7. Mark each square with the number/letter combination shown in the layout diagrams for sides 1 and 2. Or draw, color, or collage your squares at this point, following the layout for which part of the picture goes where. Make sure you mark both sides.
8. On side one, with the knife against a metal ruler for a guide, cut a horizontal flap out of the two center sections, like a squared-off letter "C," leaving one side connected.
9. Lift the flap out and fold it over the remaining middle square in the right-hand row. It will stick out to the right.
10. Fold the leftmost vertical row to the right to cover the center-left row.
11. Fold the left vertical row to the right again.

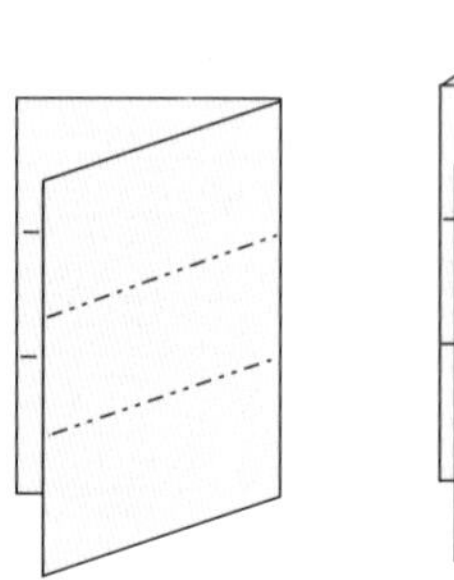

Step 5 Step 6

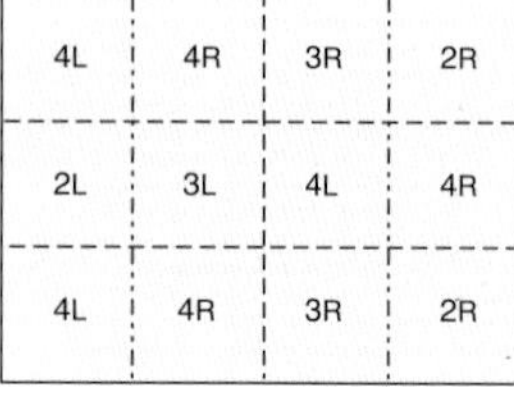

Step 7: Side 1

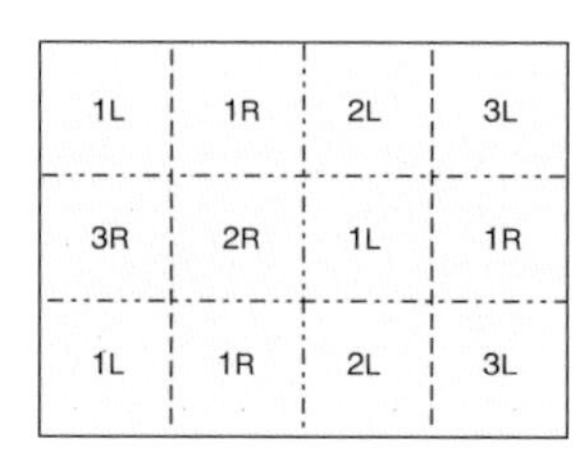

Step 7: Side 2

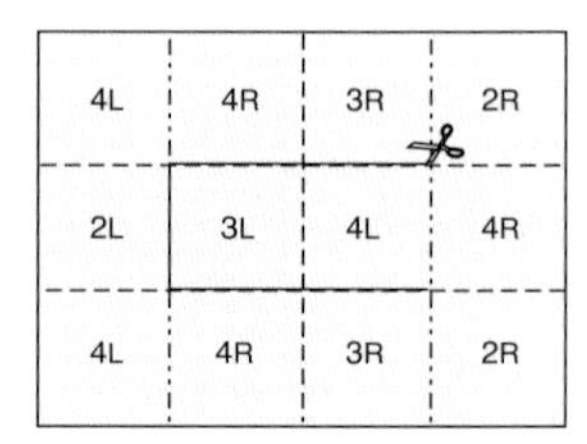

Step 8

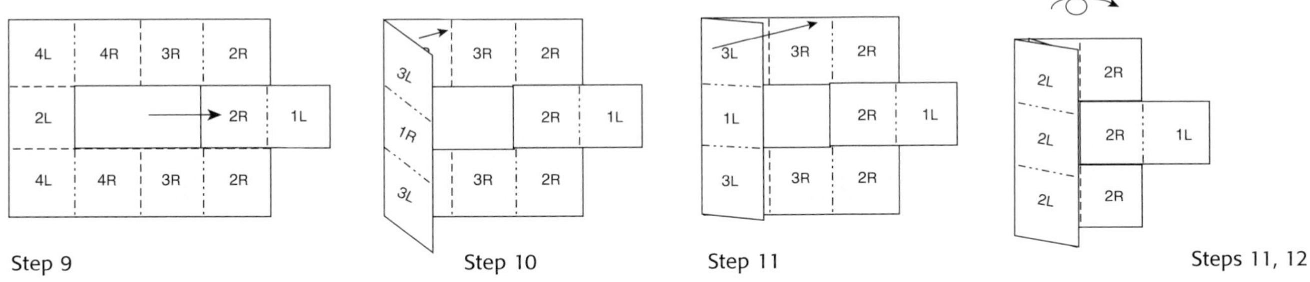

Step 9 Step 10 Step 11 Steps 11, 12

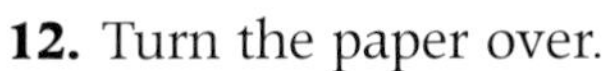

12. Turn the paper over.
13. Fold the extended square to the right.
14. Place the piece of self-adhesive linen tape along the open vertical edge in the very center. Or apply glue to a thin strip of paper that is 2¾" high and use this strip in place of the tape.
15. Turn the flexagon over again to get it into position to flex. For this layout all the movement begins with side 2.

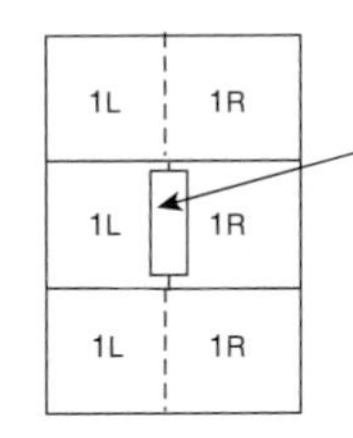

Step 13 Step 14

Activating the Flexagon
Turning the pages of this book reminds me more of separating sections of an orange or turning a sock right side out.

1. Grasp the two center squares with your thumbs and fingers.
2. Fold the right and left sides away from the center to meet in the back.
3. Open flat. We began with the 2s, now we are open to the 3s.
4. Repeat steps 1–3 one more time to get from the 3s to the 4s.
5. Reverse the steps to return the flexagon to its original position. This means that this time you'll be using your fingers to grasp the center squares at the back, and fold them toward the front with your thumbs.

Gulag Treasure, 2004; acrylic inks and gesso, stencils; tetra-tetra flexagon; unique; 5½" × 8¼"

Variation 1: Varied Height. The width of the panels (rows) must all be equal to each other, but the height of each panel may vary and be irregular, such as in Edward Hutchins's *Album.*
Variation 2: Folded Addition. Make a completely visual book using only images. Put words on a separate paper that measures slightly less than the height of the flexagon and two times the width of one column minus ½" (such as 8" × 5", grained long). Fold this paper into a very thin strip and tuck it into one of the center sections of the flexagon. It will stay there unless the reader removes it. The first one I saw like this was shown to me by Ed Hutchins; it was *Salmagundi* by Heather Hunter, made in 1998.
Variation 3: Sewn Addition. After you have made and assembled the basic Tetra-Tetra Flexagon, sew a tiny book (less than 2" in height or width) in the middle fold of 4L and 4R, the second row down. This puts a tiny book at the very end of the manipulation. Use the Single-Signature stitch from page 78.

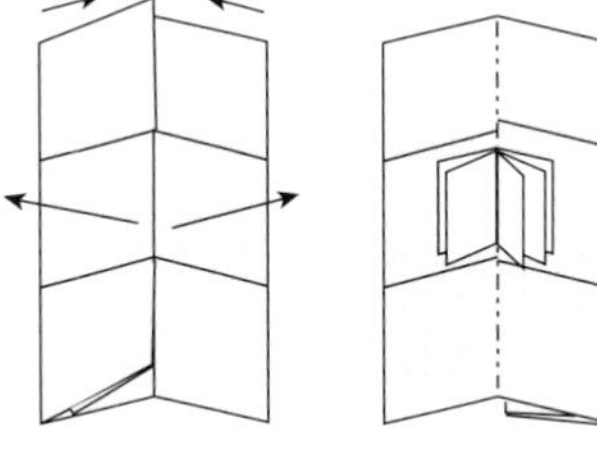

Activating the Flexagon Variation 3

Square Flexagon

Time: 10–20 minutes
Ed Hutchins introduced me to this structure, whose creator is unknown. I loved Emily Martin's *Chasing Your Tale*; her humorous story has a whimsical picture of a dog in the center of every page, which breaks in half and seems to come together again. You see the image, then it disappears and forms into something else. The really lovely thing about this one is that it keeps going round and round. You don't have to back up to put it right again.

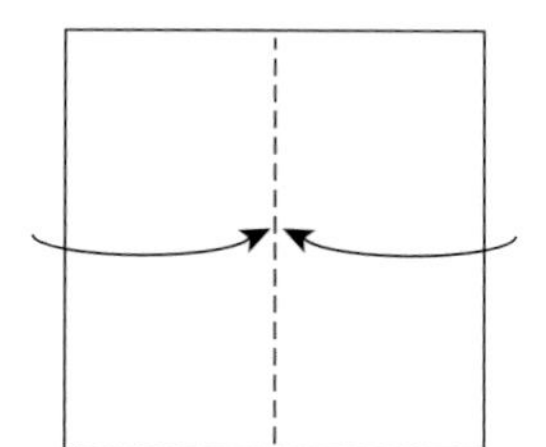

Steps 1, 2

Tools: bone folder; PVA and small brush (or glue stick)
Materials: a square piece of paper between 6" and 8½" inches

Preparation: Think of something naturally cyclical, like the stages of trees, the cycle of the sun, the phases of the moon, the seasons. Or think of something never-ending, like a person or pet's habits, buying or making food, teaching people to read, tidying your desk, caring for others. Jot down your ideas. Then pick at least four paragraphs, sentences, or words (one may be the title). Gather or create images that enhance those words (one may be the introductory image). Make the flexagon and add the words and images afterward, or use the layouts shown for sides 1 and 2.

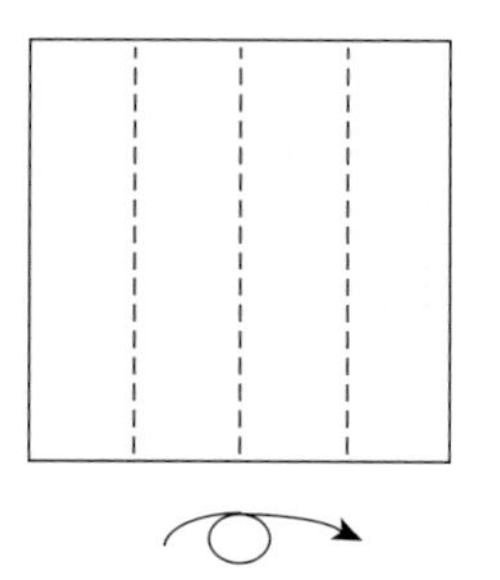

Step 3

1. Fold paper in half. Open.
2. Fold ends in to the center fold. Open.
3. Turn the paper over.
4. Fold the paper in half the other way. Fold the ends in to the center fold.
5. Cut out the four squares in the center, leaving a square-shaped opening.
6. Arrange the paper so that all the valley folds on this side are horizontal.
7. Apply glue to the top left and bottom right squares.
8. Refold the edges to the center fold, pressing down on the glued squares. Smooth them down.

Emily Martin: *Chasing Your Tale*, 2000; archival inkjet on paper; flexagon; open edition; 4" × 4"

Square Flexagon Models, 2004; gesso and acrylic inks; unique; descending squares: 6", 3", 1½"

Step 4

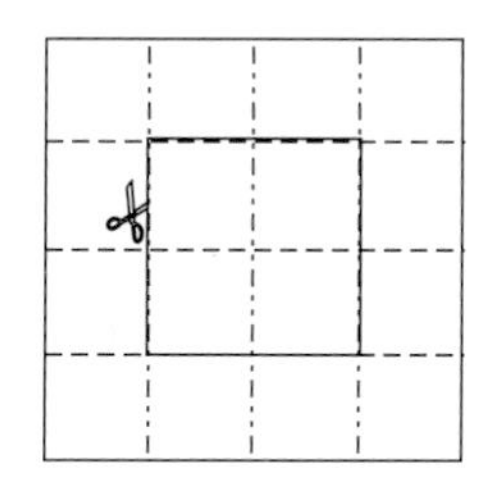

Step 5

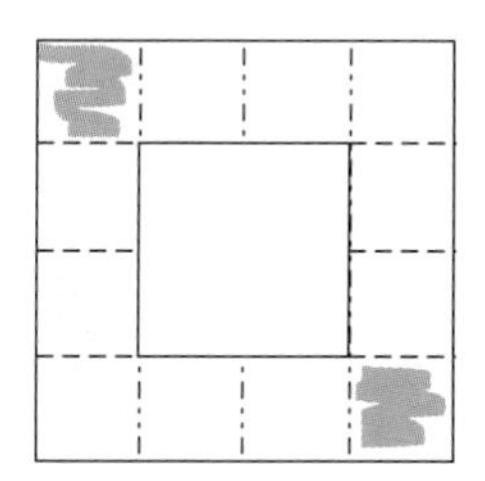

Steps 6, 7

9. In this configuration, apply glue to the top right and bottom left squares. Fold the shorter edges in toward the center; press and smooth down. Let dry, if necessary. Note: If you work with children, this is a terrific way to illustrate fractions. The square hole you cut out to make the first flexagon can be folded to another square flexagon that is one-quarter the size of the first. With the example size given here, you can fold four flexagons, each one-quarter the size of the previous one.

Activating the Flexagon

Notice the two open edges in the center. It will be easiest to open if the edges are vertical.

10. Fold the flexagon away from you, to the back, along the center fold, at the same time pull open the center edges as if you were opening any standard book. You will see that the center edges are now horizontal.

11. Turn the book so that the open edges are vertical again and repeat step 10.

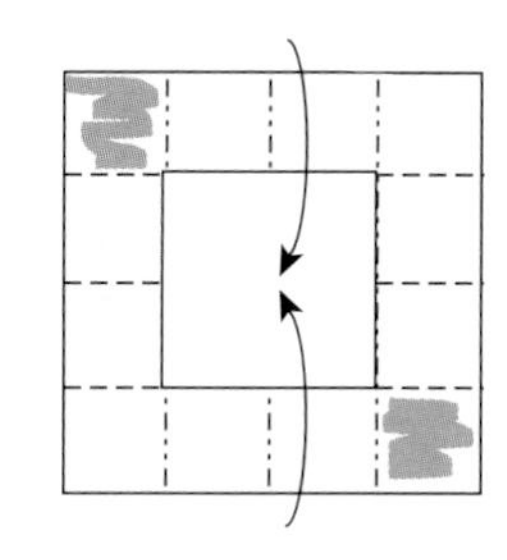

Step 8

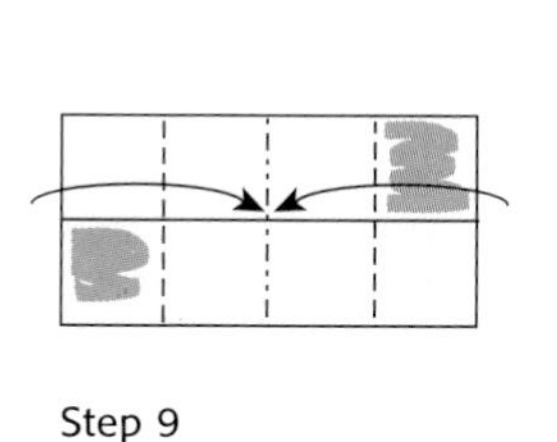

Step 9

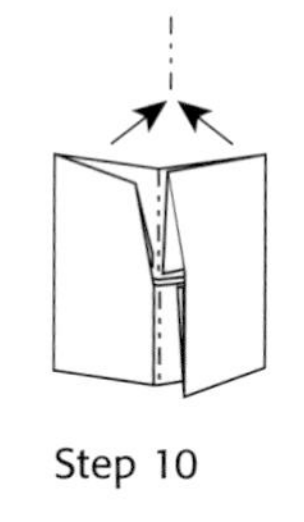

Step 10

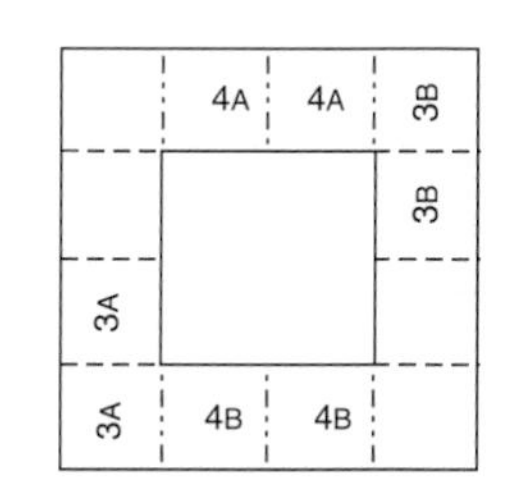

Layout: Side 1

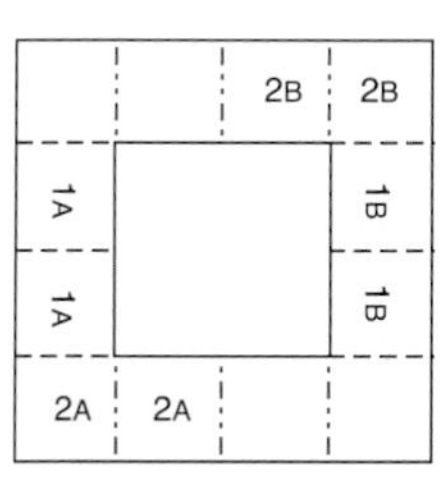

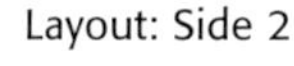

Layout: Side 2

Cultural Exchange with Flexagons

When Ed Hutchins and Steve Warren went to Mexico for a year, they made the cross-flexagon, or hexa-tetra-flexagon, *Voces de Mexico,* in honor of Mexican independence. The four faces have quotes from famous Mexicans on art and education, life, death, and politics. It was printed in red and green on white cardstock, the colors of the Mexican flag. Ed tells this story of how they used the flexagon to meet the local people:

"We gave copies to everyone who helped us on our adventure: people we asked for directions, shopkeepers, police officers, hotel staff, bus drivers, children in classes we visited, waitstaff in restaurants, visitors to the studio, people next to us at concerts. The goal was to pass out six hundred copies before we left the country. Once, while waiting for a bus in Tapachula, we were killing time in the *zocalo* [town square]. I decided to get my shoes polished, and a young boy did an especially nice job. Besides paying him and giving him a tip, we gave him a copy of *Voces de Mexico,* and he went off seeking new customers.

A little while later we were suddenly surrounded by a dozen kids asking for the *rompe cabeza* (they meant puzzle, but the Spanish phrase literally means 'head breaker'). Unfortunately, we didn't have enough copies for everyone. As we left the plaza to catch our bus, we spied the fellow who polished my shoes walking the other direction, his shoe-shine box in one hand and the flexagon clutched tightly in the other."

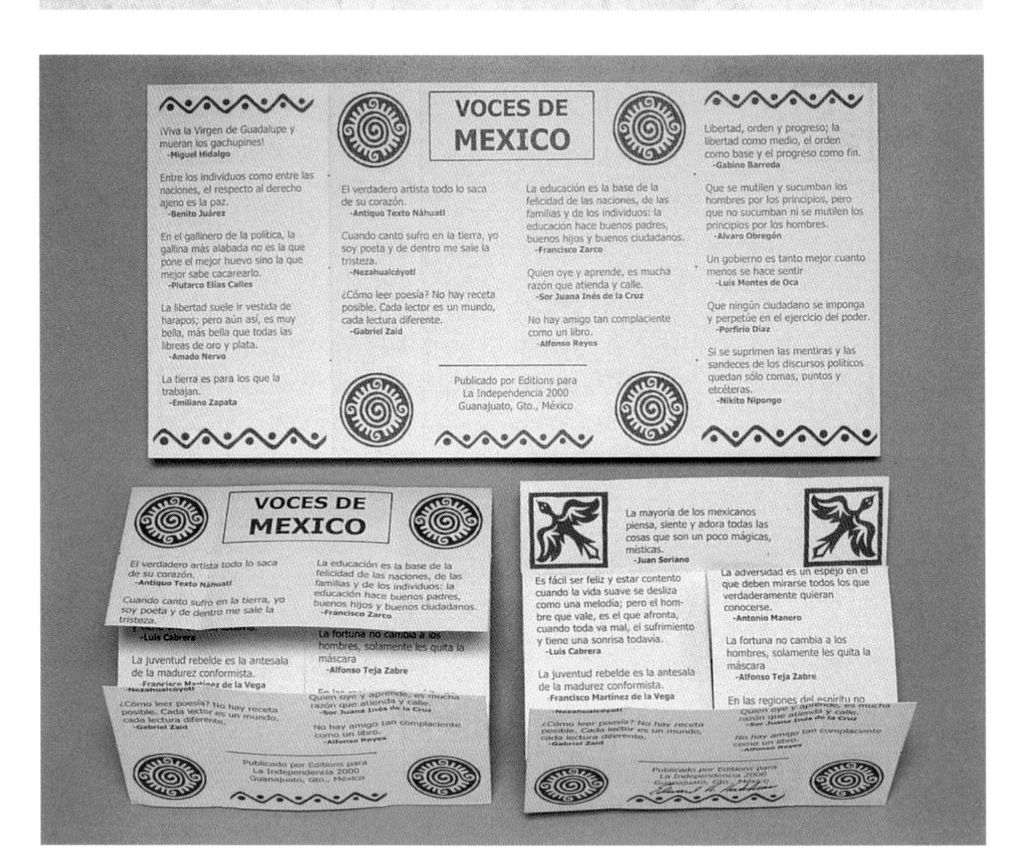

Edward Hutchins: *Voces de Mexico (Voices of Mexico)*, 2000; two-color offset printing; cross-flexagon; edition of 600; 5" × 5"

Chapter Six

COVERS AND CLOSURES: KEEPING IT ALL TOGETHER

The covers are the frame for your work and should enhance, not overshadow, the contents. A hard cover protects the book and gives it more presence, while a soft cover is suitable for informal structures and books within books. In every case, consider the front cover to be the door to the contents, setting the tone for what is inside. Let the reader know what to expect by titling your book and by adhering a tiny photograph, print, or drawing in a recess or by presenting an image in relief. The theme of the book, the structure, and the type of paper used may help you determine what type of cover and closure, if desired, would be appropriate for your project. Each closure has its own advantages and disadvantages. You will have to decide what is most important to you.

Covers and Closures
Clockwise from the bottom: *House on File; Chalk Voices; Eight Degrees of Charity; Critical Opalescence*

This chapter is devoted to hard covers. Some hard covers are specific to a type of structure; those are included with their projects. Other types of covers will function with more than one kind of book; these are included here.

Board margin

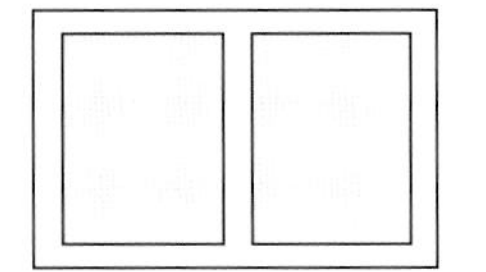

Covering material margin

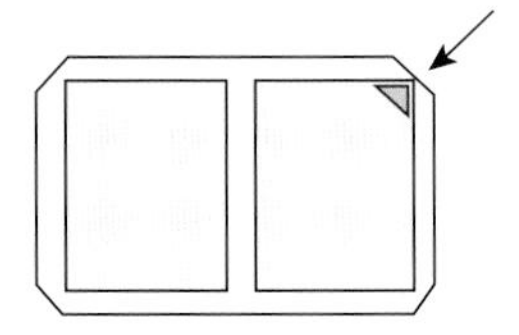

Mending a corner

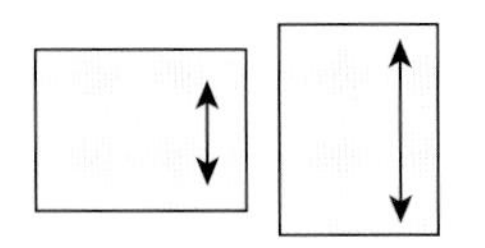

paper grains: short and long

A Few Covering Tips

- Covers are protection for your book, so most likely they will need to be slightly larger than your text block; occasionally they will be the same size, but they are never smaller. I plan for a 1/8-1/4" margin on all sides. When preparing covering material, be it cloth or paper, I allow at least a 3/4" margin on all sides.
- When you cut the diagonals at the corners of the cover, give yourself a little room—about 1/16" to 1/8" between the corner of the board and the cut; this is a bit more than the thickness of the board. If, by mistake, you cut off too much at the corners you may take one of the triangles you cut off, apply more glue, align it, and press it down over the gap. Then apply the inner cover paper over the mended corner as directed. For details about different kinds of adhesives, see page 26.
- The grain of the boards and papers will always be parallel to the spine. For example, a book with a horizontal format will have boards and papers that are grained short; a book with a vertical format will have boards and papers that are grained long.

Wrapped Hard Cover
(Non-adhesive)

Time: 10 minutes
This is the fastest and simplest way to produce a hard cover; sandwich a piece of board between two tucked-in pieces of paper. If you use it with an accordion-fold book you may need to glue the endpapers of the text block to the cover. The paper that is cut to be the exact width of the board should have the grain running parallel to the width. The paper that is the exact height of the board should have the grain running parallel to the height.
Tools: bone folder, scissors

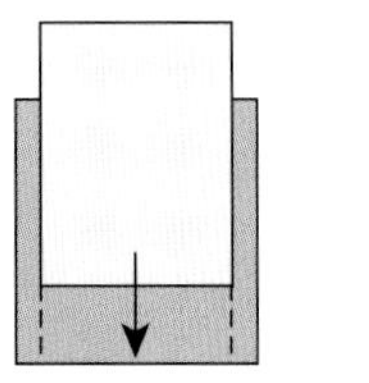

Step 1

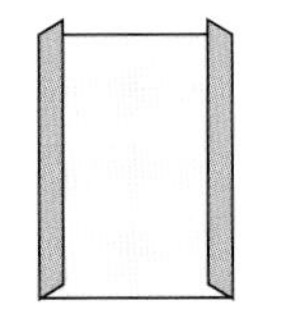

Step 2

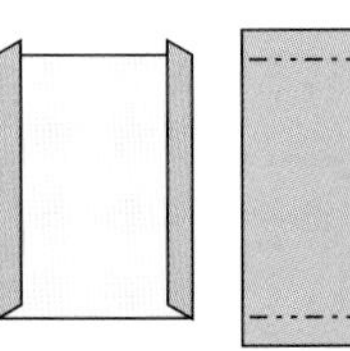

Steps 3, 4

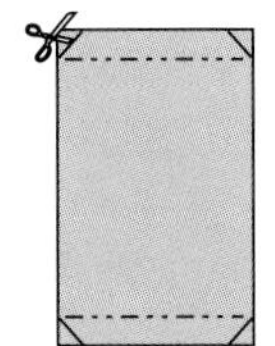

Step 5

Dorothy Yule, illustrations by Susan Hunt Yule: *Souvenirs of Great Cities: San Francisco*, 1996

Materials: two pieces of 4-ply museum board that are the same as or 1⁄8" larger than the size of your text block; two medium-weight cover papers (width of the book + 2") × (height); two medium-weight papers (height + 2") × (width).

1. Align one cover paper with the height of one board.
2. Fold 1" flaps from the right and left edges around the right and left edges of the board.
3. Align a second cover paper with the width of the board. Cover the exposed side (over the flaps from step 2).
4. Fold 1" flaps from the top and bottom, around the top and bottom edges of the board.
5. Cut slight diagonals at the corners, from the folds to the top and bottom edges.
6. Tuck the top and bottom flaps of the second cover paper into the openings between the folded flaps at the right and left sides of the first cover paper, forming a single front cover unit. (Smooth it down.)
7. Repeat steps 1–6 with the second board and the remaining cover papers to form the second cover.
8. Take the first page or panel of your text block and tuck it into the long, open edge of the front cover. Repeat with the last page or panel and the back cover.

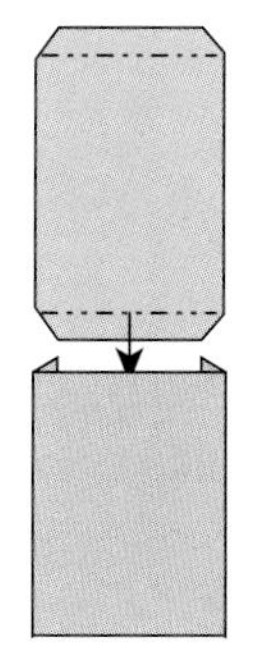

Step 6

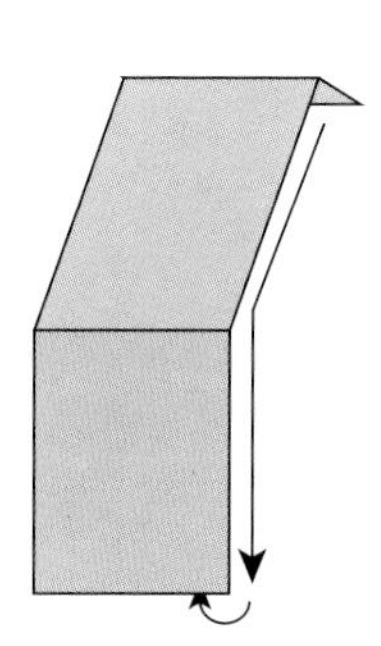

Step 6, 7

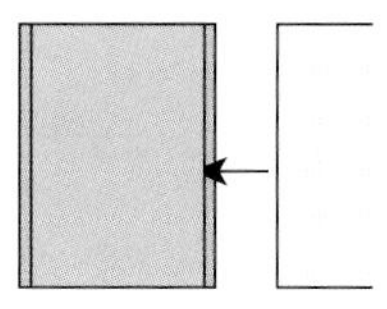

Step 8

Where, Oh Where, 2003; rubber stamps, acrylics, sewing, typewriter; unique; 6" × 6½", open

Covering Separate Boards (Adhesive)

Time: 15–20 minutes
This technique is most suitable for accordions and origami books that are meant to stretch out. Use 4-ply museum boards for books under 9" × 12"; if your book is larger, you will want to glue two 4-ply museum boards together, making an 8-ply board, which will be sturdier. For miniature books you could use 2-ply museum board.

Tools: scissors; magazines or catalogs for scrap paper; PVA; brush for gluing; waxed paper, heavy book or weight
Materials: two museum boards the same size as the text block or ¼" larger; two pieces of lightweight to medium-weight paper or book cloth 1½" larger (by both height and width) than the boards to cover them.

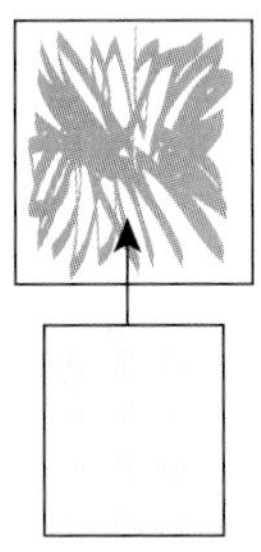

Steps 2, 3, 4

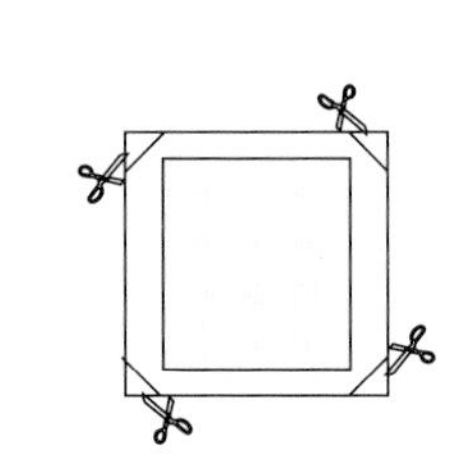

Steps 4, 5

1. Cover your work surface with layers of magazine pages. Discard any layers if they get any glue on them.
2. Arrange one cover paper in front of you, decorated-side down.
3. Spread glue evenly on your paper with the brush. Work from the center outward. Discard one layer of scrap paper to give yourself a clean surface.
4. Center a piece of board on the cover paper. Press down.

5. Cut off the corners of the cover paper, leaving at least the thickness of the board as a margin between the board and the diagonal you will cut. Discard sticky scrap paper.

6. Apply more glue on the flaps, if necessary. Fold over and smooth down each flap. Give the paper a little push in with your thumbnail when you are at two flaps that are perpendicular to each other, so that the corner tips of the board will be completely covered and the cover paper doesn't stick out.

7. Repeat steps 1–6 to make the second cover.

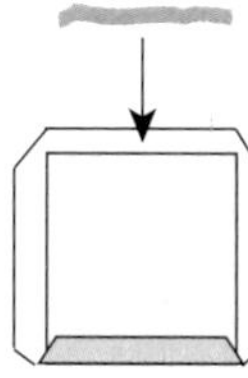

Step 6

Attaching an Accordion

8. With your project face down on a piece of scrap paper, apply glue evenly to the back of the first panel of your accordion, making sure it reaches all edges.

9. Discard the sticky scrap paper.

10. Align the folded edge of the first accordion panel with the spine edge of the board on the back of the front cover. Press in place and hold down a few seconds.

11. Repeat steps 8–10 with the last panel of the accordion and the back cover.

12. For flag books, continue with step 13. For all others, place waxed paper between the newly glued sheet and the rest of the text block. Close the book. Place the book between waxed paper and Masonite boards. Put a heavy weight on top. Let the project dry overnight.

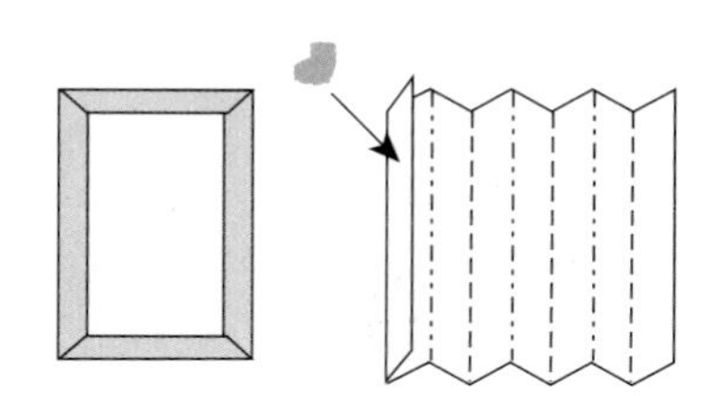

Step 8

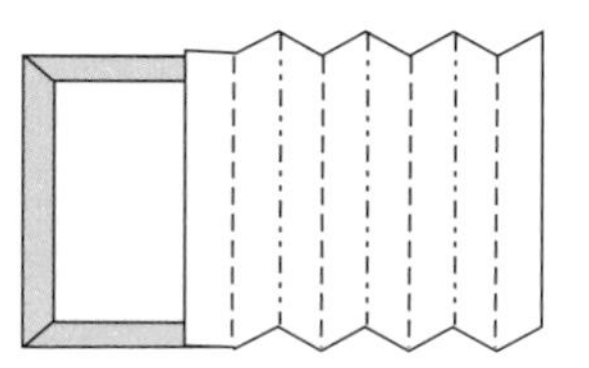

Step 10

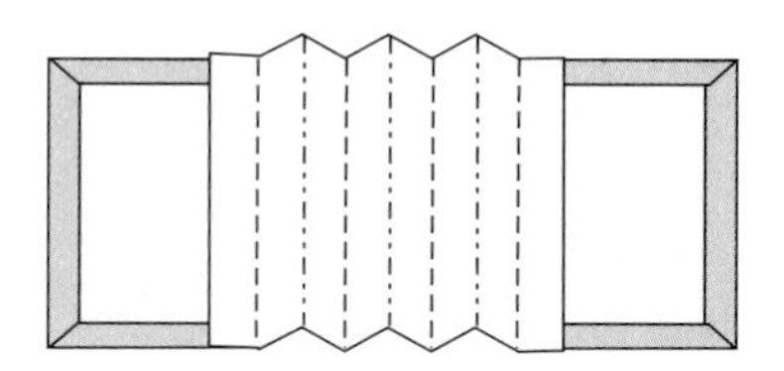

Step 11

For the flag books add inner cover papers (endpapers):

Endpapers should be ¼"–½" smaller than the size of the cover boards.

13. On a clean sheet of scrap paper, apply adhesive to the back of the inner cover paper.

14. Center the inner cover paper, glue side down, on the back of one covered board (over the accordion strip) and press into place. Smooth it down.

15. Repeat steps 13 and 14 for the other cover.

16. Place waxed paper between the newly glued sheet and the rest of the text block. Close the book. Place the book between waxed paper and Masonite boards. Put a heavy weight on top. Let the project dry overnight.

Variation: Portfolio. Cover two museum boards following steps 1–7.
(a) Apply glue to the wrong side of a piece of lightweight paper or book cloth that is the same height as your outer cover paper × two inches wide

Step 13

Steps 14, 15

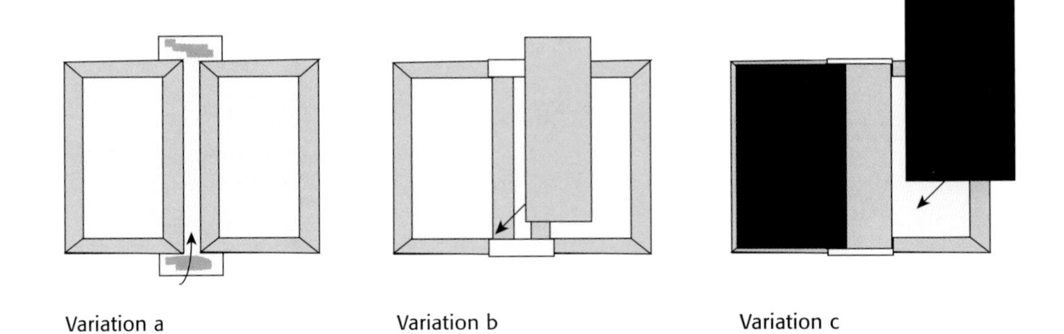

Variation a   Variation b   Variation c

(long). Center the boards on this outer cover strip with a 3/8" gap between the boards (the width of two spacing bars). Wrap the edges over the head and tail of the portfolio and press down. (b) Apply glue to the wrong side of a piece of lightweight paper that is the same height as your endpapers × two inches wide. Center it across the gap and press down. (c) Apply glue to the endpapers, following instructions 13–16.

Split-Board Binding

Time: 20–30 minutes
For this binding, the ends of your text block or accordion spine are sandwiched between two boards, hence the name "split board." You may use this for almost any type of text block: accordion or codex (one with signatures). I recommend it for accordions.
Tools: scissors; magazines, or catalogs for scrap paper; PVA; brush for gluing; waxed paper; heavy book or weight
Materials: two 4-ply museum boards the same size as the text block or 1/4" larger, two pieces of lightweight to medium-weight paper or book cloth 1 1/2" larger (by both height and width) than the boards to cover them, two 2-ply museum boards the same height as the 4-ply boards but 1/8" narrower

1. Wrap each of the four boards as you would for a Covering Separate Boards (see page 126). Instead of wrapping them, you may paint the outer boards with gesso or use a dry brush with acrylics, rubbing the paint into the board (this will prevent the covers from being too sticky).
2. Put the accordion spine or text block in front of you. The open edge should be on your right.
3. Place a piece of scrap paper between the first panel and the rest of your book to protect it. The open edge should still be on the right.
4. Arrange the front board in front of you, wrong-side up.
5. Apply glue evenly to the exposed paper, making sure the adhesive reaches all edges.
6. Discard the sticky scrap paper.

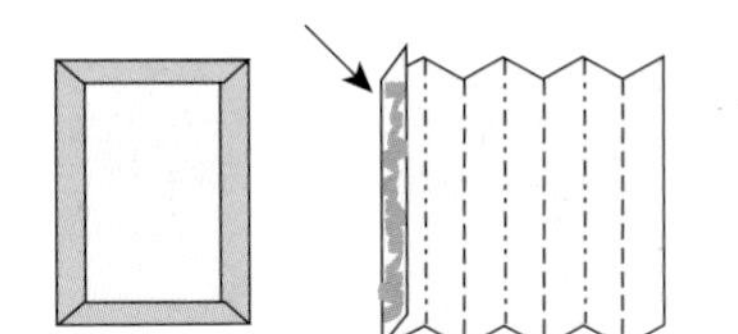

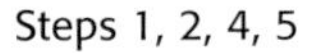

Steps 1, 2, 4, 5

7. Align the first fold from the paper at step 5 with the edge of the board nearest the spine. Press in place and hold down a few seconds.
8. Repeat steps 4–7 with the last page and the back cover.
9. Turn the remaining boards face down on several layers of scrap paper. Apply glue smoothly and evenly to the back of one of the boards. Align and press the board into place on the inside of the front cover board, sandwiching the sticky paper; align the inner board with the fore edge. The board will not align at the spine.
10. Repeat step *9* for the back cover.
11. Place waxed paper between the newly glued boards and the rest of the text block. Close the book. Place the book between waxed paper and Masonite boards. Put a heavy weight on top. Let the project dry overnight.

Left: *A Black Ribbon*, 2003; typewriter, color copy, copy transfer, tags; unique; 4½" × 7⅜"
Right: *At Circle's Edge*, 2003; paste papers, hooked rug; split-board covers and accordion; 5¼" × 7"

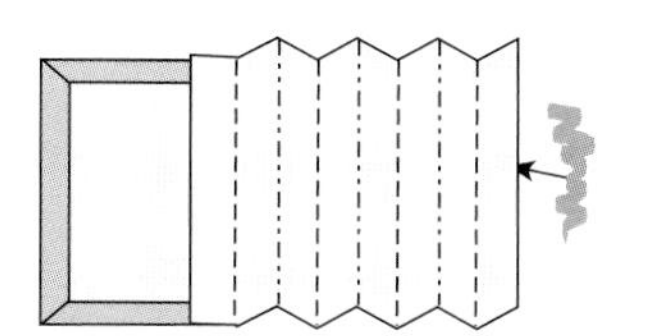
Steps 7, 8

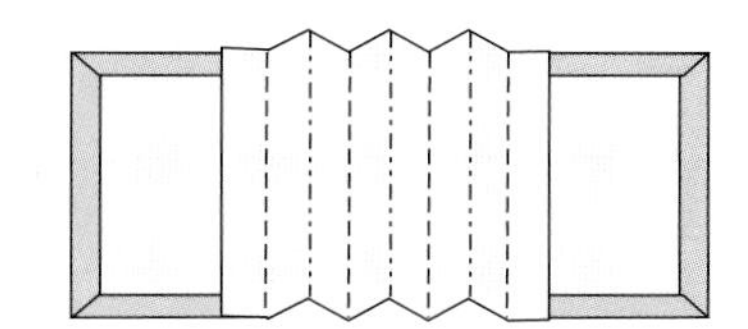
Step 8

Step 9

Step 10

Case Binding

Time: 45 minutes
This cover works best for a book with multiple signatures or an accordion made of heavyweight paper. If your text block is 1/4" or thicker, you will want a rigid spine attached to your cover to protect the pages and keep the book together. The following measurements give you a 1/8" border around the text block. I have to calculate this every time I make a new book. Copy the formula and fill in your own numbers. The example is for a text block that is 5" × 7" × 1/4". You may make this cover into a portfolio by omitting the spine piece, and allowing a 3/8"–1/2" gap between the front and back covers.

Boards should be 1/8" wider than your text block and 1/4" taller.
Cover paper should be this width:
(3/4" + width____ + 3/16" + spine depth___ + 3/16" + width___ + 3/4"), which you may round off to: 2 × (width___) + (spine depth___ + 2"). The height should be simply: (height___ + 1 1/2").
Inner cover paper (endpaper) should be this width: 2 × (width of boards___) + 1/8". The height is the same as that of the text block.

Tools: bone folder, pencil, 12" metal ruler, scissors, magazines or catalogs for scrap paper, PVA or PVA/paste combo, brush for gluing, 3/16" spacing bar (optional), waxed paper, heavy book or weight, Masonite boards

Left: *A Dime Date*, 2004; ink-written text, rubber stamps, stamps made from Model Magic™, dimes; accordion with Coptic stitch; edition of two; 3 1/4" × 3 1/4" × 7/8"
Right: *Under the Magnolia*, 2004; acrylic inks and gesso, graphite; circle accordion; unique; 6" × 10 5/8" × 3/4"; open

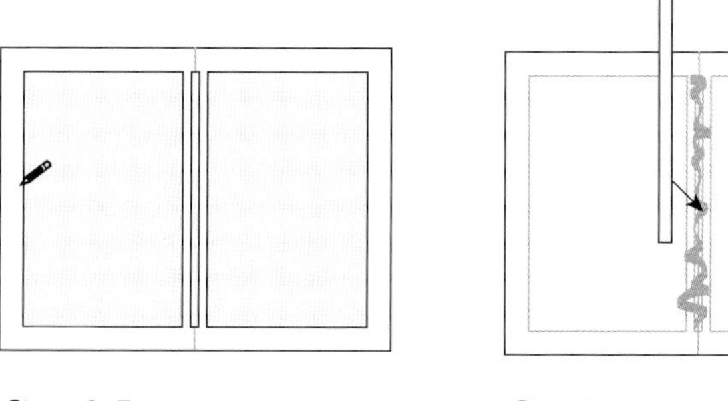

Steps 2, 3

Step 4

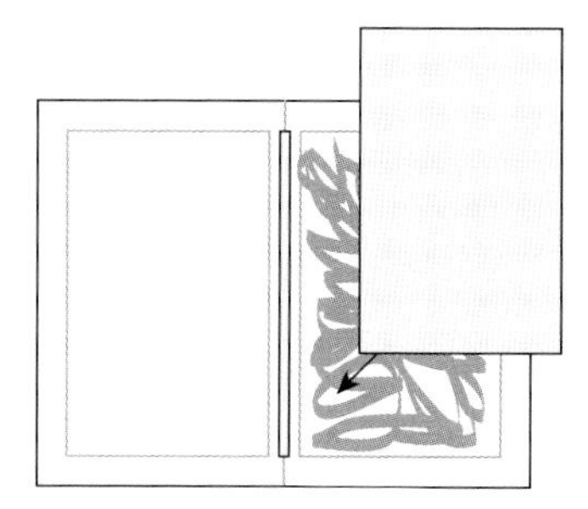

Steps 5, 6

Materials: two 4-ply museum boards 5⅛" × 7¼" (long), one 4-ply museum board ¼" × 7¼" (long) for the spine, one piece of lightweight paper or book cloth 12¼" × 8¾" (short) for the cover, one piece of decorative lightweight paper 10⅜" × 7" (short) for the inner covers
Example: 5⅛" × 7¼" x ¼" finished book (text block is 5" × 7")

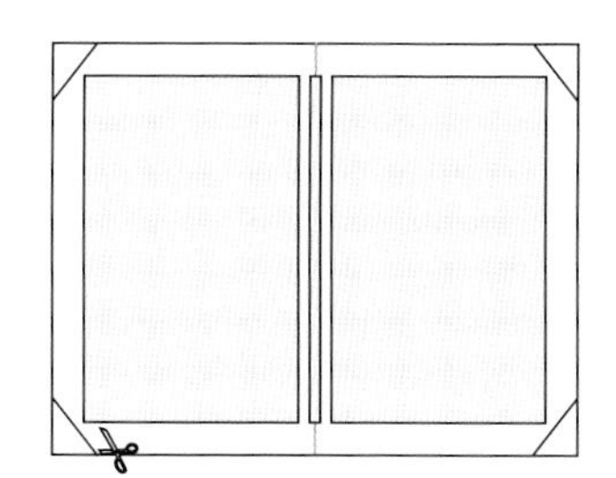

Steps 8, 9

1. Place layers of magazine pages over your work surface. Discard pages as they get sticky.
2. Place the cover paper wrong-side up. Find the center on the back of the cover paper and mark it with a pencil or fold the paper in half, widthwise.
3. Place the boards on the paper, with the spine centered on the mark or fold. Use the spacing bar between the spine and the front and back boards or measure 3/16" between them. This space between the boards ensures that your book will open and close. Using the ruler as a guide, align the boards, then draw around the boards with the pencil. (For a soft spine, measure 3/16" on either side of the fold. Draw around the boards and remove them, but don't use the spacing bar or the spine board; skip to step 5.)
4. Remove the boards. Apply glue to the center, where the spine board will go. Press the spine board into place.
5. Apply the glue on one half of the cover paper, keeping the glue inside of the drawn rectangle. It is helpful to work from the center outward, in a fanlike manner.
6. Place one board on top of the sticky rectangle. Press down.
7. Apply glue to the other half of the paper, inside the other drawn rectangle.
8. Press the second board into place.
9. Cut diagonals across the corners of the cover paper, leaving a margin the width of the board before you cut the diagonals.
10. Apply more glue and fold down the edge flaps, one at a time. I like to make the parallel flap my second turn in, but you may fold the flaps in any order. When working with perpendicular flaps, be sure to give the paper a little push in with your thumbnail when you are at the corners, so that the corner tips of the board will be completely covered and the cover paper won't stick out.
11. Move the project to a clean work surface. Smooth down the newly glued papers. You may do this by putting a sheet of waxed paper over the project

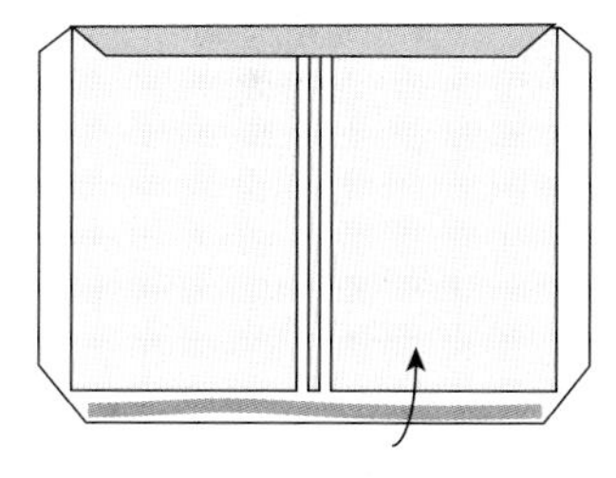

Step 10

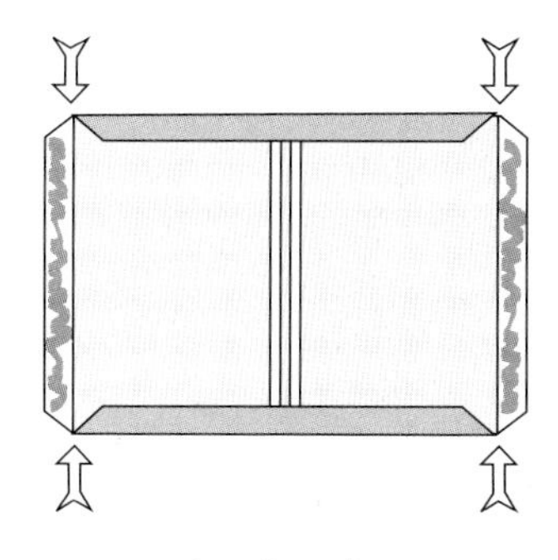

Step 10 (continued)

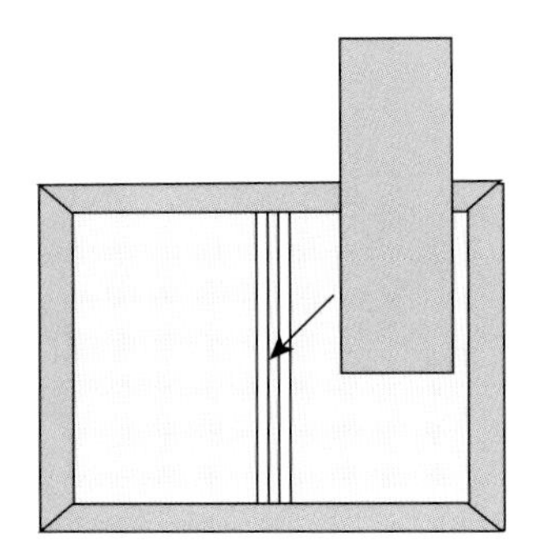

Step 13

and rubbing with a bone folder on top of the waxed paper. Proceed to step 1 of Attaching the Text Block to the Case. For an accordion-folded text block, add an inner spine-covering paper. The inner spine paper should be the same height as the text block, and it should be the width of the spine board plus two inches.

12. Put the inner spine paper wrong-side up on top of some clean scrap paper. Spread a thin, even coat of glue on the paper.

13. Center the paper on the uncovered side of the boards over the spine board) and press into place. With the bone folder, smooth the paper down into the grooves between the spine and the front and back covers.

14. Apply glue and attach the text block to the covers as in steps 1–8 of Attaching the Text Block to the Case.

Note on Spines: For other projects you will need to measure the depth of your text block before you cut a board for your spine. You may need a spine piece that is ½" or another size so that your book will close flat. The measurement of your spine is from the outside of the top edge of the text block to the bottom edge of the text block.

Attaching the Text Block to the Case

Sometimes the text block will attach directly to the hard covers. Begin with the hard covers open, wrong-side up.

1. Place a piece of scrap paper between the first and second pages of the text block. Apply glue in a fanlike manner to the back of the first page. Remove the scrap paper.

2. Pick up the text block, taking care not to get glue on the rest of the book. Arrange the now-sticky endpaper on the inside of the front cover, aligning the spine of the text block with the right edge of the board, and centering the book top and bottom.

3. Smooth down the sheet with a bone folder. Put a piece of waxed paper between the endpaper and the next free page of the book. Close the book and face it to the left, leaving the back cover open and flat.

4. Place a piece of scrap paper between the last page and the rest of the text block. Apply glue in a fanlike manner to the back of the last page. Remove the scrap paper.

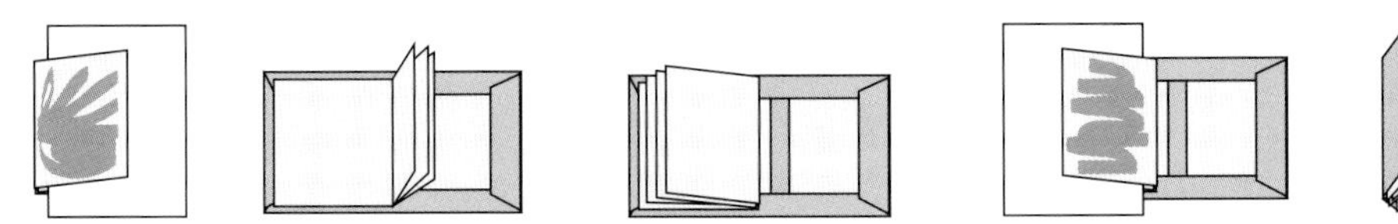

Step 1 Step 2 Step 3 Step 4 Step 5

5. You may need to close the book slightly (possibly to a 45-degree angle) to obtain the same margins as the endpaper at the front of the book. Press the sticky sheet onto the inside of the back cover.

6. Put waxed paper over the endpaper and smooth it with a bone folder.

7. Place waxed paper between the newly glued sheet and the rest of the text block. Close the book.

8. Place the book between waxed paper and Masonite boards. Put a heavy weight on top. Let the project dry overnight.

WRAPAROUND PORTFOLIO

Time: 60–75 minutes

As I was working on *Chalk Voices*, I kept running into new problems. My paper was very stiff so that when it was folded into the pop-up insert it did not stay closed. Eventually, I designed the wraparound portfolio to hold the pop-up insert. I secured mine with a little clasp, but magnetic strips, ribbons, or a paper clasp would also work. For *Chalk Voices,* the Wraparound Portfolio is merged with a folded paper that pops open like the one in the children's book *Papa, Please Get the Moon for Me* by Eric Carle. The Wraparound Portfolio is really just a Case Binding with two extra pieces of museum board.

Chalk Voices, 2003; letterpress and reduction print; pop-open insert and wraparound portfolio with single signature; edition of 30; 4¼" × 6¼"

Step 1

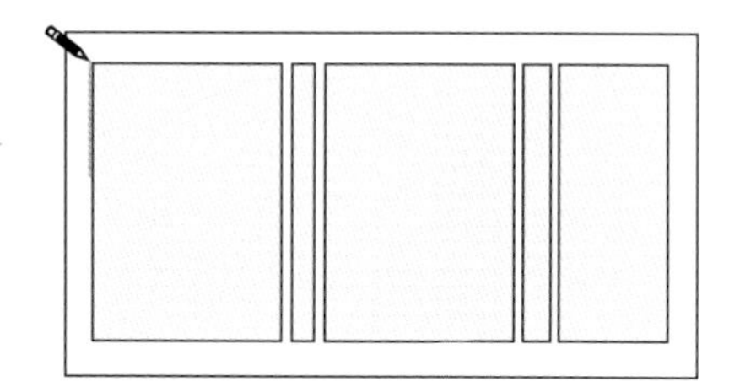

Step 2

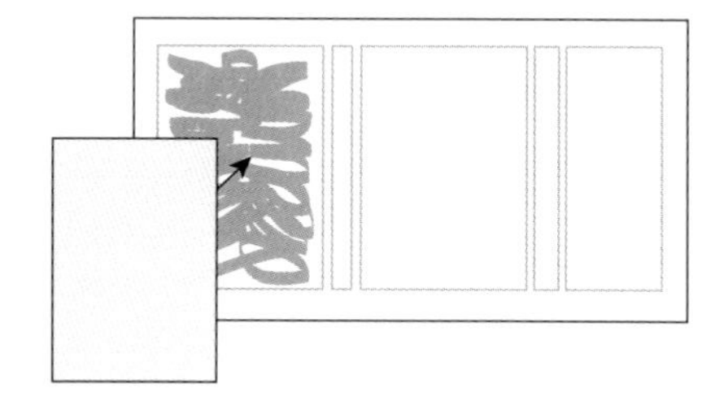

Step 3

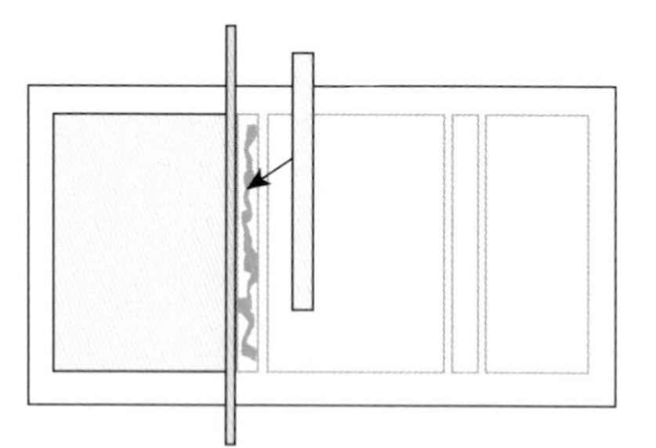

Step 4

Tools: bone folder, pencil, 12" metal ruler, scissors or art knife and cutting mat, magazines or catalogs for scrap paper, PVA or paste/PVA (if you use book cloth), brush for gluing, 3/16" metal spacing bar
Materials: two 4-ply museum boards 4¼" × 6½" (long), one 4-ply spine ¼" × 6½" (long), one 4-ply spine ⅜" × 6½" (long), one 4-ply flap 2½" × 6½" (long), one piece of lightweight paper or book cloth for outer cover 14" × 7¾" (short), one piece of lightweight inner paper 12¼" × 6" (short), 18" ribbon or a clasp (see pages 138–142 for closure ideas).
Example: 4¼" × 6½" x ⅜"

1. Arrange the boards in front of you in a horizontal line left to right: large board, narrow spine, large board, wide spine, flap.
2. Place layers of magazine pages on your work surface for scrap paper. Discard any scrap paper that gets messy. Use paste or a paste/PVA mixture. Place the lightweight paper in front of you, horizontally, wrong-side up. If you are using book cloth, place it with the paper-side up. Put the boards in order on top of the paper or cloth with 3/16" gaps between the boards and ¾" from the top of the paper or cloth and centered top and bottom. When the boards are in place, draw around each of the boards lightly with a pencil.
3. Remove the boards. Apply glue inside the rectangle you drew for the first board on the left. Press the board into place.
4. Apply glue along the narrow rectangle you drew for the first spine. Place a 3/16" spacing bar next to the first board, then place the spine next to the bar. Press the spine into place. Remove the bar.
5. Continue to apply glue, use the spacing bar, and press the remaining boards and spines in place.
6. Turn the project over onto clean scrap paper and smooth it down with a bone folder. Turn it back over to keep working.
7. Cut off the corners of the cover paper or book cloth with scissors, leaving at least ⅛" between the diagonal cuts and the boards.
8. Apply glue to one of the long flaps. Fold it over the boards, pulling very gently to wrap the paper or cloth over the edges. Discard any sticky scrap paper. At the corners, use your fingernail to neatly tuck in the tiny margin of paper or cloth so it won't stick out when the boards are completely covered.
9. Repeat step 8 with the other long flap, then the side flaps.
10. Attach a ribbon or ribbon and clasp at this point, if desired. To attach a ribbon, cut slits in the center of the cover paper or cloth in the space on both sides of

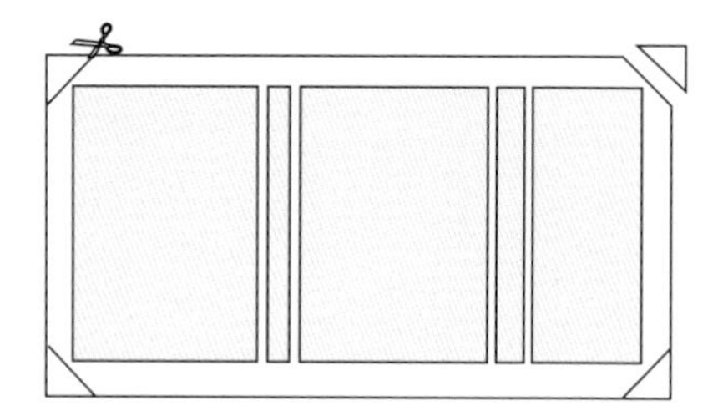

Step 7

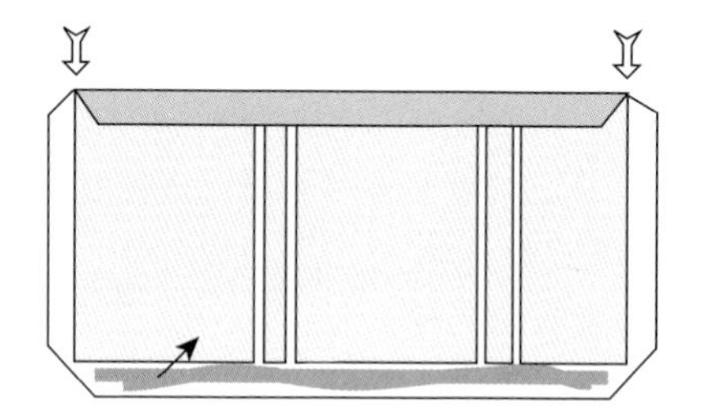

Step 8

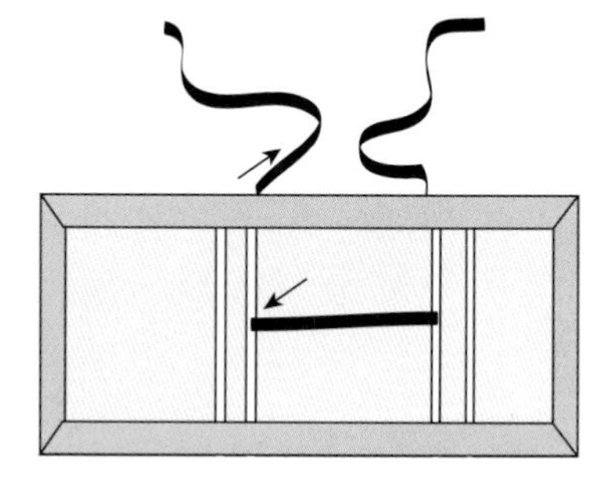

Step 10

the center board, and thread the ribbon through. If you are using Velcro or magnetic strips, add them at step 13.

11. Place the inner paper, horizontally, on clean scrap paper, wrong-side up. Apply glue evenly to the inner paper, working from the center outward.

12. Pick up the paper and, holding it in a "U" shape, center it across the exposed side of the boards. Smooth it into place with the bone folder, pressing it into the grooves.

13. Add adhesive-backed Velcro or magnetic strips as a closure if you did not use ribbon.

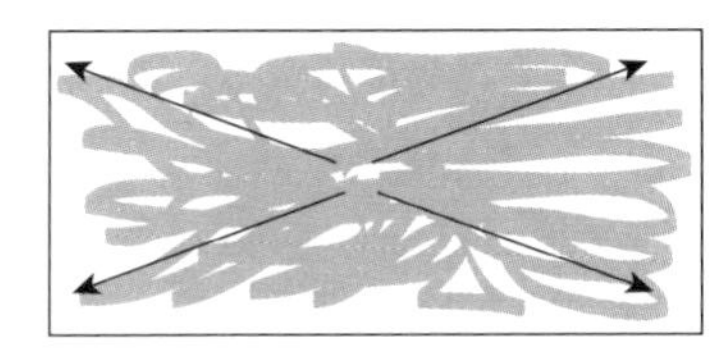

Step 11

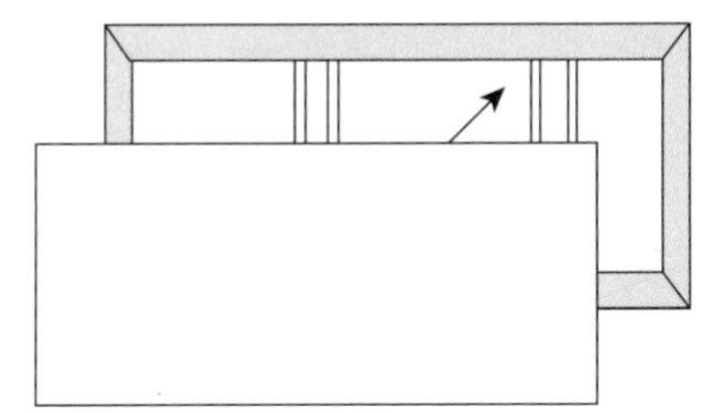

Step 12

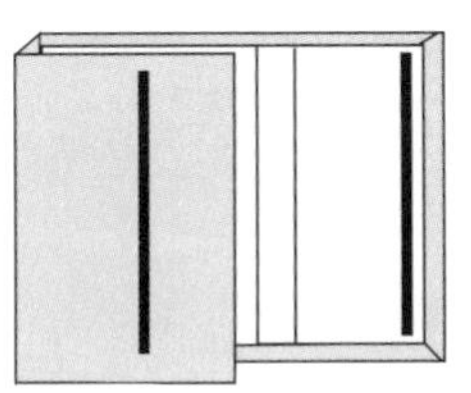

Step 13

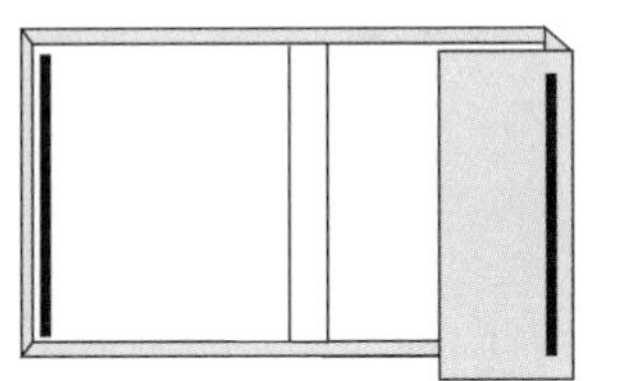

Variation

Variation: Switch the two spines so that the larger spine is on the left; the flap will be inside for a smooth, flat front cover. Use a ribbon or a magnetic strip to keep it closed.

Inner Folder Insert

Make a paper folder to secure loose objects so that they do not fall out of the open bottom of the wraparound portfolio. You can also plan to attach the insert to the front or back cover of any hardcover book; just remember to make the spine of the book cover deep enough to include it.

Tools: bone folder, pencil, 12" metal ruler, PVA, brush for gluing
Materials: one piece of medium- to heavy-weight piece of paper 4⅛" × 14⅛" (short)
Example: insert to hold 4" × 6" thin book, cards, or photos
All scores are horizontal.

Portfolios with inserts, 2003; book cloth, paper, ribbon; 4⅝" × 6½"

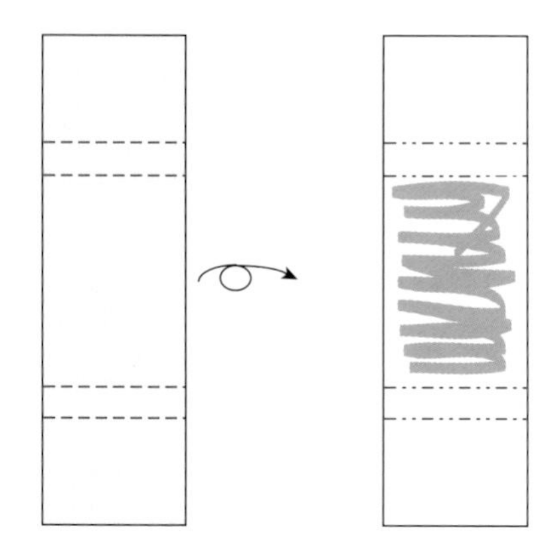

Steps 1–6 Step 7

1. Place the paper in front of you, vertically.
2. Measure, mark, and score 3" from the top of the paper.
3. Measure, mark, and score 1/4" from the first score.
4. Measure, mark, and score 6 1/4" from the previous score.
5. Measure, mark, and score 1/4" from the previous score.
6. Fold up along all scores into valley folds. Turn the paper over.
7. Brush a flat, even coat of glue in the large center segment.
8. Center this segment on the large board in the center of the wraparound portfolio. Smooth down.

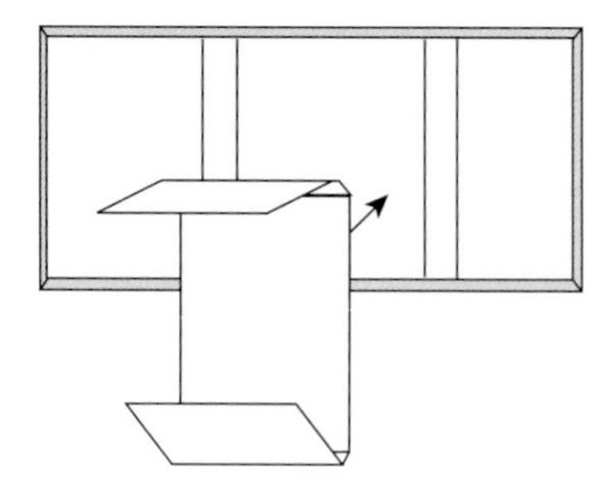

Step 8

Recesses

When you want to inset a title strip or small image on the front of your portfolio, box, or hardcover book, you can make a shallow recess in the 4-ply museum board before you cover the board. I made the flower shape for *Under the Magnolia*, then drew around it with pencil on the front-cover board. Rectangles and squares are the easiest shapes to work with.
Tools: pencil, 12" metal ruler, art knife and cutting mat, tweezers
Materials: one 4-ply museum board for the front cover of your project, the item to be inset

Left: *A Little After A*, 2003; oven thermometer, gesso, cutouts; circle accordion; 5 3/16" × 7"
Right: *Under the Magnolia*, 2004; acrylic inks and gesso, graphite; circle accordion; unique; 6" × 10 5/8" × 3/4"

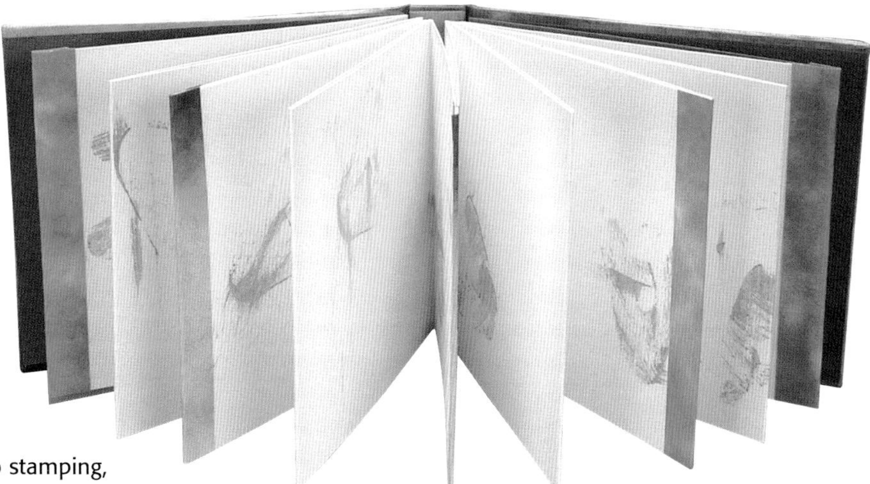

Return to A, 2003; wooden puzzle letter, gold gesso stamping, book in progress; accordion with strips; 5$\frac{3}{8}$" $\times$ 4$\frac{1}{2}$"

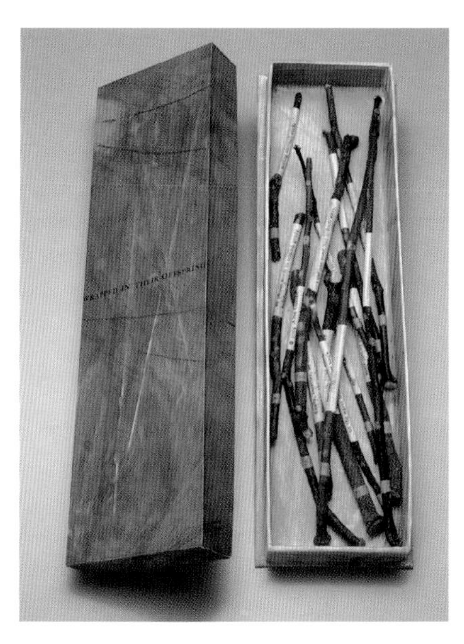

1. On the 4-ply board, measure and mark (for a square or rectangle) or draw around the shape you will be using. For *Under the Magnolia*, I drew around the little painting of the magnolia, then enlarged the magnolia shape slightly for the recess.
2. Cut into the board with your knife, on the drawn lines. You want to cut about halfway into the board, but not all the way through. Cut along the lines you drew. Use the knife to loosen the edges by digging under the surface and starting to peel up the layers with the grain. As always, the direction of the grain should be parallel to the spine of the book.
3. With your fingernails or tweezers, pull up the layers of board to make a uniformly flat recess. If you are having trouble pulling up the layers, you may have not cut deeply enough into the board or you are trying to pull it up against the grain. Correct either of these problems by going back over the edges with your knife or peeling up the layers perpendicular to the way you started.

RELIEFS

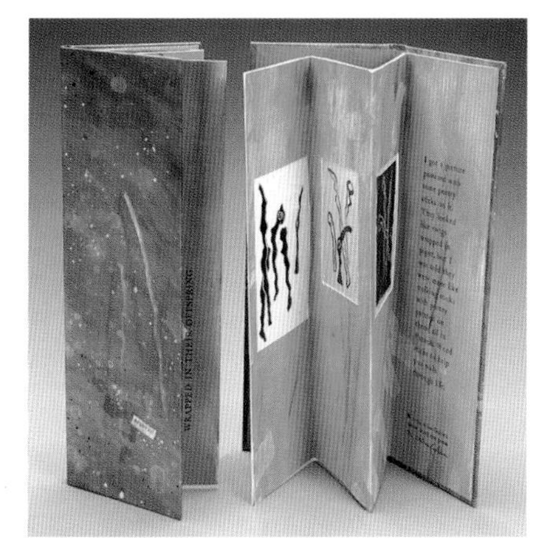

Add texture and dimension to your box or book by cutting shapes from 2-ply museum board and gluing them to the boards before you cover or paint them. Make sure the grain or the shape you will cut matches the grain of the cover so it won't warp. For the cover of the box of *Wrapped in Their Offspring* I overlapped twiglike shapes, then covered them with paper painted to resemble wood. The cover of the book inside the box has both a relief and a recess.

Wrapped in Their Offspring, 2004; acrylic inks and gesso, letterpress, camphor sticks; linoleum cuts; accordion book, 3$\frac{1}{4}$" $\times$ 10$\frac{1}{4}$", in box, 4" $\times$ 14"

Ribbons

Critical Opalescence, 2004; letterpress and mixed media; edition of 40; pamphlets, 3" × 3", 4" × 4", 4" × 7", in portfolio, 4 3/8" × 7 3/4" (photo by A. Golden)

Ribbons are popular, decorative closures, and you probably have them around the house. The only problem associated with them is that the reader may worry about tying them correctly. One friend always hands my book back to me untied; once she said, "I don't do bows." Sometimes the book just wants to have ribbons. *Critical Opalescence* needed a closure. I just happened to have a wavy, wire-edged French ribbon in a color that matched. If you plan to tie a bow be aware that the wider the ribbon, the longer it will need to be. Add the ribbons *before* you glue the endpapers.

Tools: 12" metal ruler, scissors, art knife and cutting mat, PVA, brush for gluing
Materials: two pieces of ribbon the same size; book or portfolio
Example: two 1/4" × 6" pieces of ribbon for a book of any size

1. With the knife, make a vertical slit in the front cover of the book or portfolio. It should be 1/2" from the fore edge and centered, top and bottom, and be 1/16" longer than the width of the ribbon.
2. Close the book or portfolio and mark a corresponding slit inside the back cover by pushing your knife through the front-cover slit and into the back cover.
3. Open the book and go over the slit until it goes through.
4. Use a butter knife or similar tool to push one end of one of the ribbons through the slit. You can trim any ragged ends later. Leave 1/2" on the inside of the book.
5. Push the other ribbon through the other slit, again leaving 1/2" inside.
6. Trim any ragged ends on the 1/2" side.
7. Apply glue to the 1/2" ends and adhere them to the cover boards. Press down for about 20 seconds or until they are set. You may add a small square of self-adhesive linen tape on top of the ribbons for reinforcement.
8. Apply an endpaper or endpapers as directed for the particular project.

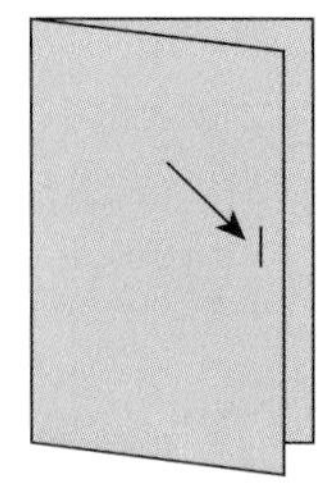

Steps 1, 2

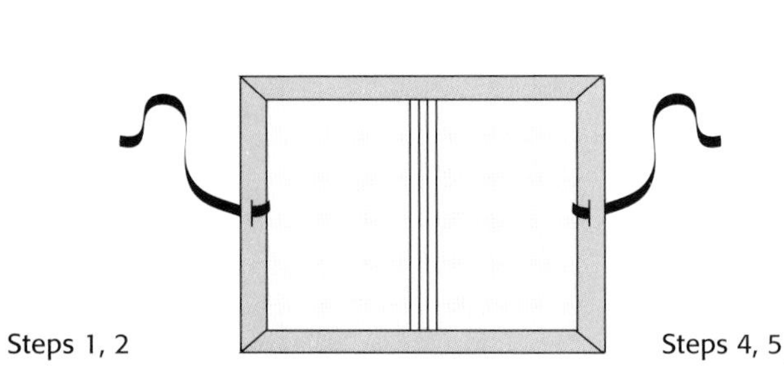

Steps 4, 5

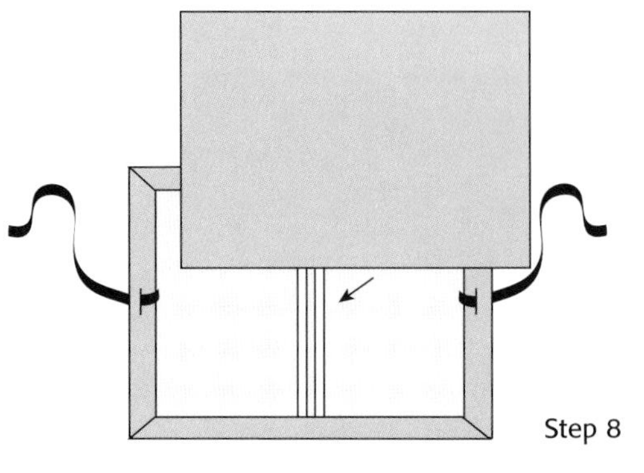

Step 8

Magnetic Strips or Velcro

Magnetic strips give the front of the book a clean look. You can find them in many office-supply stores. Use the self-adhesive kind on a wraparound portfolio or a flag file book. Cut them to the desired size. Self-adhesive Velcro may be used as an alternate. The instructions are the same. However, you may need to sew the Velcro to the boards to secure it so it does not rip.

Materials: book or portfolio, magentic strips

1. Remove the backing paper from one self-adhesive magnetic strip. Center the sticky side of one magnetic strip at the far left edge of the endpaper inside the front cover.
2. Magnetically attach the remaining magnetic strip to the first one. Align the edges.
3. Remove the backing sheet from the top strip, leaving the two strips attached.
4. Close the front cover, making sure the far right flap is folded up.
5. Press down. Check that that all magnets are stuck to the flaps.
6. Separate the two magnets and firmly press each one in place.

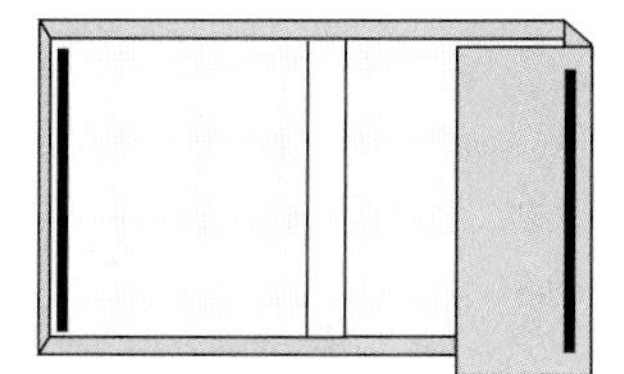

Step 6

Bone or Polymer Closures

Long and triangular in shape, the bone closure has a slit into which you thread a loop of reinforced paper or a ribbon. The bone closures I have used have a 1/4" slit, which means the finished size of the paper strip should be 3/16" wide (the starting paper is four times the width of the finished size). Make the paper strip only after you have purchased the bone clasp, to be sure you are making the correct size. As a variation, use 1/8"–1/4" ribbon instead. Skip to step 6 if you want to use a ribbon. If you are a vegetarian or object to using bone, you can make your own polymer closure in any color. I used a bone closure on the back of *Eight Degrees of Charity* (see photo on page 123).

Tools: bone folder, pencil, 12" ruler, scissors, art knife and cutting mat, magazines or catalogs for scrap paper, PVA, brush for gluing
Materials: lightweight paper 3/4" × 6" (long), 1"-long bone clasp or flat triangular polymer bead with a 1/4" slit, book or portfolio
Example: 3/16" × 6" strip

Tiny Books, 2004; painted papers; 2" square each

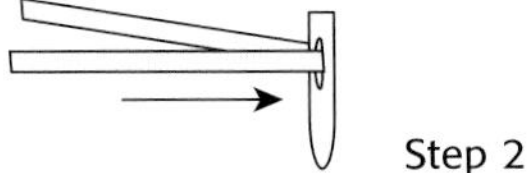

Step 2

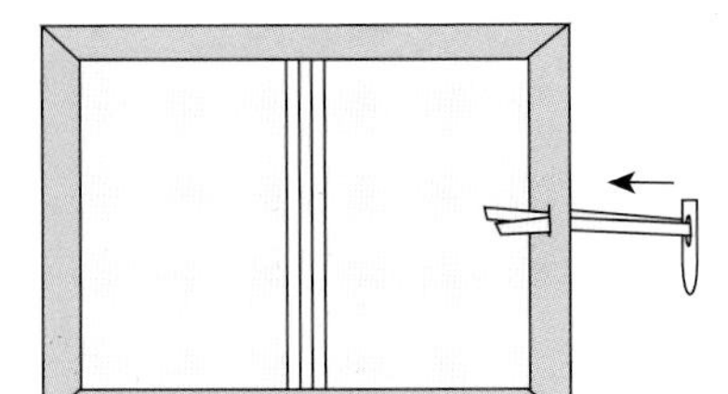

Steps 4, 5

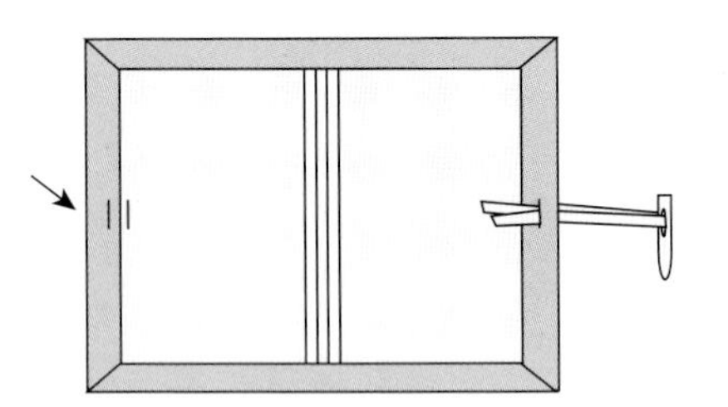

Steps 6, 7

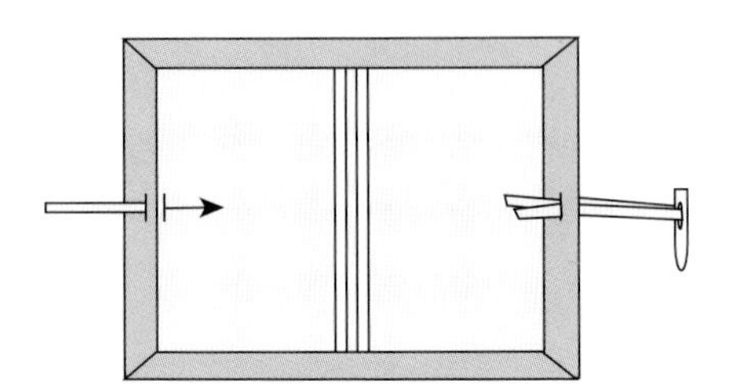

Steps 8, 9

1. Make a Paper Clasp Strip, page 141, steps 1-5, using the above measurements.
2. Thread one end of the paper strip through the slit in the bead. Leave about a 2" tail.
3. Cut the strip so that the cut end aligns with the other end. The bead will be in the center of a 4" strip. Save the cut piece.
4. With the knife, make a vertical slit through the back cover of the book or portfolio. It should be ½" from the fore edge and centered, top and bottom, and be about 1⁄16" wider than the paper strip.
5. Push both ends of the strip with the bead through the slit, from front to back. Use the dull side of the knife to push it through. You can trim any ragged ends later. Leave about ½" on the inside of the book.
6. Make a vertical slit through the front cover of the book or portfolio. It should be ½" from the fore edge and centered, top and bottom, and be about 1⁄16" wider than the strip.
7. Moving toward the spine, make a second vertical slit ¼" from the first one.
8. Using a butter knife or similar dull tool, push the leftover strip, from back to front, through one of the two front slits.
9. Push the end of the strip, from front to back, through the second front slit to create a loop on the front cover.
10. Close the book and reach the clasp around to tuck into the loop. Adjust the tightness of the loop so that it is snug but not impossible to remove the clasp. Adjust the strip that holds the clasp as well.
11. Trim any ragged ends of the paper strip on the inside, leaving ½".

12. Apply glue to the ½" ends and adhere them to the cover boards, facing their ends toward the spine. Press down for about 20 seconds or until they are set. You may apply a small square of self-adhesive linen tape over the ends of the strips for reinforcement.
13. Apply an endpaper or endpapers as directed for the particular project.

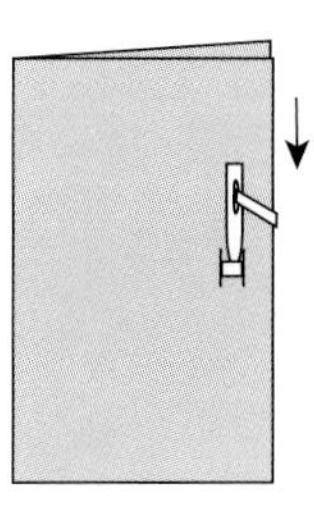

Step 10

Paper Clasp

This paper clasp is a strip that is glued into a complete loop. It remains separate from the book; you remove the loop to open the book You may also prepare the paper strip and use it with the bone closure on page 139.

Tools: bone folder, art knife and cutting mat, magazines or catalogs for scrap paper, PVA, brush for gluing
Materials: lightweight paper 2" × 8" (long); book or portfolio. You can change the width of the strip by using paper (four times the desired width) × (desired length). So, if you prefer a strip 1" wide, use paper 4" wide. Always make your folds along the grain.
Example: ½" × 8" strip

Preparing the Paper Strip

1. Fold the paper in half, lengthwise, making the paper long and narrow. Open.
2. Fold the edges in to the center fold, making the paper even narrower. Open.

Left: *Sea Star*, 2003; collage, stencil, acrylic ink, batiked paper; unique; circle-star accordion book, 7½" × 5½", in portfolio, 8¼" × 6", with paper loop closure
Right: *Healing Between the Dots*, 2004; drawings made with one ink line, gesso, acrylic inks; circle accordion with double pockets; unique; 5" × 7" book (not shown) in 5⅝" × 7¾" × 1½" box with paper clasp hinges

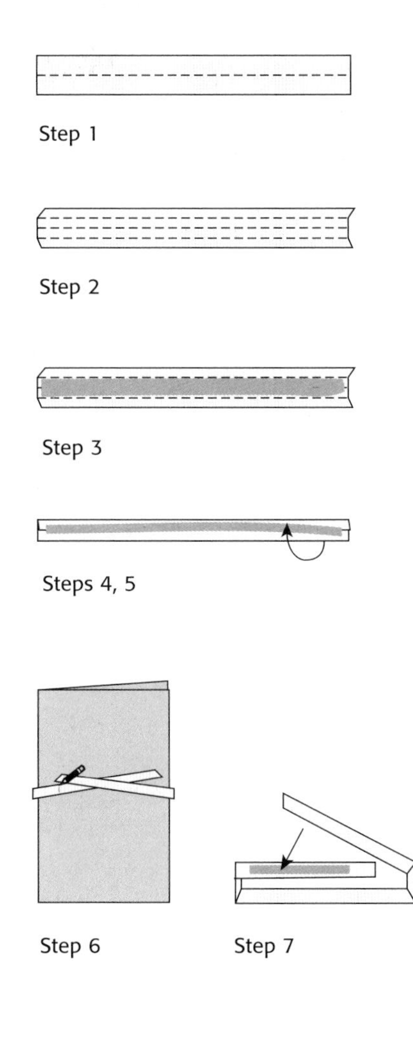

3. Cover your work surface with several layers of magazine pages. Discard any that become sticky. Spread a thin layer of glue on the center two sections of the paper. Refold the edges in to the center fold and press down.

4. Spread a thin layer of glue on top of one of these folded panels.

5. Fold the paper in half, making it even longer and thinner. Press it flat with a bone folder. Continue with step 6 for the Loop. Use this paper clasp with a bone closure (page 139).

Loop

6. Center the folded-and -glued paper strip at the back of your book or portfolio. Bring each side over and around so that they overlap each other on the front. Leave a comfortable margin (about ¼"–½") so that you will be able to get the strip on and off the book or portfolio. Mark where one end overlaps the other.

7. Apply glue from the pencil mark to the end of the strip.

8. Press the other end on top of the glue and align the edges. It will help to turn the loop so that the glued edge is next to the table. You will be able to press it down firmly in this position. Let it dry alone or wrapped around the book. If you slip it around the book, wrap the book first in waxed paper to protect it from any wet glue.

Left: *Healing Between the Dots*, 2004; drawings made with one ink line, gesso, acrylic inks; circle accordion with double pockets; unique; 5" × 7" book in 5⅝" × 7¾" × 1½" box with paper clasp hinges

Right: *Little Black Books*, 2004; paper, museum boards, ribbon; two acrylic ink-painted circle accordion books, 2¾" × 3" in slipcases, 3" × 3⅛" × 1½" with paper loop pen holders

Chapter Seven

Sorting Through the Big Box: Handling Memorabilia

One of the first things we are taught, sometimes even before we learn to walk, is how to sort. By sorting we make connections between things: what is the same, what is different, and how they are related. Often the objects we are sorting seem to have no obvious connection, yet fascinating connections may exist just under the surface. The key is to spend enough time with something to understand it fully. Whether we are aware of it or not, the process of sorting is how we learn to understand our world.

This sorting skill is useful when you start something new. You start over every time you make a book, so think about sorting before you begin. Perhaps you have a box of memorabilia: mementos from someone who has died, souvenirs from a trip you took, or random sayings and postcards that you've collected. Perhaps you intend to put them all in a scrapbook, but

Sorting
four books made from ephemera collected in 1977; color copies, acrylic inks, collage
Back: *Transit*
Front (left to right): *Israel Touring; Museum; Sugar with That*

Ephemera collected from Israel trip, 1978

somehow the time is never right to put it together or the abundance of material is just too overwhelming. Look at it now. Sort through it and discover which items are most important to you. It may help you to explain each piece to another person.

Sit down with your box and try one of the following brainstorming ideas. Most of these projects involve making photocopies or scans of the original items. You don't have to be precise about where and when you found each piece; you may interpret the objects and form them into a completely new story. See what you can learn from the process.

These books employ structures from the previous chapters. Suggested structures are given; choose any others that appeal to you.

Beginning with Categories

I finally sat down with a bag of stuff from Israel I've been keeping since I was sixteen. In addition to my bag, I still have a detailed travel journal and photographs to support my memory. My ephemera were sorted into these categories:

Money: paper money, coins, traveler's checks, receipts, bank documents
Entertainment: tickets from concerts, museums, plays, movies
Transportation: boarding passes, baggage-claim checks, bus transfers, maps
Food and Lodging: packets of salt, sugar, pepper, towelettes, napkins, bags, bottle tops
Tourist: booklets, literature, store receipts
Mail: stamps, postcards
Personal: checklists, letters received, notes to self, identification documents

SINGLE-FOCUS BOOK

Remove one piece from the box. Could you tell a whole story about just this? If you can, write it now. After you finish writing, you may put your box away and choose a book structure. If you can't tell a story with the object, put it aside, perhaps in a separate box. Continue this process if you desire more items in your book or if one story needs more than one item to be effective.

Go through your box, one item at a time, continuing to evaluate each piece and writing about it. Make a Circle Accordion (see page 32). Try making copies of the original items to attach to the pages, or use photo corners or PVA to adhere the originals.

If you cannot think of what to write, pick the piece or pieces that appeal to you most. Sometimes handling something can give you an idea. Look at the colors of the object and paint paper or make a collage to match it or enhance it. Keep working toward the visual side of the book. Eventually you will make a connection.

A Pound of Feathers has a small origami pocket at the very end containing a pamphlet with the text. I used a hard cover for *A Pound of Feathers* because I had a large piece of handmade paper with a feather in it that was perfect to cover two boards and a spine.

Betsy Davids used the story of a journey she took in search of a midden as the basis for her book *Quest for Arberth.* In a legend, that mound was reported to have magical powers. She collected ephemera during her travels in Wales and then used the copied and collaged materials to make her book, which uses paper bags as the structure.

Left: *A Pound of Feathers*, 2003; stencil and gesso; irregular accordion; unique; 6⅛" × 9½"
Right: Betsy Davids: *Quest for Arberth,* 1990/1994; mixed media with photocopies and paper bags; unique; 9¾" × 13"

COLLAGE BOOK

Museum, 2004; collage and color copies; origami pocket pamphlet; unique; 3" × 2¾"

If your objects are three-dimensional, or if you don't want to put glue on or harm the originals, consider scanning them or having them color-copied. You can enlarge or reduce them this way. You can also make a collage without fear of damaging the originals and with the knowledge that you have many chances to make the collage that you like.

Make a series of collaged cards, all the same size, and write about each collage on the back of the card. If you don't have a story, you can just write a sentence or a list of words. Try making them into a Single Flag Book (see page 57) or arrange the cards or the objects themselves on a page to make a Shorts Book to put in an Origami Pocket Envelope (see pages 104 and 106).

For a purely visual book, place many objects on a copier; make two copies. Fold one page into an Origami Pocket Pamphlet (see page 107). Put collaged cards in these pockets. From the second sheet, cut one 2¾" × 11" strip for a wraparound soft cover, and another, narrower strip to make into a paper loop to hold the book closed, like *Museum.*

If you kept a travel journal, you can photocopy pages onto good paper and use those words for the text. Experiment with making the words larger and smaller. You can also collage the words in various sizes. Before you cut

Sugar with That, 2004; color and black-and-white copy, acrylic ink and gesso; pocket flag book; unique; 4½" × 7"

up the photocopies, paint over them with a watercolor or acrylic ink wash; now you have words on a colored background that will look more integrated with the piece.

Sugar with That incorporates copies of sugar, creamer, salt, and pepper packets that are made into hanging tags for a Pocket Flag Book (see page 61). The pockets are folded from photocopied journal entries about food.

Book of Favorites

Spread the contents of the box on a table. Start by putting things back into the box that don't interest you anymore. Pick out the things that you know you can't part with, and hold onto them. If they are wildly different sizes, you may want to photocopy or scan the items, reducing or enlarging the sizes to make them uniform. You may want to arrange the items on a page, copy them, then cut the page into strips.

In either case, try making a Multiple-Flag Book using the images as the flag pages. Mount the images onto thicker paper and write on the back or type up your observations or memory of each object and use that paper as the backing for the images. Or, instead of backing the paper, you may double the width of the flag and fold it in half with images on both sides. Use up to forty-two very small images with this structure (see Mounting Paper, page 26, and Multiple-Flag Book, page 64.)

You may also have objects that are naturally long and narrow, such as tickets, bus transfers, or receipts. Photocopy these, then trim around them

Transit, 2004; color copy, ink, painted paper, book cloth; flag book; unique; 4" × 7¾"

Left: *Snapshots of Sea Glass*, 2004; color copy, foil stamp title; edition of 40; shorts book with bead, 4" × 4", in origami envelope, 4¼" × 4¼"
Right: Emily Martin: *Wish You Were Here*, 1996; postcards, tickets, envelopes; piano-hinge binding with sharpened pencils; unique; 7" × 9" × 8"

and use them as flags. If they are different sizes, make the spaces as wide as the largest item, such as the pages in *Transit.*

In *Snapshots of Sea Glass* I used color copies of pebbles and sticks and things I picked up on Glass Beach on the northern California coast. The background is paste paper that I wrote on with a waterproof pen. The story is about things we overlook and things we notice, based on, but not a literal description of, my trip.

Emily Martin went on a trip to the United Kingdom and sent herself postcards, tickets, and envelopes to be made into the book *Wish You Were Here* when she got home.

THEME BOOK

Choose one object as a theme and pull out all other materials that support this theme. They may not be items that you particularly treasure, but they just may seem to belong together. Try concrete themes such as "shops" or "airplanes" or "twisty roads." Write your feelings about the theme, what you like and dislike, how comfortable you are or aren't, then write about your connection with the object or other materials.

Make one of the books with pockets for the objects. Or sort the materials into envelopes that you label with categories, then choose the envelope that appeals to you the most.

For *Israel Touring* my theme was places I went where I needed a ticket. I folded the Check Book (see page 110) out of color copies of a map and put the copies of tickets in the pockets. On the back of each ticket I stenciled the date, then copied over my description of the event from my journal. I was much surprised to see the feelings of my teenaged self written in my middle-aged handwriting. Sometimes your choice of lettering influences how you understand the words.

Israel Touring, 2004; color copy, collage, ink; origami check book; unique; 3" × 6"

Dream Connections Book

Perhaps you have dreamed about one of the objects from your box of ephemera or about a place where one of the items has been. How does this item connect dreams to waking life? Take a big piece of newsprint or inexpensive drawing paper and write short phrases about the dream and about the object. Circle the phrases and draw lines between the ones that seem to go together. If you like, choose a six-letter word for a title and try a Side Binding with Tabbed Pages (see page 83). Copy the phrases onto your book pages.

Another approach takes a few days and a little concentration. Pick one object and study it. Put it by your bed and tell yourself "I'm going to dream about _____." Keep track of your dreams about the object for one week. Write the dreams on cards, one dream per card. Make a File Flag Book or a box that will hold your object and cards that contain your dreams. Add your waking connection, both from when you first obtained the object and what you think of it today.

Memorial Book

Mainstream culture reveals quite a bit of sex and violence but doesn't deal much with love, death, and grief. This may be one reason death is such a hard topic for so many people. Some people won't even say the word. Yet everyone is touched by it eventually. Sometimes our experience of grief

Top: *Dear Ezra*, 2004; color copies, typewritten and laser-printed text, watercolor crayon, ink, found objects; accordion with pockets; unique; 4½" × 5½" book in a hand-felted pouch
Bottom: *Dear Ezra*, 2004; open

seems to happen too early or too quickly. Maybe it is always too early for grief; no one seems to want to talk about it. After a death there is almost always stuff to sort through, physically and emotionally. Working through the stuff creatively can be helpful to the grieving process. Giving a creative remembrance piece to a survivor can help both you and the recipient.

A woman came to me with a box of things that she had kept since her father had died ten years earlier. After discussing how she wanted to remember him and what objects were the most important to her, we focused on a couple of book structures that would make the project manageable. When some of the objects didn't go together, I suggested she might make a series of books. If you decide to make a series of books, consider making them all the same size and putting them in a box to keep them together.

Dorothy Yule lost her nephew unexpectedly when he was thirty-four, and she made a book to give to the boy's mother as well as additional copies for other family members. Dorothy has been making books all her life, and her nephew had recently been asking her to make him a book; as it happened, the book she made for him was a memorial. *A Book for Ian* is a book and memento when closed, and a shrine when the accordion is opened, with the photographs tucked into slots. Dorothy writes, "When the awkward time came to say words before we gave his ashes to the sea, I offered the book to those gathered and, as it circulated so people could look at the pictures of Ian over time, I read the poem and then we tied the rose petal book around the urn, which went into the water. A copy of the book went with his remains and another copy stayed behind to comfort his mother."

Try starting with just a couple of items and maybe one or two anecdotes. Perhaps copy a series of photographs. Depending where you are in your grieving or healing process, you may want to make a book that reminds you of the good things in a person's life, the things you want to

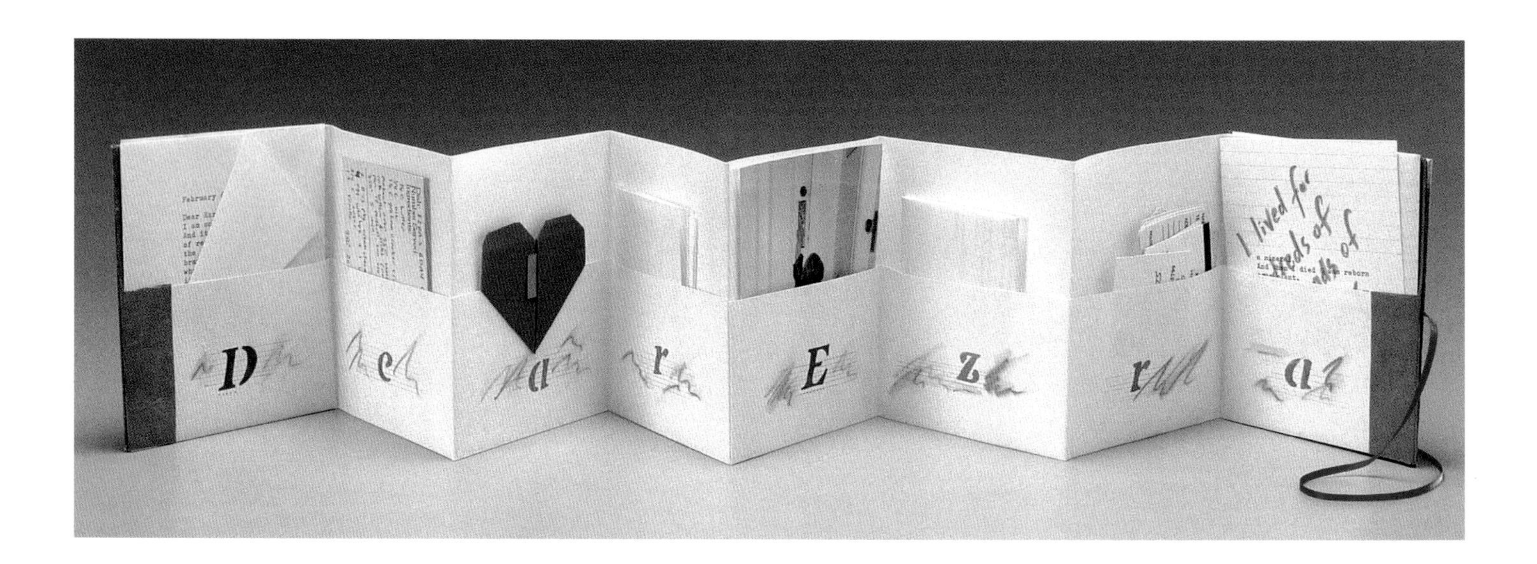

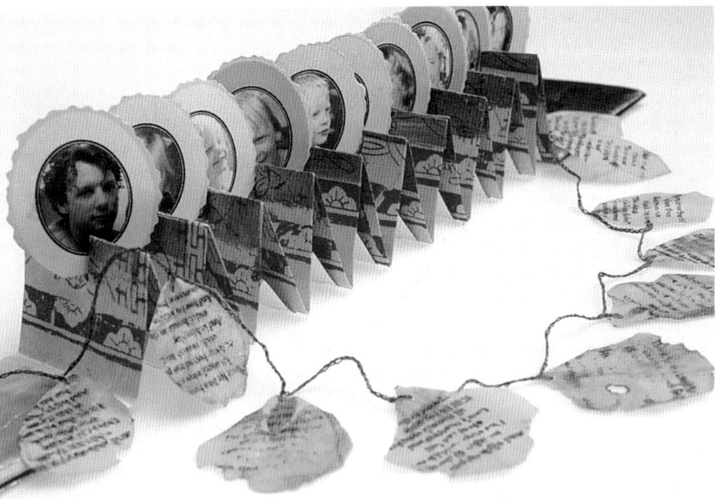

Left: Dorothy Yule: *A Book for Ian*, 2003; laser print and laser-print transfer on paper and rose petals, joss papers; accordion with portraits that swivel forward when opened; edition of 10; 3¼" × 2⅜" (photo by Russell Yip)
Right: Dorothy Yule: *A Book for Ian*, 2003; open

remember; or you may need to write about their death or your grief. To create a book that stands up like Dorothy's, work with an accordion structure; cut slits halfway across the peak folds, and make a series of cards that can be inserted into the slits. Or make a flag book or a book with pockets. I made an accordion with pockets to hold my private letters to my son, condolence messages, quotes, and business cards for services I no longer needed after he died, for the book *Dear Ezra*.

Recycled-Text Book: Sorting Through the Mail

Sometimes the mail you receive can be turned into a gift to return to the sender. Two different artists I knew were getting married and both sent fantastic announcements. Dorothy Yule, a book artist, sent an invitation that included an exquisitely made three-dimensional flexagon with a rhymed poem celebrating her upcoming marriage. Jim Hair, a photographer, had made a book from one piece of paper with photographs and a brief description of his courtship. Both of these creative packages inspired me to make nontraditional wedding albums.

You can use the same technique for other life-cycle events to which you receive a written invitation. The text comes from the invitation; you just copy and rearrange the words. Or make a book for yourself based on a letter, a short article in a magazine, or some junk mail.

Use the Circle Accordion with Pockets (page 38), but make pockets in all the pages and fold a 1" spine (instead of ¾"). You will need two sheets of

Left: *Book for Jim and Vicki,* 2004; *Book for Dorothy and George,* 2004; acrylic inks, collage, gesso; unique; 5" × 7"
Right: Dorothy Yule, with illustrations by Susan Hunt Yule: *Wedding Invitation,* 2004; letterpress from polymer plates; two intertwining ring flexagons; edition of 115; 5" square box

22" × 30" paper for the inside (which you will trim), and one sheet of 7" × 21" paper for the outside. You may use a different structure.

Preparation: Use small cardboard stencils, which you can buy at an office-supply store (hardware stores often have them, too), and gold (or black) gesso to stencil the names of the wedding couple or some key words on one side of the paper. Paint with transparent and iridescent acrylic inks over and around the names. On a computer or typewriter, type words from the received mail on one sheet of paper; use whatever fits in about four columns, 10- or 12-point type, double spaced. Cut out all the words and play with them to make new sentences and phrases. After folding up the pages and pockets, use acrylic gel medium (or PVA) to glue the words onto the pages in their new arrangements. You may paint over them, if you like. Then follow the instructions for the variation for the Circle Accordion with Pockets (see page 41).

Visual Lettering and Words on a Receptive Page

When you read a certain book, you may notice that the design is pleasant and interesting. It may be easy to read.

Visual Lettering
When you make books, keep this in mind and try to vary the reading experience. Use stencils for titles or for key words, or use rubber-stamped letters for titles and then use typewritten text. As you would be quickly numbed looking through a book that had pages and pages of just one

word, your eye can become fatigued viewing text produced by one style of lettering.

Just as your eye can lose interest looking at the same thing over and over, it can also become overwhelmed by too much stimulation. Avoid mixing too many styles. Too much information distracts the reader from absorbing the content of your book. The ransom-note style works in small doses, but the reader will give up reading after just a few words.

Moderation is best, unless you are actively looking for a collaged style. All capital letters scream out unless they are in a tiny size. But capitals look and read better than lower case letters when they have large spaces between them.

Use different media for the lettering. Try stencils, rubber stamps, typewritten text, laser-printed computer fonts, handwriting, letterpress printing (if available to you). Be careful mixing fonts within a medium. I like to use one sans serif font with one serif font and possibly one italic font. Rarely use more than three different fonts when using either a computer-generated text or only letterpress printing.

Exceptions may be made when you desire a certain look, such as a businesslike form printed one way and rubber stamps or handwritten text to fill in the blanks.

Handwritten text doesn't have to feature your natural handwriting. Look at a newspaper or book and copy out the alphabet that you see printed there. Note the shapes of the little *a*'s and *e*'s. Are the *t*'s curved at

Anchor in a Tin Boat, 2004; acrylic inks and gesso, gel pen, paper, canvas, seed pearls; file flag with ribbon loop closure; unique; 7½" × 5⅞" × 1½"

the bottom or straight? Practice. Trace it first, if you like. Practice your handwritten typeface until it feels comfortable. Try it out in a simple book.

Avoid overly stylized fonts unless they contribute to your content. The word *candy* might look great in some of the more whimsical typefaces with little balls on the ends, curlicues, or dots. Those novelty faces are rarely appropriate for a whole sentence; they would be unreadable as a complete story. When in doubt, keep it simple.

Words on a Receptive Page

To make any book, I recommend you print out or mark up the pages first. I am in awe of people who can write boldly on a white piece of paper, especially if that piece of paper is bound into a beautiful handmade book. I can't do it. I prefer to mark up my pages before I bind a book, either by a printmaking technique such as linoleum cuts, collagraphs, or letterpress, or a collage or painting technique: acrylic inks, watercolor crayons, gesso, or paste paper. In the preparation sections of the previous chapters I have given suggestions of how to paint your paper before you bind the book. Sometimes the swirls or inadvertent lines provide an anchoring place for the words; the sentences do not have to be straight.

Even if all you have are some pens and a coffee cup, you can treat the pages so they become friendlier to write on. Scribble with the pens. Make coffee circles with the cup. Keep your hands moving. In time, these marks may inspire a story.

Plan variety for your reader's eye. Use sharp edges and torn edges; drawings and photographs; painted areas with a dry brush and painted areas with fluid color; pristine color and scratched-in design. I like to see that the maker has been there via torn edge, brushstroke, handwriting, or drawing: a little chaos. Then I like to see one of those juxtaposed with either a trimmed edge, a photograph, an old engraving, or printed type: a little calm. Keep the reader interested and curious.

Book for Jim and Vicki, 2004; acrylic inks, collage, gesso; unique; 5" × 7"

Moving Forward

A friend of mine sighed and said that she wished she could compose music and write songs. She was a good vocalist. She could arrange music. She could take a march and turn it into a piece for a kazoo orchestra. I asked her why she felt she couldn't create. "Creators can pick out things from life and make them seem universal. I think about the same things, but I can't say them in that fresh way."

I believe that everyone has a talent for creating; it just shows up in different ways. Perhaps, if my friend were a visual artist she might alter books or make collages but not draw or paint the images herself.

A drawing teacher once told me that drawing wasn't about drawing, it was about looking. All art is about observation and interpretation. When you have a moment, listen to every sound, look at every face, smell and touch what you can. Endless sources of inspiration pass you by, and all because you are not paying attention.

You can sift through everything you have heard and make connections between seemingly different things. Try taking two random words or images and spin a web between them. It can be easy to find connections between them if you let your mind wander without judgment.

My teacher and friend Betsy Davids suggested that some people have trouble making things because they worry that what they have to say isn't important. But you never know when what you have to say will touch or resonate with another person.

Occasionally people talk about things that are personal and things that are universal as if these were different concepts. In reality, many of the details of a personal story are also what make it universal; the reader can say, "Yes, I have one of those," or "That happened to me, too!" If you actively strive to be universal you may end up being overly general, with no emotional content, no handle for the reader to grasp. A drawing of a rectangle is only a geometric shape; it could be a newspaper, a lunch box, or a book. It is the details that are important, especially if they have meaning to you.

Whatever you pick as your subject, whatever medium you choose, you can create something new. Because each of us is different, each of us will leave a mark that is unique. What subject should you choose? Something you feel passionate about. Remember those teachers who loved their subjects and got you to love them too? You can have an effect on yourself and on your reader, should you choose to share your work. Commit yourself to your topic; choose something and dedicate your thoughts to it. Then focus on a structure that suits your project or one that simply pleases you. Even if you are unsure of the result, keep going. The main thing is to begin. The next main thing is to finish. Anything can happen in between.

CONTRIBUTING ARTISTS

Jody Alexander is a book artist, teacher, and librarian. She has a special interest in historical bookbinding, hand papermaking, ancient communications systems, and, more recently, incorporating found objects into her work. Originally trained in art history in Los Angeles and library science in Boston, she teaches in Santa Cruz and around the San Francisco Bay Area and gives workshops occasionally at the Center for Book Arts in New York City. Her work may be found at www.jalexbooks.com.

Betsy Davids has taught writing since 1968 and bookmaking since 1972 at California College of the Arts (formerly CCAC) in Oakland and San Francisco. She and James Petrillo published collaborative letterpress editions of new writing and art under their Rebis Press imprint in the '70s and '80s. She is a cofounder of the Pacific Center for the Book Arts. Her recent work is handmade one-of-a-kind books evolving from day-to-day life and travel experience, incorporating everyday materials and text from her dream journaling practice. See an example at http://dreamtalk.hypermart.net/gallery2003/idx_davids.htm

Elsi Vassdal Ellis is a professor at Western Washington University, teaching graphic design and book arts, with a major interest in visual psychology and visual communication. She gives workshops and presentations around the country. Since 1983 she has been the proprietor of EVE press, where she makes letterpress books, currently with political themes. Her work is found in many special collections and at www.ac.wwu.edu/~eve/book_arts.

Charles Hobson is an artist and teacher who has worked with images and words since 1984 and has taught at the San Francisco Art Institute since 1990. He works primarily with printmaking techniques involving monotypes, pastels, and collage, and by incorporating found objects into his books. Usually following literary or historical themes, his books have covered topics as diverse as famous couples who met in Paris to shipwrecks along the California coast. Three of his artist's books were published as trade editions by Chronicle Books: *Leonardo Knows Baseball* (1991), *Parisian Encounters* (1994), and *Seeing Stars* (2001). His work is in several major collections and may be found at www.charleshobson.com.

Edward H. Hutchins is a book artist, graphic designer, and teacher who has given bookmaking and design classes in art institutions, libraries, and public schools across the United States, Canada, and Mexico. Since 1989 he has been the proprietor of Editions, a studio for producing artist's book multiples using a variety of media and directed at social and political issues. His designs have received awards from the American Association of Museums and the Miniature Book Society. In 1994 he was selected by the Smithsonian Institution to produce one of the artist's books for the "Science and the Artist's Book" show. His work is included in most contemporary book art collections. See his books at www.artistbooks.com.

Susan King is an artist and writer who grew up in Kentucky, did graduate work in ceramics in New Mexico, but moved to Los Angeles, where she joined the experimental Feminist Studio Workshop started by Judy Chicago, Sheila de Bretteville, and Arlene Raven. Since 1975 she has been making artist's books; in 1978 she founded Paradise Press, her imprint for her letterpress and offset books. She was studio director of the Women's Graphics Center in Los Angeles. Currently she divides her time between her studio in Disputanta, Kentucky, merging photography and writing, and teaching workshops around the country. Her writing appears in many publications, including *I to I: Life Writing by Kentucky Feminists* (Western Kentucky University, 2004). Her book art may be found in special collections of universities and museums across the country.

Hedi Kyle recently retired as head conservator at the American Philosophical Society. After a brief career as a graphic designer, her interest turned to book arts and book conservation. She is adjunct professor at the University of the Arts in Philadelphia, Pennsylvania, where she teaches book structures in the Graduate Program in Book Arts and Printmaking. She graduated from the Werk-Kunst Schule in Wiesbaden, Germany. Her one-of-a-kind constructions have been exhibited internationally and are in private and public collections. She is cofounder of Paper and Book Intensive (PBI), and has given workshops in the U.S., Canada, and Switzerland for the past twenty years.

Emily Martin started as a painter and sculptor who found books a better medium to combine words, images, and multiple scenes. She has been working under the imprint Naughty Dog Press since 1996, but has been making artist's books since the late 1970s using a variety of printing methods, including inkjet, letterpress, copiers, and offset. Her themes are often personal stories; her press is named after her dog and studio companion, Gomez. She teaches at the University of Iowa Center for the Book and gives workshops around the country. Her work is in public and private collections internationally and may also be seen at www.emilymartin.com.

Keith Smith has been teaching in universities and art schools since 1970. He lives in New York, where he makes art and write books; he also travels within the United States and around the world to give visiting artist and summer workshops. Exploring book structures, photography, and conceptual art combined with personal and political themes are important aspects of his work. Since 1977 he has published forty-two books, including nine books-on-books: these under his imprint, keith smith *BOOKS*. The recipient of two Guggenheim Fellowships, an NEA grant, and other major grants, Keith continues to create and exhibit his art. His work is collected internationally in museums and libraries. His work may also be seen at www.keithsmithbooks.com

Dorothy A. Yule is a graphic designer and letterpress printer who often collaborates with her twin sister, Susan Hunt Yule, on books produced under her imprint, Left Coast Press. Having made books since she was a child, she was finally able to pursue her interest in bookmaking in 1986 in the Mills College graduate program in book arts, shortly before the program ended. Her first childhood influences were poets like Edward Lear, Lewis Carroll, and Ogden Nash; her current subjects are often life-cycle events, written in original rhyme. She is fascinated by paper engineering and has created many unusual pop-up and movable books. Her work is in the Special Collections Department of many universities, public libraries, and museums in the U.S. and abroad. *New York,* and *San Francisco,* two books from her set of four *Souvenirs of Great Cities,* have been published in trade editions by Chronicle Books (2005).

ABOUT THE AUTHOR

Alisa Golden is a book artist, printmaker, teacher, and writer who makes handmade books under the imprint she established in 1983, never mind the press. She is also the author of *Creating Handmade Books* (1998) and *Unique Handmade Books* (2001), both published by Sterling. She teaches bookmaking in the San Francisco Bay area, including at California College of the Arts (formerly CCAC), the San Francisco Center for the Book, and in elementary schools. Her book art is collected by universities and libraries across the country and may also be seen at www.neverbook.com.

INDEX